We Marched With Mosley

The Authorised History of The British Union of Fascists

Richard Reynell Bellamy

We Marched With Mosley

The Authorised History of the British Union of Fascists

Richard Reynell Bellamy
National Inspector of British Union

ISBN-13: 978-1-913176-27-3

Sanctuary Press Ltd
71-75 Shelton Street
Covent Garden
London
WC2H 9JQ

www.sanctuarypress.com
Email: info@sanctuarypress.com

Contents

Acknowledgements

The tones of many voices can be detected in this saga of domestic politics, international affairs and two world wars. They can be heard proclaiming the various and diverging views of King Edward VIII; the Earls Baldwin and Lloyd-George; the Lords Avon, Beaverbrook, Birkett, Citrine and Morrison of Lambeth; the Generals Heinz Guderian, Sir Giffard Martel, and Sir Andrew Thorne; the historians and politicians Margaret Boveri, Sir Philip Gibbs, Adolf Hitler, George Lansbury, Richard Thurlow and Leon Trotsky; the clerics Dr. Hewlett Johnson and Baron Cosmo Lang, Archbishop of Canterbury; and the writers Beverley Nichols, George Orwell, John Rae, John Ruskin, George Bernard Shaw, Hannen Swaffer, Count Tolstoy and Henry Williamson.

As in the case of all my political writings I must make very special acknowledgements to Sir Winston Churchill, Major-General J.F.C. Fuller, Captain B.H. Liddell Hart and Sir Oswald Mosley.

Richard Reynell Bellamy

Introduction

I was born in 1901, the first of a Manchester family of eight children. We were not poor: on my mother's side we were related to the Milnes, who in the course of the nineteenth century had acquired wealth and power from cotton and commerce, much as the Mosleys had three centuries before in that area. My maternal grandfather had been co-founder of Kendal Milne and Company, Manchester's leading department store.

From an early age my burning ambition was to become an officer in the Royal Navy and this seemed likely to be fulfilled when at the age of eight I was sent to Sedbergh School with the intention that I should in due course sit the entrance examination for Osborne College on the Isle of Wight, whence after two years' training as a cadet I would graduate to the Royal Naval College in Dartmouth and in due course receive my commission as a midshipman.

Alas! At Prep school I made the mistake of winning a classical scholarship whereupon my Father, envisaging a promising academic or business career for me, transferred me to St. Bees Grammar School in Cumberland and I arrived there shortly after the outbreak of the First World War. Driven completely off my chosen course I sampled a variety of jobs before leaving England in the early 1920s to become a 'jackaroo' in the Australian Outback and later – after I married – a coffee planter in the French possession of New Caledonia. My South Seas adventures are described in my book 'Mixed Bliss in Melanesia'.

In 1930, for the sake of my year old son's health, my wife and I decided to return to England, where we landed in March 1931, after a nightmare voyage lasting 76 days in the course of which the Captain of our French ship, the Ville de Verdun, was shot dead by the Burser.

Introduction

As if this experience had not been bad enough, a few days before berthing in Marseilles my wife was struck down by a tropical bug and on landing had to be rushed to hospital for an emergency operation. Some three weeks later she was deemed well enough to complete her journey to England, where she had to undergo further surgery and many months of treatment by a specialist before she fully recovered. Due to my preoccupation with my wife's illness the brief life of Sir Oswald Mosley's New Party, founded in February 1931 and annihilated at the General Election of that year, passed me by, though I had heard of it's formation on the ship's radio.

After such a long period abroad, conditions in Britain shocked me, particularly the condition of the unemployed who by then numbered some three millions. When I had left home about a million had been without work, and that had been considered a national calamity. Now that that figure had trebled, there seemed to be a tendency to dismiss the ever-mounting numbers as a sad inevitability about which nothing could be done.

The recession – "slump" as it was then called – was particularly bad in East Anglia, where my father had retired and where I now made my own home. Hundreds of acres of potatoes in the Fens were left to rot in the ground unharvested while a few miles away in King's Lynn, foreign vessels were unloading hundreds of tons of potatoes from the Continent. What had been good arable farms in the heart of high farming Norfolk were changing hands at £2 an acre, and less; the displaced farm workers, ineligible in those days for Unemployment Benefit, were sent to work in the stone-pits for a few shillings.

In Yarmouth, fishing vessels entered port deep-laden with herring catches only to be ordered to sea again to dump their hauls, while at the same time, a few miles away, the wives and children of unemployed farm-labourers made their main meal of the day out of a single herring divided between every two members of the family. Dutch vessels were entering the Pool of London with fresh milk from Holland at the same time that English milk, already being produced in excess, not of human needs but of economic requirements, was being processed into umbrella handles. In South Wales an unemployed miner was sent to prison for stealing a bottle of milk for a hungry and ailing child. In Lancashire, children of unemployed cotton-workers were actually perishing from the effects of prolonged malnutrition, a polite term for slow starvation.

When I first expressed my opinion, in the bosom of the family, that "what this country needs is a revolution", it was not well received. My father expostulated: "My dear boy, you must not speak like that. The affairs of old England are in more capable, experienced and trustworthy hands than you imagine."

Other members of the family who could think of revolution only in terms of barricades and guillotines, or of Latin American General Officers with political aspirations, recoiled in horror from my "treasonable" suggestion. I think I was as much appalled by the complacency of the middle-class as I was by the misery among the working-class. Not that unemployment was confined to manual workers; but, as in my own case, the average middle-class family, even if considerably worse off than before the First World War, was still able to feed and shelter it's less fortunate members.

In countless working-class homes, on the other hand there was cold and hunger. Yet because the "dole" prevented the sufferers from actually dropping dead in the streets, there was wide indifference to their fate. Walter Greenwood's 1933 novel 'Love On The Dole', is as accurate a social document of those times as any future social historian might wish to consult. This disregard for the workless among the middle-classes was not due to any innate callousness, because like most of our nation they are a kindly and humane lot, but unless they lived in a "Distressed Area", there was little evidence of abject poverty.

The most acutely affected regions, such as the South Wales coalfields and the ship-building towns of the north-east coast, to name two such localities, had been officially designated as Distressed Areas, and some effort, mostly inadequate, was being made to alleviate the paralysis creeping over them. The attitude of middle-class people was largely the outcome of their environment; they lacked both experience and imagination. My own feelings regarding hunger and want had doubtless been sharpened by my experience of unemployment in Australia, where I first learned just what it was to be jobless and moneyless, and spurned by people who were safe and comfortable.

When in October 1932, after the crushing electoral defeat of the New Party and the scuttling away to safer political climes of all the amiable and well-meaning socialist intellectuals who formed it's upper-crust, Mosley launched his "British Union of Fascists", I was interested at once.

So much nonsense has since been written about that event and that organisation, that I feel a duty to state simply and honestly how it seemed at the time. The BUF, as it came to be known, was a merger of the stouter-hearted remnants of the progressive New Party with the rudderless and relatively reactionary "British Fascists" formed a decade before. Mosley published his programme in a book entitled 'The Greater Britain', when the BUF was founded. After all I had seen of the misery and muddle in Britain, this new programme appealed to my belief in my country. It was an inspiring plan for national reconstruction, which at the same time challenged the brutal and destructive alternative of communism.

I was about to apply to Mosley's London headquarters for particulars of membership, when I happened to read in that old die-hard Tory newspaper, 'Morning Post', since merged with – and smothered by the more suave and complacent 'Daily Telegraph' – that Mosley's "blackshirts" could be better described as Mosley's "boiled shirts". "Sentinel" was, I think, the commentator responsible for the article. Four years later he described the Mosleyites rather more accurately as "decent, clean-living young fellows, some of them Public School products, but most of them drawn from every rank and vocation." Back in 1932, however, he had claimed that Mosley's appeal was directed almost exclusively to Public School and ex-officer types – men who had been looking for work ever since the war ended. Ex-officers who had led platoons, companies and battalions into battle; ex-airmen who had flown their Farmans and their Sopwiths against the Kaiser's air force; and sailors who had known the rigours of Atlantic winters were now unemployed and often destitute.

Britain's now-unwanted heroes had knocked on thousands of disinterested doors, trying to sell vacuum-cleaners to hard-up housewives. They had pushed ice-cream barrows and helped to gather in Canadian harvests. They were willing to tackle any job, however menial and degrading, to get off the scrapheap to which financial democracy had ungratefully consigned them. Their education was of little help. Nor were those qualities of proven courage, leadership and self-reliance that they had developed through their wartime experiences. They were misfits in a society obsessed with making money, or irresponsibly throwing it away.

But when "Sentinel" suggested that it was mainly to these dispossessed gentlemen that Mosley's appeal was addressed, my initial enthusiasm waned. Even to my politically immature eyes it was obvious that a party confining its membership to the upper classes was not going to solve Britain's problems. However, this proved only an early example of how the press could mislead its readers about "Mosleyites".

I was still undecided when in the late spring of 1933 I received a visit in my Norfolk home from a member of the BUF, a tall, well-built, good-looking fellow dressed in a tight-fitting black fencing-jacket and breeches. Gueroult was the first Blackshirt I had actually seen, and I became very impressed by him.

He explained his French name. Apparently, his great-grandfather had fled to Britain from the French Revolution. He was himself a schoolmaster, after serving as a British officer in the 1914-18 war. He had charm, eloquence and wit; for an entire evening he captivated the family, and kept us from our beds until the early hours of the next day. Whereas the tonic of his words soon wore off where my parents and brothers were concerned, in my case the more I thought on what he had said, the greater became my conviction that Mosley had the answers to the questions of the day.

7

I was converted to Mosley's cause by the plain sense of Gueroult's statement that the New Movement's policy combined the discipline, good order and patriotism of the right with the reforms and social justice of the Left. He quoted Mosley himself: "It has become axiomatic that if an Englishman wishes to see his country great and strong, armed to defend, and the imperial possessions firmly held, he aligns himself automatically with those selfish interests which are opposed to the long overdue reforms. If on the other hand he is a social reformer, it is inevitable that he should also be a social pacifist would be prepared to see Britain defenceless in an armed world, he would let the Empire fall apart, and be ever ready to listen to the subversive voice of Moscow."

Here at last was news of a movement ready to put the "Great" back into Britain and the selfish interests into their proper place, but which at the same time could defeat the soulless materialism of the Left. It was the message I had been waiting for. I could hesitate no longer. I joined.

I had been an active member of the British Union of Fascists for several months before I set eyes on its Leader or heard him speak. The occasion was a meeting in an East Anglian market town, where I had cycled in company with other Blackshirt stewards from outlying villages.

I saw a man, tall and commanding, deep chested, brawny and athletic despite a slight limp. Dark-haired and handsome, he was stern at times, but charming and completely disarming when he smiled. Occasionally, very rarely a light would flash in his eyes. It was a phenomenon I have known in no other man; it seemed to indicate some inner force or fire.

Although converted to his creed, I still had reservations concerning this man himself. These prejudices I had in my callowness imbibed from right-wing newspapers, which had denigrated him in every way since he left the Conservative Party. When I signed my enrolment form I said to the BUF officer: "I'm joining your party because plain sense tells me that its policy is the right one, but I've yet to be convinced that Mosley is the right man to lead it."

The overriding impression that I carried away from that meeting, however, was of an array of talents seldom to be found in any one man. He showed extensive knowledge and deep understanding of the many aspects of his subject, memory for facts and figures, (for he spoke without notes), the ability to simplify difficult and abstruse matters so that slow and 'bucolic' minds could understand, and above all there remained with me the recollection of his stirring magnetism in that strong voice as he spoke on and on, without strain or affectation in polished but unaffected prose.

It has been said that he was the only member of the House of Commons excepting Winston Churchill, whose speeches were reported verbatim and without alteration in 'Hansard'. The utterances of other Members of Parliament had to be edited, sometimes drastically, otherwise the speakers would have appeared in print as semi-literate.

Listening carefully to Mosley that day, and watching him closely convinced me that in joining his movement I had accepted the leadership of one of the most talented and portentous figures in Britain.

That was in the late autumn of 1933. Since then, the world has undergone some of the greatest upheavals in all history. Among the major catastrophes attending the Second World War, the British Empire – which we had pledged ourselves to serve and defend – has been swept away, or rather thrown away, to join the empires of Spain, of Rome, and of Alexander the Great. The fruits of three and a half centuries of heroic endeavour and of glorious achievement, our priceless heritage, also our awesome responsibility, have been cast away by politicians too weary, weak, or subverted to carry on the great tradition of the Pax Britannica.

Long ago Mosley foretold: "Without some great spiritual revival, Britain is doomed." For more than four decades he strove unceasingly to implant the seed of spiritual and national regeneration. Since 1945 we have seen our country slowly sink, its power ebb, its honour wilt, and its glory fade. All that remains is an ignoble obsession with material gain, once so completely immortalised by Harold Macmillan as "never had it so good".

It has been asked repeatedly: Why did Oswald Mosley deliberately walk out into the political wilderness? "Surely," they say, "there was a place for him within one of the established Parties?"

L.C.E. Seaman provides an answer. "It was all the fault of the old and silly politicians. There can be no doubt that the political leaders of that time were unusually hostile to intelligence and ability. The most spectacular example was provided by ... Sir Oswald Mosley... His skill in Parliamentary debate, his power of oratory on a public platform, his fashionable good looks, which would have made him a box-office draw as a cinema hero, his personal magnetism and the fertility of his ideas all stamped him as a future Labour Prime Minister. Macdonald made him one of his committee of three with special responsibility for unemployment. He produced a programme. It was sensible, constructive and imaginative. His elders and betters turned it down. He resigned in protest. He made impressive speeches to the Parliamentary party and to Labour's annual conference. Party loyalty was too strong for him; his impatient autocratic temperament, his flair and his style were unacceptable to the old men of Labour, as the mercurial brilliance of Lloyd George and the impulsive energy of Churchill were to the Conservatives ... the career of Oswald Mosley, like the careers during this period of Lloyd George, Churchill, the economist J.M. Keynes, and the expert on tank warfare, Liddell Hart, all of whom were largely ignored, demonstrates that from 1922 to 1939 England's affairs were managed in accordance with Baldwin's view that the country was best served by ten men with second-class brains, on the grounds that ten with first-class brains had second-class characters."

Mosley's creation of the British Union of Fascists was as irrevocable a sundering of all old political ties as had been Caesar's crossing of the Rubicon.

We Marched with Mosley

The occasion when I first saw Mosley was at a public meeting in the Corn Hall, King's Lynn, on a cold, dull Saturday afternoon in the late autumn of 1933. Although by no means an ideal time for a political meeting, the large hall was filled.

He strode briskly on to an empty platform, thanked the people for coming in such numbers on a bleak afternoon, and then without further preamble began to state his case. He started by stressing the need for a modern movement to cope with the problems of the modern world.

It was his contention that everything in Britain had been changed almost out of recognition except the system of government, which while it had functioned well enough in the age of the stage-coach, was hopelessly out of date in the age of the wireless, the internal combustion engine, and the aeroplane. Science, he said, had outrun parliamentary democracy, which was so slow and cumbersome that it could handle no more than two major bills in any one parliamentary year. He called for a "steel creed for an iron age", and explained how the machinery of government needed to be overhauled drastically to bring it into line with the enormous scientific advances of the past century.

Turning to the men in charge of the existing machinery, he compared the elderly, woolly, wordy, pontifying Stanley Baldwin, with the tireless, thrusting, imaginative and inventive Mussolini, whom he described as a "young man in a hurry". He said mockingly of the British "democratic" leaders that they stood as much chance of competing with the Italian fascist leader as would an old plough horse entered for The Oaks of finishing first.

King's Lynn being the main market town for one of the most wholly arable farming areas in Britain, Mosley devoted most of his speech to agriculture. He told his audience, mostly farmers, farm workers and those whose livelihoods depended on the well-being of British agriculture, that their means of living were being threatened with near-extinction by the financiers of the City of London in favour of their vast financial stakes abroad, particularly in Argentina, that great producer of wheat and meat.

11

Introduction

He reminded his hearers that in addition to those imported foodstuffs from Argentina, and the butter, bacon, and eggs from Denmark, there were now milk from Holland, poultry from Poland, eggs from Turkey and China, and even dairy produce from Siberia all allowed in duty free, dumped, so that the usurers could reap their profits from the investments in those countries, while Britain's oldest industry which still employed the greatest number of people declined towards the point of disaster. The Government of Great Britain in its subservience to international finance thus denied the British farmer his birthright, which was the British market.

Mosley declared his policy for the reclamation of agriculture. It was simple; he would allow the British farmer first place in the British market, and the farmers of the British Empire second place, but foreigners none, except for those items that the two first comers could not produce.

He stated that in the present year, 1933, the latest returns showed that while Britain herself was producing annually £280 millions of foodstuffs, and importing £140 millions from the Dominions, she was at the same time importing foreign foodstuffs to the value of £220 millions. It was his intention to expand home production at the expense of the foreigner and of the foreign investor. In support of his plans he quoted expert farming opinion that British home agricultural production could be nearly doubled.

Turning to those of his audience who were merchants and shopkeepers, he reminded them that the agricultural community with prosperity restored and its purchasing power greatly increased would become insatiable customers. He declared that the only people likely to lose by the restoration of British farming would be the financiers, many of whom anyway were of alien origin, in the City of London.

At the close of the meeting several new members were enrolled; among them Dorothy, Viscountess Downe (née ffolkes), whose ancestral lands at Hillington adjoined those of the Royal estate of Sandringham. Lady Downe was not only a neighbour and former Lady-in-Waiting, but a personal friend of Queen Mary. She was something of a celebrity in Norfolk, as she managed her Hillington estate herself, efficiently, without the services of a land-agent. She dealt with her tenants personally, supervised her own forestry, and found time to sit on the Local Council. She was gallant and charming, best described perhaps as an "old darling"; one of Mosley's best recruits. Her courage, faith and loyalty were unflagging; they survived the persecution of the war years, and lasted until her death in 1958.

About the time that the Movement relinquished the famous Black House in Chelsea I was promoted to Assistant National Inspector. I was summoned to the new N.H.Q in Great Smith Street, Westminster to attend my first senior officers' conference, which was made ever memorable for me by the cold water douche thrown over us by Mosley when he announced calmly and evenly: "This struggle on which we are embarked may take us three, or it may take us thirty years, but..." and he went on to enumerate those qualities we must develop if we were to endure to make our mission succeed. As most of us had still been thinking in terms of a two or three year contest for power, this statement of down-to-earth sanity was a jolt, which was probably exactly what he intended.

I had seen Mosley on the platform many times, had known him relaxed and friendly across the supper table, and had seen him in affable conversation with followers and admirers after successful meetings and rallies; but this was the first time I had met him in council.

Now was revealed to me another facet of his character, which is his ability to probe directly to the root of most problems. At this, and at many other conferences, questions were laid before him which we, his lieutenants, had found insoluble. As each knotty point was presented, and some seemed inextricable teasers, he would reflect in silence for a moment, finger against cheek before pronouncing opinion. Then he would lean forward across the table looking directly at whoever had posed the question, and propound his remedy.

Introduction

To slow-thinking people like myself it was an exhibition of extraordinary mental ability and speed. In a flash the situation would have been clarified, made to appear basically simple, and an equally simple and obvious remedy prescribed.

In 1936 came the accession of Edward VIII and the Abdication Crisis. As the conflict of opinion and principle between ruler and elderly priests and politicians became more generally understood, the temper of the British people grew inflamed. There was a wide cleavage of opinion; the country was suddenly more bitterly divided than at any time within living memory.

The campaign initiated by Mosley was named from its slogan, "Stand by the King", which was printed on leaflets and painted on walls. There was little time in which to prepare a properly planned nationwide propaganda drive, as for once the government of Stanley Baldwin was moving with speed and determination, as it hustled its unhappy monarch and bewildered people through possibly the greatest constitutional crisis of its kind since William III landed at Torbay.

There was talk of forming a "King's Party", to consist of all those public men, newspaper owners, and organised sections of opinion such as British Union, opposed to the pressure being put by the Government on the King to get out; but nothing came of it. Time was too short. Had such an alliance been born, a strange array of associates would have presented itself. There would have been Oswald Mosley, Winston Churchill, Lloyd George, H.G. Wells, Bernard Shaw, Compton Mackenzie, and Lord Beaverbrook for once all in the same camp.

British Union brought out a news-sheet *Crisis*, which sold out as fast as it came off the printing machines, and was hawked on the streets by every available active member. I recall that my first customer was Sir Henry Wood on his way from a rehearsal of the Halle Orchestra. Every possible speaker whom the Movement could muster was pressed into service.

At the time of this heated turning-point in national affairs, I was responsible for the organisation of the Movement's public meetings held anywhere between Birmingham and Newcastle. The confidential reports on the scores and scores of meetings then held, came to my desk. I claim therefore to have been in better position than most to assess the public's reaction to the crisis in the Midlands and North.

The reports were extraordinarily unanimous. The middle-classes, particularly the lower middle-class, considered that Edward's proposed marriage was an affront to petit bourgeois respectability, and therefore he ought to go, some adding "and the sooner the better". Some conventional middle-class citizens were stupid enough to proclaim that they would not have a divorced woman for Queen, when it had never been seriously suggested that the King's prospective wife should share his throne.

This endorsed the conviction held by many members of British Union that the heritage of Praise-God Barebones and his Puritan troopers with their moral repression still lay heavily on middle-class England.

From these same reports it was obvious that the working-classes, except for those extremists who scorned everything even remotely connected with Royalty, were solidly for their King. Knowing that he understood and sympathised for them, in particular with those who had fallen on hard times, they wanted fervently to see him secure on his throne. They wished him also that happiness in his private life that could come only from a happy marriage.

To those of us who, irrespective of our political sympathies, loved our King and all that he represented, and who when we pledged his health in a loyal toast, meant it from the depths of our beings, those were agonising days.

When the news was released that the old gentlemen of the Establishment had succeeded in their vendetta, and that Edward VIII had consented to sign the "Instrument of Abdication" and to leave the Realm, the blow was sickening. I can recall tears of grief and mortification on more than one war-scarred face. At

Introduction

the same time I can recall equally clearly the genuine surprise of my own mother, an elderly middle-class lady of Liberal outlook, that anyone could get so emotionally worked up over "so selfish and undeserving Sovereign".

In contradistinction to the rumpuses attending some British Union demonstrations in London, those in the provinces were held at this time with little interference from the Left. During the first part of 1936 few reports of violent opposition came in.

Mosley continued to address great and enthusiastic meetings throughout England during most of 1937. In most places where he spoke he would put over the broad outline of his policy for Britain, then would show in greater detail how that particular locality in which he happened to be speaking would benefit from the application of that policy. At the same time he would expound his views on the burning topical questions, especially foreign affairs which Hitler, Mussolini and General Franco, not to mention Stalin, Blum and Eden had rendered particularly inflammable. Despite the fact that thousands of people had participated in great orderly rallies, and that thousands of persons, often tens of thousands of persons, had listened to him in safety and peace, a search of next day's national newspapers would reveal no mention of the event, what Mosley had said, or how his views had been received. This was the beginning of the campaign of silence. The protracted newspaper attack by defamation and misrepresentation had failed so obviously to halt Mosley's progress, that new tactics were introduced.

Henceforth the name of Mosley was taboo. He was not to be mentioned by the press or the B.B.C. except in some truly outstanding circumstance, such as a major riot or some bloody incident which could not be overlooked. This boycott did not apply to any adverse scandal likely to involve the Movement, however remotely; likewise any moral lapse on the part of some obscure member of British Union that could be made use of to blacken the reputation of the fascist Movement, would be seized upon with joy. It was only the credit page that was suppressed.

While it would have been contrary to the policy of those who directed the press to have published a headline or caption such as, "Mosley acclaimed in Accrington", it was considered ethical and desirable to print, "Fascist found guilty of being drunk while in charge of a bicycle", or, "Mosley-man admits smashing milk bottle in street."

It was strange how one was never able to read, "Conservative charged with loitering with intent," or, "Police find Liberal hiding in hen-house," or, "Labour-man accused of committing a nuisance."

Of all the hundreds of persons who passed through the Courts of Justice at this time and were sentenced, fined or imprisoned for their moral lapses and mistakes, apparently not one was connected with any of the three great established political parties. From the way the news was given out it appeared that only fascists fell foul of the law, and that all other miscreants had no political affiliations nor sympathies.

Despite the press boycott, British Union continued to grow; but there could be little doubt that its development was retarded by the silence that encompassed it. How much greater would have been its expansion had its activities been fairly publicised, it is impossible to conjecture. A number of local newspapers on the other hand, which were still independent, reported honestly on British Union activities in their areas, even when their editorial outlook was diametrically opposed to almost every aspect of British Union policy and philosophy.

'*The Eastern Daily Press*', a newspaper in the old Whig tradition, published in Norwich, gave the Movement and its affairs in the eastern counties such adequate coverage and fair reporting that Mosley deputed me when I was Assistant National Inspector, East Anglia, to call on the late Mr. Cozens-Hardy, who then occupied the editorial chair, to express on his behalf appreciation of the manner in which he maintained the best traditions of English journalism.

Introduction

The edict that Mosley and his Movement should be mentioned no more, was in after years to be instrumental in misleading a number of students of the history of the 1930s. Having searched exhaustively the newspaper files covering the years 1937 to 1940, and having found little of what they sought, Messrs Colin Cross, Benewick and other modern historians, not unnaturally assumed that there had been little or nothing to report, and that by this time British fascism must have been on the wane. This conclusion they propagated in their respective works. How wrong they were[1].

Although most early members of the BUF were not greatly interested in foreign affairs, these came to attract more and more public attention as the 1930s progressed and new "aggressor nations" tried to emulate the British and French in creating Empires of their own. We Blackshirts were mostly concerned with pressing domestic and Imperial problems for which we had devised what we believed were comprehensive and constructive solutions. We had no wish for our country to become involved in tiresome and probably intractable foreign quarrels. The last thing we wanted was a second shattering European war.

So when Italy invaded Abyssinia in 1935 and Britain's League of Nations Minister, Anthony Eden, seemed intent on involving Britain in war with Italy over this, we organised a great "Mind Britain's Business" campaign and held hundreds of packed meetings throughout Britain to protest against Eden's policies. These meetings – though seldom reported in the press – were well received and brought us many excellent recruits.

As international crisis succeeded international crisis and war loomed ever nearer our activities turned inevitably from domestic policy to campaigning for peace. Our "Peace Campaign" culminated in the (then) world's largest ever indoor meeting addressed by Mosley at Earl's Court in July 1939.

---

1   *Life of Britain Between the Wars*, pages 193-195, by L.S.E. Seaman, ed. By Peter Quennell, pub. B.T. Bacsford Ltd.

Following the great Earl's Court meeting, we held hundreds of other meetings for peace and our speakers could not have wished for more attentive and sympathetic hearings.

Despite greatly increased printings, *'Action'* was completely sold out each week, leaflets were taken eagerly from our distributors, and when Mosley spoke at Ridley Road, Hackney, it was to the largest audience ever addressed at a street meeting in Britain. On concluding his speech, he called on all present to march to Tottenham with him, in protest against war.

With Mosley in the lead, the immense crowd set out for Tottenham. More and more people joined in. The column grew longer and longer, until it extended for miles along the route. Traffic was brought to a standstill. Bystanders in their hundreds, having asked and been told what it was all about, joined in. It was a great flood of humanity, following the one man who might yet save them from war.

Mosley spoke again at Tottenham to packed thousands, who hung on to his words in forlorn hope. His parting sentence was: "Meet me again on Wednesday" – when he intended to hold another such mighty demonstration, this time in the West End.

On 1st September, 1939 the exact day for which Hitler had ordered his generals to prepare when he had learnt of Chamberlain's pledge to Poland, the German Army crossed the frontier of that luckless country. That same day, hard upon the news that the German Army was on the march, and following the Prime Minister's announcement of the details of the ultimatum he had instructed the British Ambassador to present to the German Government, Arthur Greenwood, on behalf of the Labour Party, and in Attlee's absence through illness, upbraided Chamberlain for having still left open one loophole through which Hitler might withdraw, if so minded. The possibility of avoiding war at this very last moment was too dreadful to be contemplated by the Party of yesterday's pacifists.

Introduction

The French Government was also giving concern to the advocates of war. Messieurs Daladier and Bonnet, respectively Prime Minister and Foreign Minister of France, were not rattling their sabres at all enthusiastically. Many members of their Government were so obviously reluctant to declare war that many British politicians feared that they were about to leave Britain in the lurch.

When Parliament met again the next day, 2nd September, Chamberlain shocked the Labourites by speaking again of the possibility of a conference between Britain, France and Poland on the one hand, and Germany and Italy on the other, in a final effort to avert cataclysm.

What the Parliamentary jingoes of left and right regarded as Chamberlain's almost pathological reluctance to draw the sword exasperated them to a condition of near-frenzy. It was Arthur Greenwood once more, urged on by the passionate cries of Leopold Amery, who said in effect that nothing less than war with Germany – and war at once – would satisfy the British House of Commons.

The House was all but solid for war. The few weak-kneed "Munichites", as those who had supported Chamberlain at the time of the Czech crisis were called, had been abashed into silence. Never did the Mother of Parliaments less reflect the views of the majority of the British people, nor more completely sell the true long-term interests of Britain than during the last weeks of summer in 1939.

Led by that fierce and reckless old boar, Churchill, the Gadarene swine were not only running pell-mell towards the cliff top, but were pushing their feeble herdsman along in front of them.

Studying the memoirs of the politicians who had participated in those debates, or were present during those scenes, one is left with the conviction that they were not only ignoring the true sentiments of the nation, but had allowed themselves to be overcome by a mass emotionalism, a psychological condition verging on hysteria, which was confined almost entirely to members of the Establishment and precluded clear thought or reasoning.

"Suicidal military impulses under the pressure of emotion," is how Liddell Hart described the reactions of the politicians at Westminster. The United States ambassador, Joseph Kennedy, viewing the opening acts of the great unfolding tragedy, pronounced the British parliamentarians to be "punch drunk."

On the next day, 3rd September 1939 at 11a.m., Britain declared war on Germany in fulfilment of that fatal note penned by a Prime Minister of whom it had once been said that he might have made "a good Lord Mayor of Birmingham in a lean year".

It is still fashionable to vilify the name of Neville Chamberlain as that of the man responsible for the avoidance of war at the time of the Munich Agreement. It would be much more just to remember him as the Prime Minister who tried desperately to save peace but who lacked the toughness of character necessary to do so.

1 - The "New Idea" is Born in Britain

"After a long, bitter process Mosley had discovered that the rules of the political game and the increasing conservatism of British Government militated against effective action from within the political structure. Convinced of the rightness of his policies and fearful of the consequences of economic decline, Mosley became attracted to the forms of activist mass politics in an attempt to rejuvenate society. British fascism was born of the failure of economic conservatism to check the rapid decline of Britain in the inter-war years." - *Fascism in Britain* by R. Thurlow, p.36.

The rout of the New Party at the General Election of 1931 convinced Sir Oswald Mosley that no matter how favourably new political concepts might be received, it was useless to attempt to put them across with an old-fashioned type of party-political machine in the face of the implacable hostility of the established parties with their smooth-running constituency organisations, taking their lead from central offices replete with long experience, and with enormous financial resources to draw on. He saw that new methods were essential to win elections, if the New Idea was ever to come to fruition. What dramatic means could he use to attract popular attention?

For some time Oswald Mosley had been watching the movements on the Continent. By 1932, Mussolini had held power in Italy for ten years – in which time he had achieved so remarkable transformation of every aspect of National life, both material and metaphysical, that he was attracting more and more admirers outside his own country. In Britain leading politicians and newspapers of the Right were lavish in their praise of fascist Italy and its dynamic leader.

The British Left however, never ceased from railing against

Mussolini, and the Liberals continued to deprecate him; but almost all the Right lauded his achievements, and considered that Europe was indebted to him for his victory over communism.

Where the advance of the National Socialist Party in Germany was concerned, persons and newspapers of the Right in Britain were more guarded in their pronouncements; but those who disapproved condemned Hitler and all his works more bitterly than they denounced Mussolini.

There were several reasons for this continued hostility to Germany. First, the minds of many had been so conditioned by wartime propaganda that, unable to throw off prejudices fostered seventeen and eighteen years earlier, they still regarded the German people as a race of delinquents. Secondly, the miserable, incompetent, and now obviously doomed Weimar Republic seemed to be particularly beloved by British Labourites; lastly, of course the growing anti-Semitism in Germany got a bad press in tolerant Britain.

The re-emergence of a strong and flourishing Germany seemed to those people with minds already inflamed against that country, to presage another war. Blinded by their prejudice they failed to see that such a Germany could be Europe's best bastion against Russian communism; instead they seemed bent on exciting fresh exacerbations.

Nevertheless there were in Britain prominent men, including parliamentarians, who welcomed Hitler as another saviour of western civilisation from the barbarities of bolshevism.

Winston Churchill wrote of Hitler: "If our Country were defeated, I hope that we should find a champion as indomitable to restore our courage, and lead us back to our place among the nations."

Lloyd George remarked on the happiness and contentment of the Germans under Hitler, and said of him: "Hitler is one of the greatest of the many great men I have ever met."

Therefore Mosley was in good company when he evinced admiration for the Duce and Führer, the one already in power, the other on his way to it.

He had much in common with them. All three had been initiated into that great brotherhood, the front-line fighters of the First World War. They had endured the mud and filth of the trenches, the tornados of artillery fire, the sweeping fusillades of machine-gun fire, the gas attacks, and the sickening waiting for zero hour. They had each experienced bloody wounds, and had seen soaring courage and superb endurance, had known glorious comradeship and had come to realise the illimitable potentialities of the human spirit. These experiences they held in common; also they shared a determination that the ideals that had upheld them through four and a half years of bloody sacrifice should not be in vain.

It was a German historian who wrote:[2] "The mute camaraderie of the trenches and the inconceivable stupidity of the slaughter broke down the barriers between the nations which had formerly seemed impassable........ "Reactionary [3] veteran groups in all the European countries in the 1930s had much more in common with each other than with the Left Wing pacifists or the socialists in their own lands."

The New idea in its varying forms, each adapted to the land where it originated, conceived first in the mud and blood and brotherhood of the front lines, was now being born out of the hopeless misery, squalor, and chaos of the post-war slump, as the worsening recession rolled round the globe.

From my many discussions with him from 1933 on, I realised that Mosley's fallen brothers-in-arms were always close to him in spirit. One does not need much imagination to grasp the

---

2   *Treason in the Twentieth Century*, by Margret Boveri, p.65, pub. Macdonald.

3   The New Idea could not accurately be described as 'reactionary', as its social
    outlook was as progressive as anything that emanated from the Left; it was in its
    ultra-patriotism, and in its recognition of the bonds of family and race, that it differed
    entirely from the unpractical internationalism of the doctrinaire socialists.

truth that it was the memory of them that drove him on to yet further effort, pain, and sacrifice for "the land for whose dear sake they bled."

Ever before his eyes were those memories of the immolation of his own generation, a generation of which more than one million Britons had died in battle, or from wounds received in battle. As it was the best who volunteered for the most dangerous missions, the best who led in attack, or covered the rear in withdrawal, it was the cream of the young manhood of the Empire which had perished.

It had been for the sake of the war generation, his old comrades in arms, and the ideals which had sustained them, that Mosley first entered Parliament. Ten years later, with the same mission beckoning him he wrote: "We of the War generation are marching on; and we shall march on until our end is achieved and our sacrifice atoned."

Birth, upbringing, and wealth combined with looks, charm, and wit entitled Mosley to "walk with Kings", and to spend the remainder of his days in the peaceful enjoyment of his possessions and of those country pursuits which he loves; but sense of duty unfulfilled, urged him on. Most men would have felt that the collapse of the New Party, following his irremediable breach with both the great established political parties, marked the end of his political career; but Mosley was made of more endurable stuff. Instead of announcing his abdication, he acknowledged temporary defeat, withdrew his forces, and while planning his next assault on the Establishment he rested and regrouped them.

During 1932 Mosley visited Italy, and returned impressed with the strides in material betterment and spiritual outlook being made there. Of the two movements, that in Italy was then the more impressive, as it was well established and functioning smoothly and efficiently; whereas how Adolf Hitler, and his National Socialists would operate when in power, was still a matter of conjecture.

Mosley shares the rostrum with Mussolini in Milan 1932

Beyond all other considerations, however, the tidiness and proven workability of the Corporate State appealed to him as the system of government best suited for the efficient working of a modern industrial nation. It favoured no one, and oppressed no one, but kept a fair balance between the three main sections of the community, the workers, the owners and management, and the consumers.

Mosley was influenced doubtless by the knowledge that the ties between Britain and Italy are ancient ones. Out of Italy into Britain had first come Roman government and law and order, next Augustine and the Christian missionaries, and later the Renaissance, and throughout the centuries there had been the traffic of commerce and of culture.

The spiritual regeneration of the young Germans who followed Adolf Hitler won his firm approval; but some aspects of National Socialism, such as the rising tide of hatred against the Jews on the one hand, and the revival of the worship of Thor and Odin and the old Teutonic gods, attempted by von Ludendorff and Baldur von Schirach, on the other hand, evoked no response in him.

1 - The "New Idea" is Born in Britain

The Jewish question is discussed elsewhere in these pages; but that "neo-paganism" about which the English press was to wax so hot, made little impact on the German people outside or inside the National Socialist movement.

I remember Mosley's reply to an anxious enquirer who wanted to know if the neo-pagans were becoming a threat to Christianity. He answered that supposing Lord Kitchener had been spared to live to an advanced age, and had then become a little odd in the head, and had taken to capering round Stonehenge at the summer solstice, clad in a long white night-gown, would he consider him a serious threat to the Church of England? The questioner subsided chuckling at the ridiculous picture conjured up.

On his return from the Continent, Mosley wrote of the Italian Fascist movement: "It is as remote from a stand-pat conservatism as it is from the woolly headed socialism, or the destructive communism which it overthrew... this fascism challenges alike the Right and the Left of old-world politics. It has produced not only a new system of government but also a new type of man, who differs from the politicians of the world as men from another planet."

Thirteen years' experience of parliamentary democracy at first hand, plus what he had recently seen for himself on the Continent, convinced Mosley that if Britain was to keep her place and leadership in the modern world, she too must have her version of the modern movement, and that it had devolved clearly on him to create one.

Since the early 1920s there had been several organisations with patriotic intentions but of varying lack of impact, styling themselves "fascist". Most of these groups had petered out, with the exception of the "Imperial Fascist League" which, conducted by some perfectly sincere people, seemed to have a policy neither broader nor deeper than to blame the Jews for all that was wrong. They saw the hand of the Jews in everything they did not like, just as they professed to be able to trace Jewish blood in anyone they did not like; in common with most dedicated anti-

Semites they had but one topic of conversation, and were deadly bores. They disparaged persons who did not subscribe to their own kinky views; Mosley they denounced as a "kosher fascist", implying that because he had not declared war on Jewry then, automatically, he must be aligned with what they recognised as their arch-enemy.

An organisation of rather more consequence was the "British Fascists", which had started as the "British Fascisti" in 1923, and in 1932 still had a nominal roll of several thousands distributed throughout Britain. In character it was intensely patriotic, but entirely Right Wing.

Neil Francis Hawkins, a founder member and one of the six directors of the British Fascists, had heard Mosley speak more than once, and had found himself in agreement; so when Dr. Forgan of the New Party met him on behalf of Mosley, and suggested some sort of rapprochement between the two organisations, he was prepared to listen. He met Mosley, and discovered such an identity of interest that he undertook to propose to the Council of the British Fascists that there should be a merger.

The Council consisted of six, three men and three women. The men were for amalgamation, the women for staying out. This was complete impasse. Next, the three men on the Council resigned and went over to Mosley, taking a large following with them.

The new organisation formed by the merging of the stouter-hearted remnants of the New Party with the dissidents from the British Fascists, calling itself the British Union of Fascists, but soon known as the "B.U.F.", was launched on 3rd October, 1932, with headquarters at Great George Street, Westminster.

On that same day appeared Mosley's book, 'The Greater Britain', in which he had written in the introduction:

"We seek to organise the Modern Movement in this country by British methods in a form which is suitable to and characteristic

1 - The "New Idea" is Born in Britain

of Great Britain. We are essentially a national movement, and if our policy could be summarised in two words, they would be 'Britain First'.

"Nevertheless the Modern Movement is by no means combined to Great Britain; it comes to all the great countries as their hour of crisis approaches, and in each country it naturally assumes a form and character suited to that nation. As a world-wide movement, it had come to be known as Fascism, and it is therefore right to use that name."

In the 'The Greater Britain', Mosley declared his plans for the future government of Britain, drawn as they had been from the stored accumulation of his thirteen years political experience, which had also been thirteen years of frustration and disillusion.

In the opening paragraph of Chapter One, he had written:

"In the ranks of Conservatism there are many who are attracted by the Party's tradition of loyalty, order and stability – but who are none the less repelled by its lethargy and stagnation. In the ranks of Labour there are many who follow the Party's humane ideals, and are attracted by its vital urge to remedy social and economic evils – but who are, none the less, repelled by its endless and inconclusive debates, its cowardice, its lack of leadership and decision. These elements comprise the best of both Parties: and to both Fascism appeals."

Further on in the book he emphasised that "poverty in the midst of plenty" was the outstanding problem of the age, and that this "plenty" was the result of overproduction through scientific progress in the artifices of manufacture, then called "rationalisation", now known as "automation". Man's mechanical inventiveness had outstripped his political ingenuity, hence the chronic unemployment of between one and a half million and three million workers in Britain.

He contended that in a world of rapid change only the machinery of government remained unchanged, and was now exactly one

30

hundred years behind the times. The leading politicians of the old Parties were prepared to carry on, unaware of any change having taken place.

In his book *Greater Britain*, Oswald Mosley wrote that he intended to render Britain and her Empire immune to the recurrent economic booms and slumps that, while favourable to the financiers, were so disturbing to trade and industry. He postulated that the British Empire could produce every raw material and commodity needful to modern man, and in consequence its peoples could live within an economy "insulated" from the recurrent shocks and scares of the rest of the world dominated by Wall Street and the City of London.

Elsewhere in the book he stated his intention to introduce the Corporate system of government as speedier and vastly more efficient than the democratic way, where Government was eternally hindered in its business by an opposition created for that very purpose.

Now at last Mosley had thrown down the gauntlet to the Establishment. He exposed and challenged not only the philosophy and structure of parliamentary democracy, but the premise on which it was built. He repudiated the entire edifice.

The objects of the British Union of Fascists were printed on the reverse side of the membership card issued to each new member. They were:

- To win power for Fascism and thereby establish in Great Britain the Corporate State which shall secure that –

- All shall serve the State and none the faction;

- All shall work and thus enrich their country and themselves;

- Opportunity shall be given to all, but privilege to none;

- Great position shall be conceded only to those of great talent;

- Reward shall be accorded only to service;

- Poverty shall be abolished by the power of modern science released within the organised state;

- "The barriers of class shall be destroyed and the energies of every citizen devoted to the service of the British nation, which by the effort and sacrifices of our fathers has existed gloriously for centuries before this transient generation, and which by our own exertions shall be raised to its highest destiny – the Greater Britain of Fascism."

This became the printed testimony of thousands of men and women who were to join the Movement in the next few years.

The newspapers gave considerable space to Mosley's act of unequivocal political defiance. Due to this publicity, and despite the accompanying journalistic sneers, there was a flood of enquiries, and thousands of applications to join. Those who sought to enrol were mainly ex-Service and younger men who had lost all confidence in the "Old Gang", as the leaders of the established Parties were now derisively known.

After he had assessed the reasons for the rout of the New Party, and had convinced himself of the contribution to its ruin from the softness, weakness, and even cowardice of his young intellectuals, Mosley allowed himself to become guilty of shocking heresy, when metaphorically turning his back on his weak-kneed lieutenants, he announced: "I have finished with the people who think; henceforth I shall go to the people who feel."

To these people, bewildered, disillusioned, and angry, Mosley's proclaimed contempt for the whole political set-up, echoed their own bitter and frustrated feelings. These were the men who now turned to Mosley, and placing hope and faith in him, gave him their utmost devotion. To his service hundreds of them were prepared to give their time, energies, and resources, and if called on, their lives.

It is not for the men and women of the post-Second War decades with their full employment and their full bellies, and in many cases the stagnant souls that are the natural concomitants of "never had it so good", to sneer at this fervid hero worship by men of another generation who had suffered greatly, and who then found a man of their own generation and outlook to lead them.

Those recruits to the British Union of Fascists felt that here was the man of destiny who would lead them and Britain on a great adventure to a new grandeur of spirit and nationhood.

The launching of the BUF caused even more public interest than the inauguration of the New Party. A few days after the opening ceremony in Great George Street, Londoners saw a parade of men, mostly young and well set-up, in black shirts – actually close-fitting fencing jackets of strong black corded silk – marching in columns of three.

The bearing of the marchers and their strikingly simple uniform compelled attention. In those very early days of the Movement, grey flannel trousers were worn with the black shirts; later, black trousers were substituted, and wide leather belts with large square chromium buckles replaced the original black silk cummerbunds. Grey shirts were worn by new recruits and later by members of the Youth Movement.

It was a smart and becoming uniform, but becoming only to smart figures. It was not at all kind to those to whom the years had added weight and a bulging belt-line. The jeer of "foreign symbol" at our badge – the fasces on a Union Jack – was both unfair and ignorant; particularly as it emanated mostly from those not usually concerned about matters of patriotic prestige.

The uniform drew derision, mainly from the Left, where anything savouring of militarism is ever to be denounced. Like the badge it is stigmatised as something alien and new to Britain; but, as Mosley retorted, signs, emblems and peculiarities of dress are as old as the story of English politics. Nor was it long before the followers of "Jimmy" Maxton and Sir Stafford Cripps were assuming red shirts, and disciples of Major Douglas of the Social Credit School parading the streets in blouses of green.

British political emblems, past and present, range from the red and white roses of the Houses of Lancaster and York, and the "Five Wounds of Christ" of the Pilgrimage of Grace, to the Red Flag of the Revolutionary Left, the red ties of old-fashioned radicals, down to the modest little primrose worn once a year by good Tories. The cropped heads and steeple-crown hats of the Puritans were as much a political symbol as any black shirt.

The uniform served other purposes besides inviting the ire of the opposition. It was a social leveller. All, being dressed alike, looked alike. In the service of the Movement there was little to distinguish the unemployed labourer from the comparatively well-paid artisan, or the impecunious clerk from the successful young business or professional man, or any of them from the jobless ex-officers. Partly due to the uniform, but also to the community effort and a feeling of consecration to a common cause, there grew a spirit of brotherhood and of dedication that the years couldn't dim.

When a Blackshirt put on a uniform, he did so as a declaration of his political faith. He wore it as a gesture of defiance to all those in and out of politics who were letting Britain down, and at the same time as the symbol of the regeneration of his own love and confidence in his native land. There may have been a few exhibitionists; but the overwhelming majority of those who donned the uniform did not assume it lightly but in a spirit of service and dedication.

As active Blackshirts of all ranks wore uniform, and officers their appropriate badges of rank, the uniform helped to maintain that discipline which was an important feature of the Movement, and to which recruits on joining had voluntarily undertaken to submit. Officers, irrespective of their social status outside, were saluted, obeyed and treated with respect. Naturally the better the officer, the better the discipline he exercised over his subordinates. The BUF esprit was the antithesis of the New Party, with its babbling, argumentative and captious personnel. The black shirt also had an invaluable use; it immediately distinguished friend from foe in a scrimmage.

Each new member bought his own outfit. A regulation black shirt from National Headquarter stores cost 7s. 6d., which at that time represented a considerable outlay for an unemployed family man who, according to John Scanlon, would have been drawing from the dole 18s. weekly for himself and 2s. for each child. [4] It was possible for payment to be made by instalments; but even then it remained a financial sacrifice. Yet every Blackshirt was at pains to be properly equipped and a credit to his formation.

Admission was open to all British subjects, irrespective of creed, race or colour. A candidate for enrolment had only to state that he or she was a British subject, loyal to the King and Empire, and that if accepted would obey the rules and leadership. A member in employment undertook to pay a monthly subscription of one shilling; an unemployed man or pensioner paid 4d.

As there was no quarrel with Jewry, there were Jewish members. Kid Lewis, the boxer, who was a Jew, was one of the earliest Blackshirts. I met him once, and then briefly, when I received the impression of a pleasant and robust personality. There was another tough and genial Jew I remember who gave the BUF sterling service in Manchester. He had been a pre-1914 cavalry trooper in the Regular Army and had served through the First War with credit. The anti-Semitism of the German Movement was then regarded with distaste by most British fascists, and our disagreement with it was expressed in our early literature. It was felt that it was a purely German manifestation, and no business of ours; nor did we let it influence our own tolerant attitude to British Jews.

---

4   *The Age of Illusion*, by Ronald Blythe, p.151, pub. Hamish Hamilton: "... during 1932 the dole for a married couple and their three children was 29s. 3d., but this was liable to be subjected to the Means Test."

Despite newspaper attack and denigration, the New Movement was soon well under way and expanding rapidly. Recruits poured in, and in the first few months the BUF opened branches almost daily. Soon a network of formations covered England, with offshoots in Scotland. As was to be expected, many of the top-ranking officers of the BUF, at its inception and in the first two years, were those who had held responsible positions in either the New Party or the British Fascists.

First among the officials gathered around Mosley in those early days was Dr. Forgan, who had followed him from the Labour Party to the New Party, thence to the BUF. At heart the Doctor remained a democrat, and was getting more and more out of his depth in this fascist movement with its authority and discipline, and administrative methods more akin to those of an army orderly room than to a political office. He was a kind man who lacked judgement of character; some of the more unfortunate staff appointments were rumoured to be attributable to him. It was said by the humorists that if someone minus a seat to his pants and soles to his shoes, but with a load of debt, several convictions for fraud, an abandoned wife and children who had been substituted by someone else's wife, could manage to get past the orderlies into Dr. Forgan's office, he would emerge again in due course with a senior staff appointment and, for those days, a substantial salary. Push, cheek and a persuasive tongue could impose themselves on the kind-hearted doctor only too easily. In due course he left the BUF for a more congenial occupation.

The next senior official was Neil Francis Hawkins, "F.H." to all who knew him, who had brought over a large section of the British Fascists. He was a short, thick-set, florid-faced man, courageous, competent and incorruptible; he could reduce a close friend or promote a man he personally disliked with equal aplomb.

For my part I found him difficult to get to know, although he always treated me with consideration. I was several times guest at his table, and I stayed at his Hampstead flat where, as a bachelor, he lived with his sister; but I never could feel that I had "got through" to him. Our mutual reserve might have been due to our different backgrounds, although we both originated from what I suppose must have been much the same social grade. He was an urban type, belonging to the world of city offices and boardrooms; whereas I had experienced a restless life, much of it in distant and remote places, at times completely isolated.

In a comparatively short space of time F.H. became Director General. He was entirely devoted to the Movement, and spent between ten and twelve hours daily at his office, while most weekends were given to participation in the outside activities of the Movement. He expected his subordinates to give an almost equal amount of time to their duties; those who went home after a mere eight or nine hours at their desks were labelled "clock-watchers", and denounced as unworthy of the cause they served. As many of them had wives and young families, domestic unhappiness too frequently arose. "Wife trouble" became one of the recognised occupational hazards of British fascism. A year or two later when a former Indian Army captain, Bryan Donovan, was appointed Assistant Director General (Administration), conditions for the staff workers were humanised almost immediately. I, for one, was told that I must spend at least one evening with my family. There had been no suggestion of "wife-trouble" in my home; but my wife had been remarking that since I had become a full-time fascist officer, she was not getting a super-abundance of fun out of married life.

Nevertheless, Donovan had the reputation throughout the Movement of being an uncompromising martinet. Many felt that his sense of discipline and administrative methods were not merely military but too taut, inflexible and exacting. Personally I had no objection to his precise way of issuing orders, but others of the kind who find restraint of any sort irksome clashed all too often with the Assistant Director General, and then ruefully would find themselves deprived of rank or even with membership suspended. Donovan had first shown his abilities as the District Officer of Uxbridge, then as Commanding Officer of London Command, which he made a model of its kind. He was an outstandingly capable organiser.

1 - The "New Idea" is Born in Britain

The Assistant Director General (Organisation) was another retired regular soldier, Lieut-Colonel C.S. Sharpe, who had served in Europe and Africa. He was a quiet, reserved, almost self-effacing man immersed in his routine work, who left his desk only to eat, or to return to his Richmond home. He issued terse, pointed memoranda to officers who were slow in making their returns, and in consequence was held by most in considerable awe. He never really merited the title of "His Grey Eminence" bestowed on him, unknown to himself, by those who went in fear of his rockets.

White-haired old F.K. Box, who had been Chief Election Agent for the New Party, served the BUF in similar capacity, with Bill Risdon also from the New Party, and Captain Atherley and T.L. Butler, both newly recruited to the BUF, as his assistants.

Eric Hamilton Piercy, who was also an Inspector of Special Constabulary, and had organised stewarding at the great meetings of the New Party, especially where roughhouses had been anticipated, took charge of the "I Squad" forty tough, athletic and disciplined young men, selected and trained in boxing and judo to stand up to the most vicious Red troublemakers. It was accounted a privilege to be admitted to this squad, whose members, to distinguish themselves from ordinary Blackshirts, wore black breeches and top-boots in place of the usual black trousers and shoes.

A senior officer well-known throughout the Movement was "Dick" Plathen, a former member of the Consular Service, who in 1932-34 organised all major meetings for Mosley. He was famed for his uncompromising loyalty and devotion; anecdotes concerning Plathen became legendary. Once, when a group of officials were sprucing themselves up before going on duty at an important rally, one of them noticed that Dick was industriously polishing the soles of his boots. Guffawing loudly the man drew attention to what he considered an extravagance of zeal. There were hoots of laughter, none of it ill-natured; but the object of their derision drew himself up, passed a frosty eye over his colleagues, then in his Scots' voice replied witheringly: "I am going to meet the Leader-r-r!"

Mosley and Eric Hamilton Piercy with the famous "I" Squad,
Hyde Park, London. 1934.

Mosley's Chief of Staff in those early days was Ian Dundas, who had been an officer in the Royal Navy, was the son of an Admiral and directly descended from the famous sailor of that name, "Archie" Findlay, another Scot, from assistant to Dundas became Director of Public Relations. Others on the staff included several members of the Aitken family including Commander Aitken, R.N. (Retd), and Marjorie Aitken, a trim lithe girl noted for fearlessness and the physical ease with which, thanks to her judo, she could eject truculent Reds of either sex from meetings they had been disrupting. The son of Squadron Leader Lionel Aitken, was a member of the "I" Squad and was killed in action in July, 1941. Captain Robert Gordon-Canning, M.C., soldier (10th Hussars) and poet, and educated at Eton and Sandhurst, was appointed BUF expert on foreign affairs; later he became foreign editor of 'Action'. He was one of those romantic and adventurous Englishmen who were strongly pro-Arab in sentiment. So ardently did he believe in the Arab cause that he offered his services to Abd El Krim in his revolt in the Atlas, and eventually came to serve on the staff of the Riff leader. There was a nice, worthy old soldier, Colonel Crocker of the Essex Regiment, who worked at National Headquarters for a year or two, but later went to Africa as a missionary.

George Sutton, who had served throughout the war with the Royal Field Artillery, and had been Mosley's secretary through his political career, beginning in Harrow to the end of the New Party, retained his secretarial duties, but was later appointed Director of Research.

The first Chief Woman Organiser was Lady Makgill, (nee Esther Bromley), an attractive redhead; but she did not last long. Maude, Lady Mosley, Oswald Mosley's mother, took over from her, had her office at NHQ, entered fully into the life of the Movement, and was popular with the girls; she kept a motherly eye on some of the less staid and prettier ones, and warned them of the hungry looks being cast in their direction by appreciative male Blackshirts. With the rapid expansion of the BUF, she found eventually that her entire time was being taken up by her work. She was having little or no private life, and as she was no longer young she was glad to be able to hand over her responsibilities to Ann Brock-Griggs.

Mrs Brock-Griggs, an architect's wife, was a devoted Blackshirt like her husband. A handsome young woman, she administered her side of the Movement with competence and complete self-assurance. Whenever I dropped into her office I gathered an impression of practised charm, great capability, a swift and decisive mind, together with pride and ambition, all enhanced by a well-bred elegance.

2 - BUF Organisation and Personnel

The BUF was organised on a Constituency basis with the objective of contesting for power at the polls, and not, as one newspaper was to allege, by shooting its way into office. Therefore, like the old political parties, the British Union of Fascists was constituted so that each branch or "District", as it was termed officially, conformed to a Parliamentary Division.

In charge of each district was a senior official known as the "District Officer", a local unpaid volunteer appointed by National Headquarters. The first duty of every D.O. was to expand and organise his District, so that one day the constituency which it embraced would return to Parliament a representative of the New Movement. He had his lieutenants, the Assistant District Officers (A.D.O.s), each in charge of his respective department – "Propaganda", "Transport", and "Sales" of the party's newspaper and other publications from which revenue could accrue.

Other senior officials were the District Treasurer (D.T.) and the Women's District Officer (W.D.O.). As in the army, officials were usually designated by the initial letters of their ranks or appointment.

Responsible also to each D.O. were his Section Leaders, and subordinate to them were the Unit Leaders. A Section Leader would be in charge of a considerable part of a District; there might be three or four of them under one D.O. depending on the size of the constituency and the progress made in it. The Unit Leaders were each in charge of a ward or polling district in an urban district, or of a country parish or village in a rural area. The unit was intended to consist of not less than four or five active Blackshirts, nor more than eight or nine; but there was considerable latitude as to the actual numbers in any one formation.

41

Senior to the D.O.s were the District Inspectors (D.I.s) with authority over three or four adjoining districts. Senior to them were the County Inspectors who co-ordinated the activities of all districts within the average size shire, or two or three counties combined in more sparsely populated areas.

There were also the County Propaganda Officers (C.P.O.s) each with his team of officially registered and graded public speakers. They arranged with their D.O.s to hold public meetings in village halls and schoolrooms, at local "spouters' corners", in side streets, outside factory gates during the lunch-hour, and to the long tragic queues of the unemployed outside the Labour Exchanges. The D.O.s provided the men to steward the indoor meetings and to support the open-air speakers.

All areas held classes for speakers, where they were taught the elements of public speaking and, more necessary still, were instructed in policy. It was because of some startling heresies from BUF platforms, wild assertions, promises incapable of fulfilment, and pet theories put across as official policy, that made it essential for the Movement to approve all speakers.

At the Speakers' Schools, would-be orators were properly instructed, disciplined, and when passed were granted their licences. They were also graded and indexed according to their suitability. For instance, it would not have done to have turned loose Ramsbottom, genuine fellow that he was, with his grating voice, thick accent and such pearls of speech as the "parturition of Palestine", the Jew versus Arab problem then being in the news, on to some polite suburban cultural association. It would have been equally unfruitful to have sent Dalgleish, with his almost painful refinement and precious manners, to address Liverpool Dockers during their dinner-hour. While he could have captivated the earnest spinsters of both sexes of the cultural association, Ramsbottom's raucous plea for more bread and butter would have been understood outside the dock-gates.

All these officers, speakers and ordinary members were unpaid volunteers, who devoted anything from one to seven nights a week to the Movement, often their full weekends as well. Unemployed members gave even more of their time. They neither expected nor received enumeration for their services, except a refund of travelling expenses when on duty. If this took them far from home, they did occasionally have a meal at BUF expense.

Besides the paid permanent staff at NHQ, there was a limited number of outside staff officers. At one time there must have been about a dozen full-time paid organisers, whose task was to create formations where none previously existed. If one of them by his own drive and personality succeeded in building up round himself a considerable following, but at the same time failed to discover and train a local natural-born leader, he had largely fallen down on his job. The emergence of the right local leadership was the only true key to success. All too often, after months of effort, the Organiser from NHQ, having apparently built a sound District, would be posted elsewhere to repeat his performance, and the formation would promptly collapse.

"Danny" Gill, "Rimbo" Rimmington, Fryer who was also a master mariner, Milligan who had been a tea-planter, Miller another sailor, and Hillman, were hardworking and conscientious Organising Officers who achieved results after contending with every imaginable difficulty; but others (who shall be nameless) had short reigns, long remembered for debt and scandal.

At one time there was a considerable panel of paid Staff Speakers, some of whom, like Douglas Revett, were sterling characters as well as accomplished orators. As eloquence and sincerity do not necessarily coincide, several were little more than glib adventurers, to whom speaking for the Movement represented paid employment when jobs were scarce. Orators of this kind would have spoken equally convincingly in aid of "Moral Re-Armament", "Peace Pledge Union", "Milk for Spain", or Lord Beaverbrook's "Empire Crusade", as they did for Mosley's "Greater Britain".

When a sufficient number of volunteers from Districts had been passed out from the Speakers' Schools, the entire corps of staff speakers was disbanded. "Struck down" was the current term in BUF jargon; the Movement having already adopted a phraseology of its own. Those who were genuine still adhered to the party, giving their services free; but others departed gnashing their teeth, and foretelling the imminent doom of the cause they had until yesterday so persuasively proclaimed.

Liaison between BUF Districts and NHQ was furnished by the National Inspectors and the Assistant National Inspectors, eight or nine in number, each responsible for a considerable geographical area. Thus while an A.N.I. covered the relatively unimportant region of east Anglia, one N.I. centred on Birmingham was responsible not only for that city and the surrounding Black Country but for the entire Midlands. The counties of Lancashire and Yorkshire were each national inspectorates; while another N.I. covered Northumbria. There were, of course, others in the South and West.

The Inspectors were mostly former commissioned officers of the three fighting Services, and were a little older than the majority of members. Three of them, Captains Bentinck-Budd, Priestly and Abbott, had each been partially incapacitated by extremely severe war wounds, but which did not prevent them from performing first-rate work. Captains Armstrong, Vincent Keens, John Hone, Dunkerton, Wright, Vincent Collier, also Peter Symes, and Peter Whittam, were all ex-officers.

John Sant, John Garnett and I (promoted to the Inspectorate in 1935) had been under military age during the war. Except for us, the Inspectors when assembled on ceremonial occasions could put up an imposing "fruit salad" of military decorations.

After this long period of time I cannot call to mind more than a few of the antecedents of my colleagues, most of whom had led eventful lives. It was Charles Bentinck-Budd whom I knew best, and with whose story I am best acquainted.

When the First World War broke out Bentinck-Budd had been in camp on Salisbury Plain with his school's contingent of the Officers' Training Corps. Immediately, he broke out of camp and proceeded to London, where he presented himself at an Army Recruiting Office. And so it was that within a couple of days of the Declaration of war, and after a little mild perjury concerning the date of his birth, Budd became a trooper in the 5th Dragoon Guards.

He was sent out to the Western Front early in 1915. During the Second Battle of Ypres in the spring, his conduct was so outstanding that he was commissioned in the field at the age of seventeen by the Commander-in-Chief in person. After a short course at Saint Omer, he was gazetted to the 2nd Battalion, the Buffs. That same autumn he was seriously wounded in the head, and repatriated. After prolonged hospital treatment in England, he was invalided out of the Service and put on half-pay.

Inactivity being quite unacceptable, he went to Liverpool and signed on board a merchant ship, as a seaman before the mast, and in due course he found himself in Boston, Massachusetts, where he jumped ship and enlisted in the American Army, exactly as he had set out to do. After some initial training at Fort Slocum, New York, where with the adaptability of youth he soon adjusted to the new life, quickly picking up the drill and equipment. On passing out he was posted to the 2nd Regiment of Engineers, stationed at El Paso, Texas.

Here in time the extent of his incapacity from wounds was discovered, and he was mortified that he could not be sent overseas. He was, however, offered a place at West Point, with the object of becoming a commissioned officer and instructor to the vast United States conscript army then being raised. It was active service again that Budd wanted; so he turned down the offer, took his discharge, and made his way to Galveston, Texas, where he hoped to take ship to Archangel, so as to join the White Russian forces in their struggle with the Bolsheviks. But no vessel bound for northern Russia came in. The British Consul, hearing that a penniless Englishman was on the beach, found him a job censoring Royal Navy mail from the West Indies Station, then put him aboard a homeward-bound British merchantman, where once again he worked his passage.

Oswald Mosley inspects a parade of BUF cadets

On arrival in Liverpool he was arrested as a spy from South America, and locked up. So certain were the security and counter-espionage people that he was an enemy agent, that they accused him of being a number rather than a name. However, the War Office was able to extricate him from that mess, and to restore him to his friends and relations, and even let him wangle his way back into the army and an overseas posting.

John Hone, who had been in France with the first Territorial troops to see active service, was eye-witness of a charge by French cuirassiers, wearing their plumed helmets and steel breastplates, armed with sabres, against German infantry with magazine rifles and machine-guns. Magnificent, but not war! As a civil engineer, he subsequently travelled widely, and once hit the headlines when his floating home, a Thames sailing barge, had foundered in a gale in the Irish Sea, and he and his wife were picked up by a steamer in the nick of time.

Dunkerton, a tall, silent and impressive man, was rather a mystery. His uniform fitted him superbly, and he was alleged to have been seen apparelled in some spectacular martial cloak. It was said that his magnificent, commanding presence, heightened by a monocle, was so awe-inspiring that red roughs were reduced to amazed silence. With the proud, disdainful demeanour of the bad baron in a Christmas pantomime, he would sweep untouched through a mob.

John Sant, a genial and boisterous giant, had had an extraordinary upbringing. His father, who had been a British consular official in Constantinople in 1914, disappeared on the outbreak of war with Turkey, and went underground. Obviously he was a British secret agent. Owing to the war the English school in Constantinople closed down; so John ran wild in that exciting city, until the Turks – with that out-of-date sense of chivalry that they have not yet learnt wholly to discard – picked him up and packed him off to their own Military Academy. They did this because they felt it would be unworthy to let the son of a former respected foreign official grow up into an unlettered savage. At the Academy, a Turkish equivalent of Sandhurst, he received the best all-round education then available, crammed into him for no fee whatever. He was housed, fed, and clothed gratis by his country's enemy for the duration of the war.

If it had not been for the slump, John Garnett, the son of a cotton magnate, would have put in no more than a few hours daily at his father's office, then ridden off to hounds, flogged one of the upper reaches of the Ribble, the Calder or the Lune, or sat in a butt on a Pennine moor waiting for the driven grouse, according to season. The collapse of "King Cotton" had robbed him of his pleasant heritage, and had driven him into rebellion against those parties whose neglect and supineness had made possible such a calamity, not just for John Garnett but most of Lancashire.

These were my colleagues, men who had rallied to Mosley, and because of their proven ability, including initiative and determination, had been selected as his lieutenants. Were these the "thugs and morons" of the lying enemy propaganda from Left and Right?

They were men endowed with practical intelligence rather than any dubious gift for splitting hairs in debates on political theory, or for the careful sifting and weighing of high-faluting abstractions, so dear to the highbrows. Quite simply they realised that Britain was sick, and felt that Mosley was the only man ready to apply the drastic remedies needed to restore her.

They were followers such as these that Mosley had in mind when, after the break-up of the New Party, he announced: "I have finished with the people who think: henceforth I shall go to the people who feel." Whatever the average BUF staff officer may have lacked in rarefied intellectualism, he more than made up for in guts, good sense, faith and loyalty.

3 - The Star Case

The Great George Street H.Q. building soon was crowded to bursting point, and quite inadequate to cope with the rapid expansion of the Movement. After a brief spell at 12 Lower Grosvenor Place, new premises were acquired within less than a year of the BUF's first birthday. These were the former Whitelands Teachers' Training College, situated in King's Road, Chelsea, a vast building soon to become another over-crowded hive vibrant with activity.

This came to be the almost legendary "Black House". It possessed offices, classrooms, a lecture hall, a large canteen, kitchens and dormitories. It contained storerooms, printing shops, mechanical transport workshops, and a transport yard.

Day and night it buzzed with activity. Typewriters rattled in administrative offices, printing presses clattered out *The Blackshirt*, the first BUF weekly paper, but later its house-sheet, when *Fascist Week* became the official newspaper for sale to the public. In one lecture room a lesson on election law would be in progress; in another aspiring speakers would be put through their hesitant paces; elsewhere the tough men of the "I Squad" were being taught boxing and judo. Cars roared in and out of the transport yard; and all the time there was a constant stream of callers and enquirers, some of whom were well-known figures in the literary, professional, business and sporting worlds.

The general enthusiasm within the Movement was surpassed only by the optimism. Wildly hopeful but ill-informed enthusiasts confidently predicted that Mosley would be in power within twelve months; those more sober members who thought it might take him a year or two were dismissed as pessimists.

The British Union of Fascists was still in its infancy when Jimmy

Oswald Mosley, Lloyd George, and Jimmy Maxton

Maxton, leader of the Parliamentary group of ILP members from Clyde, challenged Mosley to debate publicly with him. As Maxton was an honest rebel, respected by politicians of all parties, Sir Oswald accepted willingly.

An exciting and somewhat heated evening ensued at the Friends' Meeting House in Euston Road, with Lloyd George in the chair. This disputation had widely publicised repercussions which ended most satisfactorily for the BUF. These arose when 'The Star' not only misrepresented what had been said on that occasion, but followed up its biased version of the evening's event with comments so damaging that Mosley took legal proceedings against the Daily News Limited which owned the paper.

On 25th February 1933, 'The Star' had printed: "Sir Oswald Mosley warned Mr. Maxton that he and the fascists would be ready to take over government with the aid of machine-guns when the moment arrived." It added: "Mr. Tom Mann was recently thrown into prison on the mere suspicion that he might say something ten times less provocative than Sir Oswald Mosley's words." [5]

---

5   The veteran British Syndicalist and later Communist leader who preached and

We Marched with Mosley

What Mosley had actually stated was that in the event of Red Revolution in Britain, he and his followers out of patriotism and loyalty to the Throne would, if necessary, take up arms in their defence; something quite different to what '*The Star*' had alleged.

The late Norman Birkett K.C., later Lord Birkett, acting for the publishers, cross-examined Mosley for hours on end, to find for once someone outside the legal profession who was his match in skilled use of words and argument.

During the day-long verbal duel, the following exchanges took place:

Birkett: Suppose a Communist Government was in power with the assent of the King?

Mosley: A Communist Government?

Birkett: Yes. Would you still face them with guns?

Mosley: That is a hypothetical question on as wild hypothesis that I have ever seen.

Birkett: If a Communist Government is called to power with the assent of the King, would you shoot them down?

Mosley: It is possible to put a question on ever increasing hypotheses which leads at last to an absurdity. You might as well say that if His Majesty the King of England enacted the law of Herod that every first-born shall be slain, would you, in those circumstances, be a revolutionary? The question you have put is an hypothetical absurdity.

Birkett: Can you answer it?

Mosley: You cannot answer questions which are by their very nature absurd.

organised violence for the overthrow of the State.

Later during cross-examination Birkett put the following question to Mosley:

Birkett: It is the first time in this country, is it not, in our peaceful evolution of late years that a political leader has used language saying 'I am going to judge the moment when I use guns in the street'?

Mosley: No. Lord Carson said hundreds of things far worse than that when he was a leader at the Bar.

Birkett: It is the first time in this country, is it not, in the government of our country that any leader has said 'I will judge when the guns will shoot'?

Mosley: When did I say that I should be the judge?

Birkett: Well, who?

Mosley: It does not require much judgment. If I saw a policeman knocked down with two toughs stamping on him, it does not require the exercise of judgment to know whether or not one ought to intervene.

Mosley, in fact, fully established the point that the fascists intended not only to adhere strictly to the law but also to uphold lawful authority. Rather than threaten an elected government under the constitutional monarchy, the fascists, as law-abiding patriots, were prepared in an emergency situation, which was by no means improbable in the political conditions of the time, to assist in the defence of the State against an attempted violent revolution by the communists.

As for Mosley's personal credibility, Lord Chief Justice Hewart, who heard the case, said in his summing up: "You have heard the plaintiff's evidence. Did you, or did you not, believe him? Whatever you may think of his answers, did he or did he not appear to you to be a public man of no little courage, no little candour, and no little ability?"

We Marched with Mosley

Mosley not only won his case against the proprietors of 'The Star', but was awarded £5,000 damages, and costs, which in a protracted hearing of that kind must have represented a considerable sum of money. The fact that one of the most irreconcilably hostile newspaper opponents of the new movement should become one of the largest single contributors to its funds was greatly appreciated by all of it's members.

4 - The Death of Cynthia Mosley

In May 1933 Mosley suffered an incalculable loss. His wife died. Lady Cynthia was not only lovely to look at, but splendid in personality. She was kind and brave, loyal and wise. Everyone in and out of politics who had known her, were shocked, and felt for her husband and three children. Elinor Glyn said of her: "Those whom the gods love die young.'... Perhaps her greatest quality was courage – the courage which bears pain without complaint – the courage which can stand fast for a principle amid a storm of disapproval from the crowd, and from loved ones as well – the courage to stick to noble ideals against countless worldly influences."[6]

The Labour correspondent of 'The Observer' was moved to write: "The death of Cynthia Mosley removes from politics an extraordinary gracious and charming personality. She was a most beautiful woman, and in addition had been given the balanced sanity of many gifts – patience, the unrelenting strength of life, the divine relationships of life's continuity. Cynthia Mosley's death is a tragedy, her life a service, possibly a sacrifice. Thirty-five years old, the mother of tragedy and death, she leaves behind her three children, one a year old.

"Then she leaves a man of destiny – to fate, and this is the greatest tragedy of all. She came out of an environment of pomp, pride, and arrogance, but she came out chastened and beautiful – and to a wonderful womanhood. Pride of place, position, acknowledgment, repulse, repudiation; all these ranked in relentless order, to uplift or appal. She never wavered in loyalty, dignity, or patience. She stepped from grandeur and its blazing ephemeral uncertainty to the gutter and the hovel with a humility which killed cynicism and wrath. The wrath of the

---

6   *Sunday Graphic & Sunday News*, 21.5.1933.

Cynthia Mosley speaking in support of the BUF in East London

gutter has originated revolutions, but she met taunt and gibe with angelic sweetness; she saw, she knew. Her nature, stirred to the depths, saw the oneness of life, in relationship to the mothering of the world; and she stood abashed and humbled. "Her physical womanhood was the exquisite loveliness of her sex; there was nothing so compelling as her subtle womanhood, which was pronounced even to her gayest moods. There was a rocklike steadfastness in her loyalty and discipline, even to a party which too often had no mind for definiteness.

"There will be a tragic biography written of her some day. It will be a story of the cancer of our civilisation, the thorns with the roses of life, the sneer with the cheers, the spite with the flunky acclaim, the hollowness of pomp and position. The life of Cynthia Mosley is the story of one who came out of life's paradise to be the friend of the humble and the meek, the poor and the desolate, the mother-woman who understood the Nazarene's injunction 'to suffer little children'." [7]

---

7   *The Observer*, 21.5.1933.

A memorial service held in St. Margaret's, Westminster, was attended by the lowly and great, statesmen and parliamentarians of all parties, and by many Blackshirts in uniform, all united in sorrow and the rendering of their tributes to a woman the like of whom none of them probably would see again. To perpetuate her memory a crèche named after her was founded in Kennington where, among the many notable persons who participated in the service of dedication, were George Lansbury and the Archbishop of Canterbury.

5 - The Tithe War

In 1933 the BUF became involved in the "Tithe War", when many farmers, particularly in East Anglia, were about to be forcibly distrained upon by the ecclesiastical commissioners.

In Mosley's opinion tithe was an anachronism which should have long been dispensed with, in favour of some more equably levied form of financial support for the Established Church. He contended that it was unfair that Britain's state religion should be maintained by one section only of the populace, and that section probably worst hit by the hard times.

Tithe, as the material mainstay of the Church, had been instituted centuries ago, when farming had been England's main industry; in medieval times agriculture, which embraced also the famous wool trade, far exceeded in importance every other industry within the realm. Prior to the dissolution of the monasteries by Henry VIII, this tribute had been paid entirely in kind, when the yeomen and franklins and the lesser tillers of the soil handed over to the reeves and stewards of the ecclesiastical establishments a tenth part of the produce of their holdings. Their corn, their pulses, their wool and their flax had been received into the great tithe barns, buildings of sturdy beauty, many of which survive to this day. The toll then levied was not to make clerics fat, but to maintain those services of poor relief, the care of the infirm and the aged, hospitalisation, and of education, then in the hands of the monks, but now the responsibilities of local government, defrayed out of the rates. Farmers had long ago ceased to pay their dues in kind, but they alone were bound legally to disburse large sums of money for the upkeep of the national church.

For the purpose of tithe collection in latter times, land had been assessed according to its estimated corn productions; but this rating had been agreed on during the "golden days" of farming, when corn prices had been high. Now in 1933-34, because of foreign dumping, wheat, barley and most other fruits of the soil stood at some of the lowest figures of all time. Faced with disaster, nagged at by their creditors, and fearfully aware of the imminence of bankruptcy, farmers in Norfolk and Suffolk in particular turned their grumbling protests to acts of defiance. East Anglians took the lead in this rebellion, not only because they had been more affected as corn and beef farmers by the slump than the dairy, pig, fruit and vegetable producers of the Home Counties, Midlands and West, but because stubbornness and rebellion are inherent among all true natives of these two eastern counties. So they dug in their toes, and refused to pay.

Bailiffs, escorted by police, appeared on the farms of non-payers, and seizing livestock and tackle, caused them to be sold locally by public auction. At the sales, attended in force by friends and neighbours, would-be bargain hunters were intimidated by the overwhelming hostility, and made no bids. What offers were made were so paltry and then generally on behalf of the victim that the ecclesiastical commissioners got no satisfaction.

When because of local indignation the bailiffs started to distrain on animals and machinery to be sold in markets two or three counties distant, where they would not be recognised, the Blackshirts offered their services to the oppressed farmers. The BUF sought legal opinion, and was advised that if its members happened to be on the farm with the owner's consent, and abstaining from force but by their passive presence hindered the bailiffs, they would be within the law.

So parties of Blackshirts converged on farms in East Anglia, where the bailiffs were expected daily. One small party camped in a barn at Fincham Hall, ten or twelve miles from King's Lynn, then farmed by the late Leonard Mason, who believed that a flock of his lambs was about to be seized. When the servants of the commissioners came with their transport, the Blackshirts intended to kick a football about near the lorries, making it impossible to load the animals.

Most of the excitement of the "Tithe War" took place at Wortham on the Norfolk and Suffolk borders, near the pleasant little town of Eye, where the farm of Mr. Rash, husband of the well-known East Anglian novelist, Doreen Wallace was under threat of distraint. On this farm a larger party of fascists, commanded by Dick Plathen, worked hard to frustrate the ecclesiastical grabbers. They felled trees across the private road leading to the farm premises, dug trenches, and put up barbed-wire, so that access to the farm livestock was almost impossible.

Locally there was tense excitement, which spread until the interest became nationwide. Newspaper reporters and photographers descended on the place, and visitors came from afar to look at the siege preparations. Mr. Rash was a popular employer and neighbour, so the villagers lent a hand and vowed that the bailiffs would go away empty-handed.

Then the powers-that-be struck. Police reinforcements were brought in, and proceeded to arrest the Blackshirts, obviously on the instructions of the Home Office, under an obscure, long-forgotten, centuries-old statute which some pertinacious lawyer had delved for and found among the archives. I cannot recall the Act, or the actual charges, but I seem to recall that the accused were charged with "conspiring to cause an act whereby mischief might be... etc., etc."

The fascists, taken aback for they had been relying on their legal advisers, were put into motor-coaches and driven off under strong escort to H.M. Prison on the heights of Mousehold Heath. In due course, they stood lined up in the Assize Court, where having pleaded guilty, but in consideration of their good characters, their misapprehension concerning the illegality of their actions and their undertaking not to renew their efforts to circumvent the employees of the commissioners, they were bound over. Most East Anglian parsons were acutely distressed at the heartless exactions. At the same time several of their number were becoming financially embarrassed through the refusal or inability of their parishioners to pay up. One Norfolk clergyman, Rev. Molyneux, the rector of Marham, told me he doubted if he could carry out his duties much longer, if two or three local farmers of large acreage continued to default.

The Church suffered too. In several parishes where the tithe question had been vexed, the number of worshippers dropped, as in their eyes the Church of England had become identified with Shylock.

The mass arrest of the Blackshirt tithe warriors might have seemed to outsiders to be an ignominious end to an irresponsible adventure; but a most unjust and indecent state of affairs had been amply spotlighted. Never again did the Church of England through its commissioners exercise such tyranny over honest and hardworking men already on the verge of bankruptcy. "They" had had their lesson; and it was the BUF which had administered it.

6 - Friends and Supporters

During its first few years the BUF attracted a number of prominent persons of all classes and from all sections of the community, most of whom were to remain loyal friends.

Major-General J.F.C. Fuller, C.B., C.B.E., D.S.O., the distinguished soldier and even more distinguished military historian and critic, was one of the best-known men publicly to align himself with Mosley. His articles published in the 'Fascist Quarterly' made valuable contributions to the thinking of the Movement, especially in the formulation of defence planning.

Colonel Fuller, as he was in 1916, had been a creator and pioneer of the original Tank Corps. That fine fighting soldier and Royal Armoured Corps leader of the Second World War, General Martel, has nothing but praise for him. In his memoirs he records that Colonel Fuller's arrival as Senior General Staff Officer to the Tank Corps was a "splendid appointment", and he speaks of the "valuable help which he rendered to our cause and to the Army for many years to come". [8]

Martel laments repeatedly how the authorities continued to ignore Fuller with his great gifts: "I fear the Army failed to obtain anything like full value from 'Boney' (General Fuller's nickname among his contemporaries) that they might have received, but it is not easy to fit an outstanding genius into an inevitably cumbersome machine like the Army... At this time (the pioneer days of the Tank Corps) our band of 'crusaders' was starting to form. Our leader was undoubtedly Colonel Fuller, and he was fully supported by Captain Liddell Hart, Colonel Lindsay, and myself..." [9] Elsewhere in his book Martel reflects

8   *An Out-Spoken Soldier*, by Lieut-General Sir Giffard Martel, p.14, Sifton, Praed & Co.

9   Idem, pp. 36-37

ruefully and with every justification on "the great work which 'Boney' did for the Army" and that its value was "more fully realised by other European countries than our own".

General Sir Andrew Thorne, who was British Military Attaché in Berlin from April 1932 to May 1935, in a letter to Lord Hankey, wrote that he had been "impressed by the extent to which both Liddell Hart's and 'Boney' Fuller's books were being studied by officers of all ranks and arms in the German Army. "I knew," wrote Thorne, "both Blomberg (Minister for War) and Reichenau (Chief of the Defence Staff) very well, and they were both engaged in translating books by these two authors for use of non-English-speaking German officers." [10]

Colonel Khandyeff of the Bulgarian Army, who had been attached to the German Army during the 1930s, wrote in August 1939 concerning "the activity of General Guderian in developing the tank forces, and said, 'His faith in armoured formations was such that he took immense pains to plant the same enthusiasm in the people under him. His gods were General Fuller and Captain Liddell Hart. Liddell Hart, he considered, was the best analytical brain in the world." [11]

After the war, Guderian confirmed that Colonel Khandyeff's account was correct. Furthermore, when Rommel summed up his campaign in 1943, he stated: "In Germany, thanks largely to the efforts of General Guderian, the first traces of modern leadership in tank warfare began to crystallise in theory before the war. This resulted in the training and organisation of tank units on modern lines. The British Army, however, remained conservative and its responsible authorities rejected the principles of mechanised warfare which had been so eminently developed and taught by Englishmen in particular."

A paper entitled 'Vers l'Armée de Mètier' by General, then Colonel,

---

10   Reproduced in part by the late Captain B.H. Liddell Hart, who was kind enough to
       lend me a selection of his pamphlets and papers. R.R.B.

11   Also from the Liddell Hart papers.

Charles de Gaulle on the use of armoured fighting vehicles in the field seems to have been inspired by the writings of Fuller and Liddell Hart. At the time of the great German break-through in the late spring of 1940, de Gaulle appears to have been about the only French tank commander who appreciated modern tactics, and used his vehicles according to the dicta of the two Englishmen.

Once at Geneva in the lobbies of the Palace of the League of Nations, General Fuller and Captain Liddell Hart had the rare "distinction" of being sought out by Karl Radek, then foreign editor of 'Izvestiya', and greeted as fellow revolutionaries, for they too, said Radek, thought in terms of the future.

In addition to other qualities unappreciated by his superiors, Fuller possessed a lively sense of humour. Martel, for instance, narrates how 'Boney' out of sheer devilment once submitted an anonymous essay on naval tactics in a Royal United Services Institute competition, in which incidentally he nearly gave himself away by referring to one of His Majesty's ships as "it", but timely erasure and correction covered the cloven hoof of the landsman. It was only after his contribution had been awarded high praise, top marks and first prize, was it discovered amid dismay and consternation that the author was a "pongo" named Fuller.

Another early and enduring friend of the Movement was Sir Alliott Verdon-Roe, who was famous as the first Englishman ever to fly, in an achievement almost remarkable as that of the Wright brothers in America. He earned further fame for his name by those highly esteemed aircraft, the Avros, that he turned out in quantity for the R.F.C. in the First War.

Airmen in particular were prepared to accept the New Idea. Survivors of the Flying Corps and of the earlier intakes of the Royal Air Force enrolled in the BUF in proportionately larger numbers than did ex-servicemen of the other two arms. By the very nature of their vocation, airmen – like General Fuller – "thought in terms of the future". Also, of course, Mosley's record as one of the first hundred pilots and observers to fly in battle placed him in the eyes of airmen on a high pedestal. His was the sort of peacetime leadership they had long wanted and waited for.

Vice-Admiral G.B. Powell, R.N. (Retd.) was another outstanding recruit. In the Service he had been popular on the lower decks, and so when he was made District Officer of Portsmouth, his name brought local prestige.

It would be no exaggeration to write that retired regular officers of the fighting services at one time flocked into the Movement. They were men brought up in the tradition of service to their country, rather than of profiting from their country, and having served it during their working lives, now deeply conscious that something was terribly wrong, offered it further service in their retirement.

One prominent retired soldier in this category was Lieut-General Sir George Fletcher MacNunn, K.C.B., K.C.S.I., D.S.O., Legion of Honour, etc., who had served in six campaigns, including Burma, the North-West Frontier, South Africa and the First World War, and who had been in turn Quarter-Master General of the Indian Army, and Colonel Commandant, Royal Artillery. From 1932 to 1938 he was Commander of The Royal Hospital, Chelsea, home of the famous Chelsea Pensioners and a few hundred yards from the BUF's "Black House". He was an authority on the peoples and religious cults of India, author of many books and our adviser on Indian policies.

Mosley had many followers in what, in those days, was still known as the Merchant Service. I can recall by name several Master Mariners in the BUF, including Captains Nott and Frank Clifford of the Cunard Line. Several great landowners and many smaller squires supported Mosley, and at one time farming members were legion. Law and medicine were both well represented, with at least one consultant from Harley Street.

Several clergymen joined, mainly from the Church of England.

Nonconformist ministers, however much they may have agreed with our social programme, were shy of aligning themselves with an organisation in revolt against the accepted order of things; this attitude has since developed in another direction. Nonconformity was then permeated by that "Liberalism" which, while upholding the sanctity of property and the righteousness of profit-making, was intolerant of authority, except that of Mrs Grundy, ever to accept willingly a form of government that was authoritarian.

Priests of the Roman Catholic Church, on the other hand, more often expressed in private their approval of our ideals and most aspects of policy, notably our support for the corporate state and opposition to atheist Marxism, than did the clergy of the Protestant denominations; but they neither joined, nor offered material support. Doubtless, centuries of persecution in this country had taught them the need for caution, although it was the 'Catholic Herald' which said:

"Even in England the growing strength of the British Union of Fascists is a hopeful sign... it stands for the small owner as opposed to big business, and its policy is the nearest approach to the social theory of the encyclicals we have yet been offered by any prominent political party." 10.6.1938.

While a few wealthy men did at one time help to support the Movement, the great captains of industry, the tycoons, remained aloof. They had become too much part of what is now known as the Establishment, and therefore regarded Mosley and his followers as dangerous fanatics bent on destroying the status quo, which still operated satisfactorily in their favour.

Small businessmen and shopkeepers, faced with ruin through the diminution of the purchasing power of thousands of former clients through unemployment, and now faced with the new cut-throat competition of the chain-stores, were ready to join in their numbers and to discuss their cause with friends. They may not have been the sort to demonstrate in the streets; theirs was the hidden support that could become invaluable in a crisis.

A loyal and gallant lady, no longer young, who worked very actively for the BUF, was Lady Pearson, the widowed sister of Brigadier-General Sir Henry Page Croft, for many years Conservative M.P. for Bournemouth, who was later made Baron Croft. Lady Pearson, who lived in Kent, became our prospective parliamentary candidate for Canterbury.

Several leading suffragettes, including such well-known militants as Norah Elam and Mary Richardson, came in when they realised how positive was Mosley's attitude to the political aspirations of women, and understood the important place reserved for women in the Corporate State, with their full representation therein.

It has been extraordinary how the deliberate misrepresentation of women's role in British fascism, disseminated by hostile propaganda, was widely believed at the time and remains generally accepted today. Not long ago I was told in all good faith by an educated woman, a doctor, old enough to know better, that we had believed in the subservience of women.

A famous pioneer feminist to become a devoted member was Commandant Mary Allen, who had launched the first women police in Britain shortly after the First World War. She was very much a character. She wore her hair cut short like a boy's, carried a monocle, and went about in slacks, long before they came into vogue for women. She was a stern upholder of morality; organised vice was an anathema to her. But she was no grim puritan, for she had a lively sense of humour and was excellent company.

Less famous but also a faithful and lifelong supporter of Mosley was Maud Hollington, who celebrated her 100th birthday on July 20, 1987, when she received a congratulatory telegram from the Queen. Several figures in the literary world, attracted by the New Idea, felt sympathetic to Mosley and his Movement, among them Ezra Pound and Wyndham Lewis.

George Bernard Shaw, always friendly to Mosley, said of him in his pamphlet '*In Praise of Guy Fawkes*' that he was: "a very interesting man to read just now: one of the few people who are writing and thinking about real things, and not about figments and phrases. You will hear something more of Sir Oswald Mosley before you are through with him. I know you dislike him because he looks like a man who has some physical courage and is going to do something; and that is a terrible thing. You instinctively hate him, because you do not know where he will land you. Instead of talking round and round political subjects and obscuring them with bunk verbiage without ever touching them, and without understanding them, all the time assuming states of things which ceased to exist from twenty to six hundred and fifty years ago, he keeps hard down on the actual facts of the situation."

One can almost hear the Irish voice of this eminent thinker giving this accurate analysis of Mosley's typically trenchant style of concrete political prose.

Ezra Pound, the American poet and reformer, and great wit, was an open sympathiser with the New Idea in its British and Italian forms, and regularly contributed shrewd, brilliantly humorous and forceful articles both to the BUF press, and to the Union Movement journals after the last war.

The youthful E.D. Randall, poet and intellectual, became the Movement's popular song writer. Another friend was another young poet, Roy Campbell, who thus became the bug-bear of so many other poets who twanged their lyres and sang ceaselessly in praise of all things pink and beautiful. His two lines:

> "The vultures on the cook-house rest
> Like poets in the B.B.C. ..."

did nothing to endear him to his own generation of mostly incarnadined versifiers. Sir John Squire became interested in the Movement; likewise Major Francis Yeats-Brown, author of 'Bengal Lancer', and one time editor of 'Britannia and Eve'. From a very different background, John Scanlon, former ILP intellectual, and author of 'Decline and Fall of the

Labour Party' and 'Pillars of Cloud', became BUF industrial correspondent, contributing to '*Action*' under the pseudonym of John Emery. Various academics and writers such as Wyndham Lewis contributed occasionally to the Movement's periodicals, especially '*British Union Quarterly*'.

Beverley Nichols was another convert. Utterly disillusioned with post-war Britain, he had cast around for some ray of hope. He told of this search in his '*News of England*', until at last he encountered Mosley, of whom he wrote: "He is the only man I know who has in him the qualities of that hero for whom this country has waited so long and waited in vain."

Nichols wrote for the Movement until told in unmistakeable terms that his continued association could lead only to his literary ruin. It was conveyed to him that nothing from his pen would be printed in the women's glossies, nor in the popular press, until he disassociated himself from the fascists. As he would have been committing financial suicide in remaining with the Movement, his departure was understandable.

The only English author of real prominence fully to accept Mosley's political doctrine and who was prepared to stand by his allegiance cost him what it may, was Henry Williamson, then farming at Stiffkey in north Norfolk. Right up until his death in 1977 he remained one of Mosley's most loyal and devoted friends and supporters.

Williamson's approach to the New Idea was identical with that of Mosley; for he too had served throughout the First World War, when he had grown to admire and to hold in affectionate regard his fellow front-line soldiers on both sides of no-man's land. His sufferings, those of a hyper-sensitive spirit, had inspired in him high ideals of brotherhood and fellowship; which he had since seen befouled by the financial vultures who presided over the so-called plenipotentiaries of peace at Versailles, where they had been assisted by mean and ignoble politicians bent on vengeance.

Since the end of the war he had seen the England for which

he had fought and bled, and endured mental tortures and nightmares, and for the sake of which so many dear friends had died, exploited on behalf of the usurers and of those hard-faced men who had so sickened Mosley at his first coming to Westminster. He more than most men was ripe to receive Mosley's message. Like Mosley, most of his life since 1918 had been animated by the spirit of dedication to the memory of his own slaughtered generation. Williamson's disillusionment with the brass Hats of the military was expressed in '*The Wet Flanders Plain*' and '*The Patriot's Progress*'.

His sequence of novels, '*A Chronicle of Ancient Sunlight*', centred on the semi-fictitious Philip Madison, contain the most evocative of all the written descriptions of the battlefields of Flanders and the Somme, and of the true soldierly spirit of that war. Their 15 volumes constitute a landmark in English literature, and commemorate for all time the horrors and the heroism, the squalor and the glory, of those epoch-changing four and a half years.

7 - Enter Lord Rothermere: Olympia

In January 1934, the Movement received sudden added impetus when Lord Rothermere, brother of Lord Northcliffe, founder of the '*Daily Mail*', brought his newspaper into open support. This declaration of sympathy with the aims of the Blackshirts from a great national journal was immensely gratifying. We could sense at once the more favourable attitude of the general public, after he published his article "Hurrah for the Blackshirts!"

Members in uniforms were stopped in the street and congratulated on their intervention in the stagnating political life of Britain. Staunch Conservatives were heard to say that while not wanting Mosley in power, they would certainly like to see him and sufficient of his followers in Parliament to startle the lethargic Baldwinites into doing something.

It was pleasant to feel such widespread approval after having been little more than objects of interest or derision, but the sudden unexpected popularity brought problems with which the organisation was then ill-prepared to cope. Substantial sums of money came in; and another great influx of recruits. While some new members remained completely loyal throughout the Movement's existence, others proved to be fair-weather friends who disappeared at the first sign of trouble. Others turned out to be adventurers and bandwagon climbers, identical to those types who caused similar problems in Fascist movements on the Continent, and who afforded to opponents of fascism everywhere, by accident or design, examples of those charges of malpractice, peculation, bullying and brutality which were eagerly sought and quickly magnified by the democratic press.

The Movement's hierarchy decided to put on a show of strength by holding a large demonstration in Hyde Park. On 9th September 1934, a sunny Saturday afternoon, some five thousand

Blackshirts assembled on the Embankment and marched behind the BUF's band to the Park with Mosley leading the column.

For many BUF members this was their first introduction to the organised opposition, which they viewed now with horror and revulsion. The members of my own small contingent from south-east Norfolk, mostly ex-servicemen who were also unemployed farm-workers, declared in all truthfulness that they felt physically sickened by the proximity of those noisy and noisome disciples of Karl Marx. If any British left-wing intellectuals – teachers, poets, undergraduates – were present that day, they had rendered themselves inconspicuous, leaving the foremost ranks of the Red Front to as hideous an assemblage of members of the underworld as could be imagined in nightmares or painted by Bosch.

Very few English features could be discerned amongst an array of dark and alien visages. Many menacing creatures were prancing, gesticulating obscenely, and screaming abuse and hate. They maintained in a never-ending depressive chant their latest slogan, which went: "Red Front! Red Front! Red, united, fighting, Front. The only front to stand against the Blackshirts!"

This description of the communist forces gathered in Hyde Park may seem exaggerated. Actually they had to be seen to be believed; they were the very dregs of the populace not only of the Capital but of every great city in Britain, who it transpired later had been recruited and transported together to stop Mosley on that occasion.

A crowded rally, the first of three such demonstrations to be held in the Royal Albert Hall, terminated in scenes of such enthusiasm that Mosley decided on the ambitious step of following it up with a grand meeting in June, 1934, at Olympia, at that time London's largest hall, with seating capacity for 15,000.

This time the Reds were determined that Mosley should not be allowed to get away with a peaceful and successful rally. They organised to break it up. Newspapers and periodicals sympathetic to the Left appealed to their readers to turn out in force and "smash the Fascists". The *'Daily Worker'* published detailed instructions how the anti-fascists were to assemble in Hammersmith Road near Olympia on the evening of 7th June[12].

Five columns of marchers were to converge on the area from different points, and those workers who did not knock off from their jobs in time to march were to travel by underground and take advantage of the cheap tickets available for organised parties. The *'New Leader'*, official organ of the ILP, said: "The workers are going to be all out at Olympia... Get to work at once... get as many as possible to come along to Olympia."[13] Maps were published to show how to get to the hall, and the *'Daily Worker'* plainly threatened: "Inside the large Hall, and outside, the challenge of Mosley will be met... the workers' counter-action will cause them, the Blackshirts to tremble."[14]

The "counter-demonstrators" were not relying either on their vocal cords or their fists to stop the meeting, as was evidenced by the nature of the wounds and injuries sustained that evening by our stewards and supporters; and by the candid confession of participants on their side, such as Philip Toynbee, a product of Rugby School who became an active communist, in his reminiscences[15] of buying knuckle-dusters and attacking a steward.

We collected a strange assortment of weapons from the "gentle hecklers" during the course of the evening. Apart from coshes, iron bars, knuckle-dusters, and razors usually wielded by reds, and prised from them after sanguinary struggles with the stewards, this time could be included a cobbler's awl, a short-handled chopper and a curry-comb (anyone with stable experience can appreciate the possibilities of this as a weapon).

One Blackshirt, "Bill" Eaton, my friend over many years, at

---

12   *Daily Worker*, 26.5.1934.

13   *New Leader*, 1.6.1934.

14   *Daily Worker*, 7.6.1934.

15   *Friends Apart*, by Philip Toynbee.

whose wedding I was best man, was felled by a weird contrivance consisting of a tin can swung round on the end of a short length of wire with a loop for a handle. To lend weight and impetus the can was filled with sand, and to make it more interesting, numerous holes had been punched in its sides, and nails, points outermost, inserted through the holes.

The Reds were not at all nice about whom they struck, nor where, nor with what. One girl Blackshirt had her glasses smashed into her eye, and another had her face slashed savagely from eye to neck with either a knife or a razor. Many of the "workers" defended "democracy" with their feet, so that most of our injuries were kicks in the groin. The first aid posts were full of writhing, retching fascists.

Nonetheless the unarmed Blackshirts proved tougher than the Reds, for all their assorted armoury. Singly and in patches the communists and their friends were disposed of by the stewards. A fascist barbarity practised that night was the severing of the interrupters' trouser braces and the removal of vital buttons, before thrusting them out towards the street. There is little fight left in a man those mind and hands are fully occupied with the preservation of propriety; in such circumstances "be it never so humble, there's no place like home".

One memorable incident occurred when the BUF Director General, Francis Hawkins, pursued a persistent troublemaker across the girders in the lofty roof, tackled him in that dizzy place, and brought him down for ejection into the street.

Having seen yelling, kicking, struggling comrade after comrade removed with diminishing tenderness, any opponents remaining in the hall decided that silence was wisdom. Mosley was then able to proceed with the business of the evening without further interruption, and the audience was able to hear the speech they had every right to hear in peace and comfort.

Next day Britain resounded to indignant voices denouncing the fascist atrocities. Apparently Mosley planned to attain power by booking large halls, inviting the public to enter them, and then unleashing his black shirted thugs to beat up his helpless audiences so savagely that they would be sure to vote for his candidates at the next election.

In particular, Sir Gerald Barry and the Very Reverend "Dick" Shepphard fulminated against the fascist violence they claimed to have witnessed that evening. A few days later Mosley was invited by the B.B.C. to reply to the accusations already made over their network by Barry. He accepted the offer under the impression that they would confront each other, and debate the issue before an unseen audience of hundreds of thousands. However, on arrival at Broadcasting House, Mosley was ushered into a room containing a microphone, but no Gerald Barry. He said his piece, then departed, only to discover later that his adversary had been sitting in an adjacent room where he had listened in to his statement, to be allowed to return in due course to the microphone where he could further unburden himself, without the necessity of defending his allegations to Mosley's face.

Mosley was given no opportunity to reply again, or indeed to put his case at all over the radio thereafter. It appears that Mosley, as a fascist, was deemed by Sir John Reith and his leftward-leaning liberals of Broadcasting House to have forfeited his right to normal courtesy or human usage.[16]

The reports of "fascist brutality" were thus allowed to reach inflated proportions, because the broadcasters all too rarely permitted them to be punctured with hard facts and simple statistics.

Undoubtedly many Reds were thrown out with little ceremony and those who resisted with violence were ejected with violence; the stewards used a legal right and a moral duty to protect the meeting from organised disruption. The medical evidence of injuries produced afterwards shows clearly which side was the more aggressive and vicious.

---

16   Sir John Reith, later Lord Reith, famous head of the B.B.C. for many years.

A number of prominent persons, not all of whom could be suspected of viewing the affray through glasses of Tory blue, spoke up on behalf of those Blackshirts who were getting such a public trouncing in the newspapers and over the radio for the vigour with which they defended free speech and themselves. For example, Hamilton Fyfe, former editor of the 'Daily Herald', in a letter dated 13th June, stated that while no one would be likely to accuse him of pro-fascist sympathies, he considered it unfair and unwise to organise interruption at Olympia, adding that on their way to disrupt the meeting the interrupters were shouting in unison "some slogan I could not catch. They were clearly in a fighting mood, and they got what they wanted."

C.W. Lowther, a former Conservative M.P., wrote personally to Mosley to say that the stewards "seemed to be very decent folk, a very good type of British youth. I saw no ejections that were not perfectly justified. I have suffered at several elections from organised interruptions, and I think that you have hit upon the proper method of dealing with it."

Lord Strathspey of the Upper House felt obliged to write: "We were very glad to see that such a firm hand was taken to preserve law and order. If Blackshirts were rough, it was only in self-defence, and for the protection of the thousands in the hall. Furthermore they only gave the wild hooligans what they asked for, and what they right well deserved to get."

H.W. Beaumont M.P., wrote that no one present "can doubt that the interruptions which were dealt with, were skilfully organised with the object of preventing Sir Oswald Mosley from speaking... I was pleased to see the organised hooligans dealt with in the only manner they can understand." [17] And Sir G.K. Gratton-Doyle, M.P., also stated publicly: "I have no use for Fascism or dictatorships, but less sympathy... for those who think that the Red hooligans who were present in their organised hundreds were not treated with sufficient leniency." [18]

---

17   *The Times*, 8.3.1934.

18   *The Times*, 19.6.1934

Patrick Donner, M.P., in a letter to the '*National Review*' stated:[19] "To describe as certain sections of the press have done, organised gangs of hooligans as 'hecklers' or 'genuine interrupters', who attempting to elicit further information were brutally assaulted and forcibly ejected, is to give a wholly erroneous impression of what actually occurred... The fact is that many of the Communists were armed with razors, stockings filled with broken glass, knuckle-dusters and iron bars: that they had marched from the East End, the police kindly escorting, with the avowed purpose of wrecking the meeting. A friend of mine saw a woman Fascist with a razor cut across her face, and with my own eyes I witnessed gangs of Communists resisting ejection with the utmost violence."

Such statements of fact from highly placed, responsible eye-witnesses went largely unheeded amid the welter of accusations fabricated by the communists and their "fellow-travelling" friends.

From his own immense experience of political meetings, both peaceful and violent, Lloyd George saw the matter in true perspective.   Writing a fortnight later, when the argument as to how beastly the Blackshirts had been was still raging, he marvelled at the ability of one politician to gather fifteen thousand people into one place to listen to him on a fine June evening, and wondered too why the fury of the champions of free speech should be concentrated exclusively "not on those who deliberately attempted the public expression of free speech", but against those who "fought, however roughly, for free speech". He felt that men who enter meetings with the deliberate intention of suppressing it have no right to complain "if an exasperated audience handles them rudely". [20]

Those were the days, let it be remembered, when it was fashionable to have leftward leanings. Besides, no stick was too dirty with which to belabour a "fascist beast". Therefore the

---

19   *National Review*, 18.6.1934.

20   *Sunday Pictorial.*

Reds and their friends were able to make the loudest outcry, and in consequence were the more widely believed. They made Blackshirt synonymous with blackguard.

Before Olympia many of our men had been attacked while selling papers or out walking alone and in small groups. After Olympia there was an increase in violence, especially armed violence, not so much at indoor meetings as at street marches. In Manchester a column of Blackshirts, coming away from a rally addressed by Mosley in the Belle Vue Gardens, was bombarded with potatoes in which razor blades had been embedded (soon to become a favourite weapon). Several fascists were wounded, and one young drummer suffered a dreadfully gashed face. The people who threw these missiles did so from side streets where, having discharged a quick volley, they would turn about and run.

The expansion and development of the BUF at a rate that could only be described as fantastic gave concern to the government and alarmed the established political parties.

Both the Special Branch and MI5 contrived to have their spies enrolled in the Movement. [21] Whether or not all the government snoops were discovered, I cannot say; but as we had nothing to hide, and as it was advantageous to know who were the outside agents, there were no dramatic exposures nor denunciations. One at least of these undercover agents liked us so well what he found that he threw himself wholeheartedly into the life of BUF and rendered it valuable service for six or seven years.

When the old parties found that fascists were unshakeable in debate, for theirs was a cast-iron policy, simple, uncompromising and indestructible, and that the Blackshirts were prepared to stand up to armed attack with their bare fists, they tried to disrupt

21   "The second MI5 report on the activities of the BUF argued that the Olympia meeting on 7 June, 1934, which so alienated influential opinion, actually increased support amongst those who were concerned about political disruption by left-wing activists. For two days a representative cross-section of working-class men, ex-officers, and public schoolboys queued from morning to night at the Black House to join an organisation which they saw as being dedicated to preserving freedom of speech." – *Fascism in Britain* by R. Thurlow, p.94.

and weaken the Movement from within. They planted their stooges in our ranks, not only to keep their masters informed of BUF strength and plans, but to sow the seeds of dissension and to undermine authority. These tools of the "Old Gang" were usually a dirty-minded lot who could think of nothing more original than to whisper accusations of sexual perversion against almost every senior officer. If their fabrications had not been so nauseous, they could have been funny – they were so ridiculous. If there was one stain from which British fascism was free, it was sexual vice.

One rather more ingenious and less contemptible attempt to spread confusion occurred when a rumour which became known as "The Great General Fuller Sedition" was spread within National Headquarters by these agents-provocateurs. It was put around that General Fuller, not approving of Mosley's leadership had decided to assume it himself. The only person who knew nothing about this was General Fuller!

8 – Exit Lord Rothermere: The Jews

"I have seen the '*Daily Mail*' abandon its support of Sir Oswald Mosley in the Thirties under the pressure of Jewish advertisers." - Randolph Churchill, *The Spectator*, 27th December 1963.

At this period the prevailing mood of the Movement, fanned by Lord Rothermere's encouragement, was one of boundless optimism. It seemed as if the Blackshirts had recaptured for themselves the spirit of 1914: that ill-founded confidence that had buoyed everyone, except Lord Kitchener, with the reiterated promise "it will all be over by Christmas".

Members spoke of "when we are in power", as if triumph were only a few months distant. Those who considered "victory within three years" were derided as pessimists. Mosley himself set no date; so those who foresaw everything culminating quickly and gloriously had only their own wishful thinking to blame for subsequent disappointment.

For all his zeal and help, Lord Rothermere failed to absorb the real meaning of the cause he was espousing, or to understand the implications of its policies. He remained what he had always been, an unwavering reactionary. He would doubtless have continued to support the Movement without fully understanding its mission, however, but for a rude blow delivered by his advertisers.

A nationwide catering firm told him that there would be no more full-page advertisements for their Swiss rolls and other mass-produced food products, if he continued to support Mosley. In common with other newspaper barons Lord Rothermere was used to having his own way, and was most annoyed that anyone, even fellow magnates, should presume to dictate to him what he might or might not print in his own '*Daily Mail*'. The story is that he was prepared to tell the predominantly Jewish board of directors of that firm to go to hell, when he received similar messages from others of his advertising clients, mainly proprietors of the numerous hire-purchase furnishing firms.

This was called the "freedom of the press", and was hailed as a most desirable attribute of freedom of expression in a free country by the late Wickham Steed, whose manner of reasoning in this instance appears a trifle illogical.

It was not lost upon Mosley that these people who were threatening to use the boycott weapon were either Jews or under Jewish influence; which had also been blatantly the case in much of the attempted suppression of free speech at his public meetings. Whatever may be thought about the rights and wrongs of this matter, the main facts are not in doubt.

Anti-Semitism had never been one of Mosley's political planks, or even interests. He had neither threatened nor attacked Jews; although he had long denounced international finance, and the power that financiers were able to exert upon governments and nations by their manipulation of currencies and exchange. We have already seen how the Wall Street bosses put the half-nelson on Ramsay MacDonald's government in 1931, and other examples could also be cited. It so happened that many of the international financiers, the Rothschilds, Lazards, Sassoons, Oppenheimers, Joels, Beits, Barnatos and Warburgs, among others, were either still practising Jews or of Jewish extraction.

Lord Rothermere could have brought out his paper with blank spaces where advertisements normally would have appeared, and published the reason. This would have been a salutary shock to those powerful, if obscure, beings who have exerted so much control over our destiny from their offices in the City, and their luncheon tables at the Savoy, without revealing themselves. The great newspaper proprietor now had the opportunity to expose one method by which both the Establishment and public opinion can be influenced; but faced with loss of revenue he capitulated.

In this particular case Hitler can be cited to confirm the English experience, for he later observed about the power of the Jewish advertising agencies that he "found it singularly significant to see how both Hugenberg and Lord Rothermere were compelled to abandon their attempts to support a reasoned national policy, because the Jews threatened to cut off their advertising revenue. Lord Rothermere, who had at the time just published two articles in support of the Mosley movement, himself described to me at the Berghof how the Jews went to work, and how it was quite impossible at such short notice to take any effective counter-measures" [22]

This episode was not alone in making Mosley feel that he had incurred the displeasure of the Jews. The severing of the 'Daily Mail's' support was the first time that money-power had declared itself quite so directly opposed to the Movement; but the mounting number of acts of violence against Blackshirts by Jews had created an acute suspicion of the hostility that many of them felt towards advocates of the New Idea. Much has been said and written on this sensitive issue, and it is essential for readers to try to cast their minds back to the situation as it actually faced us many years before the Jewish tragedy in the last war. The simple fact was that Jews, often the same ones, were to be seen more and more frequently in opposition at our meetings.

Why were the Jews so hostile to us? At one extreme, a large number of them had been engaged in various practices in the financial sphere which fascism proposed to end. At the other, a disproportionate number of Jews were involved in communism in this country as in others. Our vigorous opposition to both these anti-European forces may in itself have driven other Jews to join their fellows in common resistance to fascism, and it was perhaps understandable that fear of persecution in National Socialist Germany intensified this resistance to the point of frenzy, although in actual fact the BUF consistently expressed its disagreement with Hitler's "racialism".

---

22 *Hitler's Table Talk*

If only responsible British Jewry through its spokesmen and publications had decisively condemned those disgusting tactics and helped to prevent the accompanying violence, Jews in Britain would have found themselves faced with much less suspicion and hostility, which was felt by many besides BUF supporters and their friends. By its unrelenting denunciation of the New Movement before the war, and by the comparative silence which seemingly condoned the shocking acts of violence, British Jewry unfortunately tended to draw on itself the dislike of many fair-minded and otherwise tolerant people.

When this question could no longer be ignored, Mosley took up the challenge, and although he replied with vigour, he also showed restraint. He condemned neither the Jewish race nor the Jewish religion; but he denounced roundly the proven malpractices of many Jews. While assuring those Jews who lived peaceably within the law, and observed the customs of the land, that they had nothing to fear, he warned those others who took advantage of British hospitality, and especially of loopholes in the law, to mend their ways. He cautioned them that they must cease to behave as if they constituted "a state within the state". Their Talmudic law should not take precedence over the law of the land, and they should not regard themselves as belonging to a privileged race. If they behaved themselves, their rights as members of the community would be respected, but if not, they would have to take the consequences.

Mosley came to realise that what most of them had long demanded, a national home, would provide the solution to their problem, if Jews insisted, as they did, in maintaining their "apartness" from the people in whose land they resided.

Palestine, he considered, could not become their national home, as it was already occupied by Arabs who had lived there for as long as the English had been in England. The Holy Land would remain a spiritual centre for Judaism, and for the Christian and Moslem religions, but the great majority of Jews would be resettled in other habitable areas of the world in fertile living-space adequate to their numbers. A conference of European

East London crowd salutes Mosley

governments, who then controlled enormous areas of under-populated territory within their empires, could have settled this question, and incidentally averted the appalling suffering of Jews during the war.

9 - An Attempted Frame-Up: Reorganisation

There was one incident that proved to what lengths the powers-that-be, either the government of the day or those other powerful yet anonymous forces that help to constitute the Establishment, were prepared to go in their endeavours to halt or discredit Mosley.

There had been a successful and orderly meeting in the Pier Pavilion, Worthing. Mosley, and those Blackshirts who had been stewarding the meeting, were leaving the hall to have a meal in the town before going their separate ways, when they found their road blocked by a large, unlovely and menacing crowd, the foremost ranks of which, encouraged by voices demanding blood, surged forward to set about Mosley, who for his part stood his ground, squared up and defended himself with his usual skill and vigour.

He and his men held off several hundred attackers, behind whom they recognised well-known Red agitators and organisers of violence from East London and elsewhere, until sufficient police arrived to clear the street, when all dispersed quietly.

To the utter amazement of everyone who had participated in, or who had witnessed the scene, Mosley and three of his senior officials, Francis Hawkins, William Joyce (who was Director of Propaganda) and Bentinck-Budd, were served with summonses to appear at Worthing Police Court on charges of riotous assembly. Once again the targets of organised violence were being accused of the crimes of their opponents.

Mosley, however, under prolonged cross-examination by Mr. John Flowers, K.C., prosecution counsel, was able to expose the trumped up "case" against him. A.K. Chesterton has provided a lengthy account of the hearing which includes the following significant dialogue:

Counsel: Do you suggest that this prosecution is an after-thought?

Mosley: I should put it higher than that.

Counsel: Whose after-thought do you suggest?

Mosley: Far be it from me to know.

Counsel: Do you suggest that it is an after-thought of the police?

Mosley: I would suggest that it is an after-thought of the authorities behind the police.

Counsel: Who are you suggesting are the authorities behind the police?

Mosley: The police, as I understand it are controlled by the Government of the day; are they not?

Counsel: Are you seriously suggesting that this prosecution has been brought by the Government of the day?

Mosley: I believe it had been brought about by political considerations.

Counsel: I want to be quite clear as to your meaning. I suppose you mean by that that some political party has influenced the police of West Sussex to institute this prosecution. Is that what you mean?

Mosley: I suggest that, yes. I can give no other explanation for the bringing of this case.

Counsel: Are you suggesting that the individual members of the Worthing Police have given false evidence against you?

Mosley: That was my impression, yes.

Counsel: Are you suggesting that?

Mosley: I certainly think that their evidence was contradictory and false.

Superintendent Bristow, who had been in charge of police outside the Pier Pavilion, gave evidence that members of the mob were all "very nice people". Mosley's derisive comment from the box was: "I do no think that the song 'We want Mosley, dead or alive' is a song that is universally known among very nice people."

Despite the corroborative evidence of witnesses who testified to the "violence and obscenity of the mob", Mosley and his three officers were committed by the Worthing magistrates to the County Assizes. When eventually the case came to the Assize Court at Lewes, it was not only dismissed in scorn by the judge, but the defendants and their counsel were never called on to answer the charge.

"Whatever intention lay behind the prosecution," wrote A.K. Chesterton, "it was frustrated by British justice, which today in its higher reaches at least, is one of the few honest institutions left to the British people."

The end of the 'Daily Mail' alliance, plus increasing pressure from Jewish interests, made retrenchment necessary. Henceforth Mosley and the BUF had to stand alone; with no press-lord to champion them, they had to withstand attack from every quarter. Funds shrank, the rate of recruiting diminished, and membership dropped.

The BUF was subjected to gross misrepresentation and abuse. Public halls in areas controlled by councils with Labour majorities were refused to the Movement on trivial pretexts. Labour councillors in particular seemed to have strange notions as to the exercise of their duties to the public; they held the view that policies which they themselves disliked or feared should be

suppressed by action in the council chamber, even though local
fascists contributed to the payment of rates for the provision of
such facilities.

Public opinion was fomented against the Blackshirts, and
physical assaults became more frequent and dangerous. Open-
air meetings often ended in trouble, affrays and minor riots. BUF
members had been made the Ishmaelites of British politics. It
was "underhand, unfair, and damned un-English", as a First Sea
Lord had once described submarine warfare when first seriously
mooted in the days of Edward VII; but it served one good
purpose, for this was the testing time of the Movement.

Now scrambled to safety all those erstwhile members who had
been pleased to be identified with Mosley when the climate had
been mild. Those worthy of the cause stuck it out, and found
that the almost universal hostility put more iron into their souls,
out of which were forged those bonds of brotherhood that were
to endure for a lifetime.

A National Headquarters Staff, reduced in numbers, but
increased in efficiency, was installed on three floors of a large
office block, Sanctuary Buildings, in Great Smith Street,
Westminster, a stone's throw from Westminster Abbey, and
little further still from our ultimate objective – the Houses of
Parliament, popularly known as "the gasworks". This new office
was no social centre, but a place of business and administration.

There was change all round. '*The Fascist Week*', which first
appeared on 11th November, 1933, and was edited in turn by
Rex Tremlett and W.J. Leaper, was replaced from 23rd May,
1934, by '*The Blackshirt*'. '*Action*', published from 21st February,
1936, became Britain's best-selling political weekly. (The name
of the New Party's paper had also been '*Action*').

The successive editors of the revived '*Action*' – Harold Nicolson
had been editor of the earlier one – were A.K. Chesterton, a
rightwards-leaning firebrand who, metaphorically speaking,
preferred writing in vitriol to ink, a style which never left him

even after he left the Movement; John Beckett, the former Labour M.P., who wrote to give the masses what he thought was good for them and was at the same time easily assimilable; Geoffrey Dorman, primarily an airman (ex-R.F.C.) and an authority on aviation, who was an easy-going humorist, writing to evoke laughter rather than wrath or tears; and lastly there was Alexander Raven Thomson, a Scottish graduate in philosophy, the BUF's chief intellectual, and in Mosley's words an "exceptional thinker" who "towered above the M.P.s I had known in the Labour Cabinet of 1929."

10 - Abyssinia

More bricks, real and metaphorical, were thrown at British Blackshirts when Mussolini, weary of a troublesome neighbour to his African possessions of Eritrea and Somaliland, and glad of a justifiable excuse to extend his imperial frontiers, at the same time hoping to find oil, decided to march into Abyssinia.

There had been innumerable raids from across the Abyssinian border by shiftas, or armed bands, composed sometimes of large numbers of warriors in search of slaves and cattle. Complaints through the usual diplomatic channels to the Emperor, Haile Selassie, were less than fruitless, as that individual seemed to single out for especial approbation those Rasses, or local chieftains, responsible for the raids. Mussolini's patience gave out.

So when there was a bloody incident with more than a hundred deaths, over the rights of Somali nomads from Italian Somaliland to water their livestock at wells in a place called Wal-Wal on the Emperor's side of the ill-defined border, where their people had drawn water probably for more than a thousand years, Mussolini reacted drastically.

The British Foreign and Colonial Offices had been rather more patient, and had allowed those parts of Kenya adjacent to the Abyssinian border to become a depopulated wilderness for a depth of a hundred miles owing to the depredations of the slave-raiders. Notes of protest, couched in the nicest diplomatic language, had been passed to the Abyssinian government in Addis Ababa, the capital, where at least three Cabinet Ministers could neither read nor write, and two other statesmen of greater erudition could just manage with great mental and physical effort to scrawl their signatures on documents of State.

Haile Selassie - slave owner, despot and paedophile

The raids continued, and subjects of His majesty King George V had been carried off in chains, to be sold, mutilated, castrated, or forced into concubinage, according to sex, age and desirability.

Sir Edward Grigg, a former Governor of Kenya, later to become Lord Altrincham, made this state of affairs known to the Commons; Winston Churchill, too, denounced Abyssinia as a backwater of barbarism, and declared her unfitness for a place among the civilised nations. Nevertheless, indignant M.P.s whom no one would readily have suspected of sympathising with slave-raiders and slave-owners gladly espoused the cause of the gallant little Christian Emperor with the appealing black eyes, who had become the innocent victim of fascist rapacity.

Haile Selassie appealed to the League of Nations at Geneva, where he found the British Foreign Minister, Sir Samuel Hoare, later Lord Templewood, not particularly helpful. Sir Samuel, in his anxiety to avoid any possibility of armed conflict between Britain and Italy, concocted with Pierre Laval of France some sort of middle-road plan which, while it pleased neither Mussolini nor the Emperor, quite infuriated the bellicose pacifists of this country.

Prime Minister Baldwin, who for all his outward phlegm appeared to live in perpetual terror of vox populi, prevailed on Sir Samuel to resign from office. Poor Sir Samuel already considerably physically shaken from a nasty fall on the ice in Switzerland, and quite overcome by the scorn and hostility that his sincere effort for peace had evoked, departed from his place on the front bench amid the floods of tears considered appropriate to such occasions.

Hoare's successor in the Foreign Office was Anthony Eden, a well-meaning idealist whose good looks and immaculate attire had made him the hero of every spinster in Britain. It was the 'News Chronicle', after one if its polls of public opinion, that announced that they were women rather than men who favoured Eden. On the Continent his looks had earned him the name of "Lord Eye-lashes"; while Mosley somewhat unkindly alluded to him as "that tailor's dummy stuffed with straw".

Notwithstanding the derisive opinions of those coarse-grained persons who were unimpressed by his general elegance, (someone once referred to him as "a most ladylike young man"), he long remained to the dewy-eyed a reincarnation of Saint George.

The Emperor found a champion in Eden, who seemed to have an almost psychopathic antipathy to dictators, unless they happened to be of the Left.

So strange had become the political alignments of the 1930s, when the neat orange volumes of the Left Book Club stood on nearly every fashionably "thinking" person's bookshelves; and when almost every place of learning in Britain was engaged in the mass production of pink internationalists, and of out-and-out communists like Anthony Blunt, Guy Burgess, Donald Maclean and "Kim" Philby,[23] that Anthony Eden, a Tory Minister of the Crown could in practical effect veer far to the Left, and be esteemed for it. Despite the dreadful purges by Stalin then

---

23 These three traitors were graduates of Trinity, Cambridge, as was Alan Nunn May, the nuclear scientist who defected to Russia.

in progress, Eden was able to maintain a tolerance if not an affection, for Russian communism; yet at the same time he could evince detestation of the New Idea, and open opposition to it wherever it emerged. He was one of the persons responsible for promoting anti-fascism into a creed which automatically put its votaries among the politically elect and saved.

This reached its peak of imbecility during the last war, when a declaration of loathing for Nazism was deemed equivalent with devotion to Britain. The British people have paid dearly for this outlook, which explains their Puchs, Pontecorvos, and Blakes, poor rootless creatures whose anti-fascist hates were considered to render them worthy of trust and British citizenship.

The New Idea born of the First World War had no more confirmed opponent than Anthony Eden, despite the originally favourable personal impression Hitler made on him. Eden was prepared to risk war in the Mediterranean on behalf of the despotic ruler of one of the most backward corners of the globe.

The League, hitherto controlled largely by the powers with great possessions, who self-righteously opposed those poorer countries that wished to expand, a case of "haves" versus "have-nots", was now also becoming an instrument of Soviet design to extend communism from Russia to the world. Leon Trotsky in his exposure of the ruthless Stalin wrote concerning the League: "Today there is a Tower of Babel at the service of Stalin, and one of its centres is Geneva, that hot-bed of intrigue."[24]

In Britain, the press, most politicians, and the League of National Union, campaigned against Italy with vigour, making every appeal to sentiment, and little to reason. They worked themselves into a frenzy of righteous wrath as the Italian fascists prepared to invade the last free and independent native kingdom in Africa, with its gentle, noble and enlightened ruler, whose adoring subjects exercised a simple and archaic form of Christian worship.

24   *Spanish Arena*, by William Foss and Cecil Gerahty, p.132, pub. The Right Book Club.

The anti-fascist propagandists recalled the fabled glories of the ancient kingdom of Prester John, and credited Haile Selassie with them.

Therefore, when Lady Simon, addressing a meeting of the League of Nations Union in Manchester on behalf of the Anti-Slavery Society, announced that she had been praying for the day when one of the European Powers would occupy Abyssinia, and free the estimated two million slaves held there, she put her audience in a dreadful quandary. It was most awkward and uncomfortable. Here was an audience of middle-class "liberals", negative do-gooders, whose ears had long been stuffed with nonsense, having to listen to a practical good-doer, primed with unpleasant and unpalatable fact, who was telling them that which they were loathe to hear. Their minds, sealed with prejudice, refused to assimilate the truth when they were shown it, because they had no intention of rejecting their preconceived ideas concerning either the wickedness of Mussolini or the gentle Christian virtues of Haile Selassie.

Then someone from the body of the hall stood up and ventured to remark that surely so progressive and informed a person as the Emperor could be depended on to bring about the necessary reforms. Lady Simon feared not, as she had been reliably informed that next to the "Christian Church" of that country, Haile Selassie was the greatest slave-owner. The Emperor was reported to own vast estates in the fertile Tigre region, cultivated entirely by slave labour. The audience remained polite, but the atmosphere froze.

It had been as long ago as 30th July, 1923, that Marquis Curzon of Nedleston, the father-in-law of Oswald Mosley, and at that time Foreign Secretary, in reply to a question from the Earl of Beauchamp in the House of Lords on slave-trading in the Horn of Africa, had stated that the British Minister in Addis Ababa had officially enquired of Ras Tafari, then Regent, later to become Emperor Haile Selassie, if he would accept co-operation from the League of Nations in suppressing slavery. Ras Tafari had declined.

A few years later two British officers, Major Darley and Dr. Dyce Sharp, reported one specific instance when Haile Selassie had been pleased to accept from a prosperous subject seeking favour a gift of 140 slaves, "children of both sexes between six and fourteen years of age". Following this disclosure, a report was sent to the Foreign Office on 8th April, 1932, above the signatures of Mr. Charles Roberts, Mr. Travers Buxton and Sir John Harris, on behalf of the Anti-Slavery Society, uncompromisingly stating: "The Emperor would hardly be in a position to know the actual number of slaves he owns himself... He receives gifts of slaves every year."

On 2nd August, 1935, in a speech at Oxford, Sir John Harris made known: "There are British subjects held as slaves in Abyssinia, and if part of the Italian grievances against Abyssinia are due to countless raids on her boundaries, it must be remembered that just as many raids were committed when the Abyssinians violated our frontiers and entered British territory." One newspaper reported this under the caption, "Mussolini Wages a Battle, which is also Ours", which was unusually truthful reporting for those times when the white-washing of Haile Selassie and the blackening of Mussolini were deemed essential to preserve and furbish up "democracy".

When the Italians launched their invasion, the outcry in London and Geneva reached a crescendo. The Emperor, who had been on the point of opening negotiations with Mussolini, and even to cede most of the territorial conquests made by his predecessor Menelik II, retaining for himself and his own people, the Amhara, their rightful homeland of the high central plateau, was persuaded by warlike voices raised on his behalf at Geneva to reject the terms.

Anthony Eden demanded that the League of Nations should invoke "sanctions" against Italy; this meant the diplomatic and economic boycott of that country by all other nations. Some League zealots even called for the drastic measure of closing the Suez Canal against Italian shipping. As every soldier and every gun for his Abyssinian venture had to pass through the canal, Mussolini would have regarded its closure as an act of war.

The prophets of the press and wireless got busy, and in addition to calling Mussolini rude names, foretold every possible disaster for the fascist bullies. They asserted with certainty that the invaders would be defeated by the waterless wastes of the Ogaden, and by the wild mountain ranges leading to the central plateau. With the absence of roads their transport problems would be insoluble. They would be decimated by tribal guerrillas, under the brave Rassess; stragglers would be mutilated by the ferocious Danakils, who adorn their necks with the dried genital organs of their victims; and the wounded would be devoured by the giant striped hyenas peculiar to that part of Africa. Disease and sunstroke would carry off the remainder. In fact, Haile Selassies's well-wishers promised him a walk-over.

The British Fleet was concentrated at Alexandria to be in a position to cut the Italian supply route at a few hours' notice. The possibility of war drew ever closer.

Sir Walter Citrine, the trade union leader, supposedly moderate in his views (hence doubtless the knighthood and later a barony), was quoted by General Fuller as having told the Trades Union Congress: "Here is your chance. You may defend Russia by defending Abyssinia."

'*Action*' reported Citrine as telling the T.U.C.: "Hitler and Mussolini are committed to a certain course and that nothing but force would restrain them. So we have to envisage the League of Nations having to take decisive action of a military character,"[25] In response to this speech, Mosley commented: "One thing only matters to the old parties, and that is to check the spiritual revival of Europe. The Labour Party now openly declared that "war alone can do it."

By their attitudes and pronouncements those responsible for the aims and policy of the Labour party proved irrefutably that contention, then voiced by Mosley for the first time, but which he was to repeat over the next few years, that "all wars are good

---

25   *Action*, 18.9.1937

to some Labour leaders, provided three conditions are fulfilled. First, that the war served the interests of Soviet Russia, and not the interests of Great Britain. Secondly, that the British troops have no arms with which to fight. Thirdly, that the Labour leaders are not included with the troops."

Unfortunately for the League-lovers and kindred souls, Britain was in no position to fight any major power. The very people who screamed the loudest to stop Mussolini were those most responsible for the deliberate run-down of Britain's fighting services. The Lords of the Admiralty had to warn the Prime Minister that in the event of hostilities, the Royal Navy would be unable to prevent the Mediterranean becoming an Italian lake. The Government also woke up to the realisation that the R.A.F. which in 1919, with 22,600 aircraft, 180 squadrons, and a personnel of approximately 300,000, had been the world's mightiest, [26] now ranked fifth or even sixth. [27]

To complete the picture of Britain's "armed might" in the Mediterranean, wherewith to deter Mussolini from his evil course of bringing civilisation to Abyssinia, the only anti-aircraft gun that could have been made available for the defence of Malta was that piece of artillery which reposed in the Imperial War Museum, London. [28]

Only two years previously, in 1933, an East Fulham by-election had shown the depth to which pacifism had penetrated, when the National Coalition vote dropped by 19,000 in a straight fight

---

26   *Dowding – The Battle of Britain*, by Robert Wright, p.38, pub Macdonald.

27   The person most responsible for the decline of the Royal Air Force was Churchill who was "War Minister and Air Minister" combined from 1918 to 1921, the crucial period for the reconstruction of the forces. The Air Staff had evolved a plan under which the post-war R.A.F. was to consist of 154 squadrons, of which 40 were for home defence. Under Churchill's aegis this was whittled down to a mere 24 squadrons with only two for home defence, and the plan for state-aided airways covering the Empire was also discarded. When he moved to a fresh office in 1921, *The Times* has this comment on the fruits of his regime at the Air Ministry: "He leaves the body of British flying well-nigh at that last gasp when a military funeral would be all that would be left for it." *Churchill at War*, by Liddell Hart, pub. In Encounter, April 1966.

28   *Our Times. 1900-1960*, by Commander Stephen King-Hall, p.157, pub. Faber & Faber.

between Alderman William Waldron, a prominent local Tory, and John Wilmot of the ILP. George Lansbury as Labour Party Leader spoke on Wilmot's platform in the town hall, and wrote him the usual official letter of encouragement and support, declaring:

"I would close every recruiting station, disband the Army, and dismiss the Air Force. I would abolish the whole dreadful equipment of war, and say to the world 'do your worst'." [29]

Britain had been reduced almost to impotence by the pressure exerted on a series of spineless governments by the Peace Pledge Union, the League of Nations Union, the National Peace Council, and by all those well-meaning, progressive-minded and bemused persons, particularly the educationists, who looked to Russia and the League to conduct suffering humanity to some new golden age. The person promised so much, and on whose behalf so many rusty and blunted sabres were being rattled, had reached his throne by guile rather than by dynastic right. Ras Tafari, to give him his original name and title, had been no more than a provincial tyrant, comparable to some powerful Norman baron in post-Conquest England. He was, however, distantly related to Menelik II, and could therefore boast of his alleged descent from the Queen of Sheba, by her passing love affair with King Solomon.

When King Menelik II died in 1911, his grandson Lidj Yassu, who was only a child, had been declared king. He was soon pushed off his throne to make room for his Aunt Zaudita, who was proclaimed Queen, with Ras Tafari as prince regent. Shackled in chains of gold the poor little ex-king was imprisoned in the ancient city of Hara; while the affairs of his kingdom, now nominally his aunt's, were in the hands of the Regent, who upheld his mediaeval system by mediaeval methods.

A French traveller, Marcel Griaule, who was a recognised authority on Abyssinia, once witnessed the execution of a wretched man who had accidently incurred displeasure; having been swathed in

29 *Britain's Locust Years, 1918-1940*, by William McElwes, p.221, pub. Faber & Faber.

strips of cloth soaked in wax and honey, he was burned alive, a leaping, capering, shrieking pillar of fire, kept in the centre of stage by a ring of spear-men, who were actually the household eunuchs of the potentate who had ordered the execution.

Griaule did not reveal the identity of the man responsible for the atrocity, and who presided personally over the dreadful scene, but tactfully referred to him as "the Prince". De Manfried, another Frenchman, held by many to be the greatest European authority on that part of the African continent, writing in the Paris publication, 'Voila', in August, 1935, declared without fear of contradiction that Griaule's prince was in fact the Prince regent, Ras Tafari, now known as the Emperor Haile Selassie. Professor Baravelli, an Italian authority on those parts, held no doubt in his mind that it was Ras Tafari who had been responsible.

Thanks to modern techniques in brainwashing, the printing and broadcasting of mendacious news and slanted views, this African tyrant who had strayed into the twentieth century was now being idolised and championed by ignorant British sentimentalists, most of whom had not known previously of his existence, nor had they much idea where he held sway. The Empress Zaudita died suddenly, as inconvenient persons are prone to die inexplicably in those less regulated lands where coroners' inquests are unheard of. Ras Tafari, modestly styling himself "Haile Selassie, King of Kings, Conquering Lion of Judah, and Emperor of Ethiopia" was graciously pleased to fill the vacancy.

When the Italian invasion was launched, a strong detachment of troops under General Graziani was projected towards Harar with the undeclared but obvious intention of freeing Lidj Yassu, now middle-aged and fat, and placing him as a puppet-ruler on the throne of his grandfather. As the Italian column approached the city and its capture seemed inevitable, the unfortunate pretender was suddenly stricken with some mysterious illness, and died. His departure from this world, while having much in common with the manner of demise of Aunt Zaudita, deprived Mussolini of a highly valuable propaganda piece.

After a campaign lasting seven months, with more road-making and bridge-building than actual fighting, the Italians entered Addis Ababa. They claimed that within that time they had liberated two million slaves, but estimated that there yet remained many thousands more to be freed. The Anti-Slavery Society had underestimated the number of human beings held in perpetual serfdom in the Christian Realm of the King of Kings.

While the Italian troops and auxiliary services cleaned up and disinfected his former capital, which had been pillaged by the Abyssinians themselves, Haile Selassie sat in the captain's cabin of the British warship which was carrying him into exile, counting his thalers or Maria Teresa dollars. If I remember rightly the newspapers reported that he had been able to bring away with him some seventy coffers of gold coin. Ladislas Farago, the Hungarian journalist who had visited him in his palace shortly before the war with Italy, had noticed how he "loved money". The Emperor's secretary who accompanied him into exile, when interviewed by the special correspondent of the '*Daily Herald*', stated that his master had between £4,000,000 and £5,000,000 deposited in London banks, while his Empress's own fortune was distributed among banks in Cairo, Jerusalem and Paris. As the vessel conveying him steamed northwards through the Red Sea and the Suez Canal, she passed fleets of Italian transports heading south, bearing those colonial administrators, medical officers of health, scientists, engineers, mechanics and agricultural experts, priests, nuns and nurses, who hoped – and to a large extent managed – to bring the benefits of civilisation to one of the darkest places in Africa. This was the ruler and this the regime that the Old Gangs in their vendetta against the New Idea were prepared to risk war to defend.

Anthony Eden's diplomacy was responsible for making an enemy of Mussolini, who previously had held Britain in high regard, and had been anxious to cement further the age-long friendship between the two peoples. Now, bursting with anger and indignation, he could not understand why he should be prevented by Britain from bringing peace and order to a barbarous land, exactly as Britain herself had done on so many occasions.

What Mussolini failed to realise was that the imperial concept in Britain, and the proud national spirit that had animated it, were nearly dead. All will to imperial greatness was being snuffed out by the teachers of leftish views who had invaded the schools and universities, by the deluge of books and pamphlets emanating from the publishing houses of Victor Gollancz and others, and by newspapers like the 'News Chronicle' and the 'Daily Herald'. The former, with its bitter fellow-traveller cartoonist, Low, was especially responsible for bringing the British imperial concept into disrepute. Low was content to ignore Russian Red imperialism in Asia and on the Baltic. He refrained also from ridiculing international bankers, unprincipled company promoters, or captains of industry even when they were known to exploit workers, but concentrated his venom for the demolition by ridicule of those servants of the state whom he exemplified in the apocryphal Colonel Blimp.

Colonel Blimp and his kind had served the Empire faithfully for generations, concerning themselves not with personal gain but with the development and administration of distant and backward lands. They had sweated in the Indian Civil Service, and under the Colonial Office had administered justice in West and East Africa, the Sudan, Malaya and many other far-off places. They had daily faced danger and disease; they had protected the poor and the weak from the dacoit and the thug, as well as from the tyranny of local despots; they had fed the hungry in time of famine; and they had punished the transgressor with impartial laws, for neither reward nor honours, but in pursuit of an ideal along the narrow path of duty.

A small minority of the Blimps may have been pompous, humourless and narrow-minded; but they were almost without exception brave, honourable and just, and did not deserve extermination as a breed by a warped and embittered cartoonist of destructive outlook, employed by a cocoa-capitalist journal. The 'News Chronicle' of those days was so "liberal" in its outlook that it appeared prepared to sanction almost any policy so long as it attacked the "Right".

If Mussolini had kept himself better informed of political trends in Britain, he would not have been surprised at the general reaction here to his venture in empire-making. In his ostracism he was driven to seek the friendship of Hitler. Thus by the genius of Anthony Eden, Britain's Secretary of State for Foreign Affairs, was born the Berlin-Rome Axis, and Europe pushed several degrees nearer the Second World War.

In Britain almost all sections of the community, victims of lying propaganda, became filled with loathing for the Italian "fascist beasts" and their Duce, who were being accused of trampling underfoot an ancient Christian kingdom and its brave, freedom-loving people. Almost every wartime atrocity was attributed to the Italians, none to the Abyssinians. The press made no mention of the Egyptian doctor of the Red Crescent Field Ambulance, who tried in vain to prevent the torturing to death of some Italian prisoners by their Abyssinian captors.

In actual fact, many of the Somali, Nilotic and negroid peoples went over to the Italians in order to avenge themselves on the cruel, proud Amhara, who had conquered and enslaved them. The Amara overlords, Haile Selassie's own people, who considered themselves a white race, had overflowed from their homeland, the Ethiopian plateau extending from Addis Ababa north to Adowa, and since 1897 had conquered and held in servitude some thirty other tribes and races. This historical background and these topical facts were withheld from the public, which was regaled instead with fantasies and fictitious accounts of Gallas, Dinkas, Danakils and Somalis rallying around their gallant Emperor.

The rapid advance of the Italian armies were ascribed by the anti-fascist propagandists to their use of poison gas. They did use mustard-gas released from aircraft, not on towns and villages, nor even on military encampments, but they laid carpets of it to protect their flanks exposed in battle, and on those bridle-paths over which the Abyssinian troops were supplied.

This stratagem incapacitated the pack-animals of the supply trains. It is not a nice expedient, but as it was a non-lethal gas, it was considerably less unpleasant than those forms of retaliation practised on the few Italians who fell alive into enemy hands.

A variety of causes contributed to the defeat of Abyssinia, which was swift and complete. There was the hatred of the subjected peoples for the Amhara, who had enslaved them several decades before, and there were those Amara chiefs, such as Ras Gugsa, who went over to the Italians because of personal grievances against Haile Selassie. Other factors included the tactical errors of the Abyssinian army commanders, who persisted in giving open battle, only to be defeated time and again, when they could have inflicted infinitely more damage with few losses in guerrilla warfare.

Mustard-gas and aerial bombardment, and other civilised refinements, contributed to the Italian victory; but the war was won mostly by the amazing speed with which roads were made and bridges built in appallingly difficult terrain. These engineering feats were made possible only by the crusading fervour of an army of dedicated zealots.

This was the spirit of fascism, which gloried in hardship and danger in service to its country. It was identical with that spirit which had animated Garibaldi's red-shirted legionaries who had, in the words of that inspired patriot, "marched and fought all day on the thought of Italy, and a bunch of grapes".

The Abyssinian war was won by men who General Fuller had seen in the field, and had laughed at their "long beards and short rifles", but described as "spiritually exalted".

11 - Mind Britain's Business

While the invasion of Abyssinia was in progress, almost every pacifist in Britain was clamouring for war against Italy in the interest of peace; which was not strictly logical, but people who throb with emotion seldom pause to think.

General Fuller wrote: "In Great Britain the truth concerning the war was rigorously suppressed, and through a criminal propaganda the country was thrown into a state of hysteria in which the Established Church joined hands with the atheists in Moscow in supporting a barbaric slave state against a Catholic people."[30]

Pierre Laval was able to steer France away from the likelihood of armed conflict with Italy; but in Britain, Anthony Eden was never more applauded than during those months when he was demanding sanctions, regardless of their probable cost. There is no knowing where his indignation might not have dragged his country but for Mosley, who, holding great meeting after great meeting not in defence of fascist Italy but for peace, persuaded Britain not to interfere in a matter which was no concern of hers.

It was in these circumstances with the imminent danger of Eden involving his country in war with one of her oldest friends, that Mosley initiated his "Mind Britain's Business" campaign. Hundreds of meetings of protest against Eden's policies were held throughout the country. Mosley himself addressed crowded meetings three or four times a week; every registered speaker in British Union spoke night after night on the same urgent theme, and at the same time massive poster parades were staged in London and the chief provincial cities warning the

30   *The First of the League Wars*, by Major General J.F.C. Fuller, p.156, pub. Eyre & Spottiswoode.

nation of the dangers that Eden, his prompters, and his followers were so recklessly incurring. This campaign was responsible for a noticeable improvement in the attitude of the public to the Movement. The anti-fascists of whatever hue, were as confirmed as ever in their hostility; but the open-minded, the undecided, and those who doubted the wisdom of such a war, were relieved to find that there was one serious political body determined to prevent it.

This was the beginning of what can only be described as the "breakthrough" of British Union. Despite the press, the B.B.C., and all the political hysteria, the people of Britain did not want to go to war with Italy, nor with any other country.

Without any of the media of mass persuasion the Movement's propagandists suddenly became aware that they were being listened to, and heeded. For the first time Mosley found himself addressing vast and enthusiastic audiences in the East End of London. In Victoria Park, Bethnal Green, he spoke to a crowd of more than one hundred thousand persons who acclaimed his views with enthusiasm.

In Norwich, an open-air meeting on the market place on a Sunday evening drew an estimated ten thousand persons. The meeting was orderly; but afterwards there were scenes caused by enthusiasm rather than antagonism as men strove to break through the crush to shake Mosley by the hand, and the streets were blocked and traffic brought to a standstill by the crowds which accompanied him back to the Royal Hotel.

This was so far Mosley's biggest meeting in the provinces, and coming immediately after the great Victoria Park rally, augured well. Those who had followed Mosley's fortunes since New Party days, and the birth of the BUF, knew that here at last was the beginning of mass support.

One crowded meeting during the "Mind Britain's Business" campaign, held in the bath-hall of some municipal baths in Nottingham, was memorable for a determined attempt by the

Red Front to wreck it. Several hundred Reds were inside the building, while thousands surged around outside, chanting: "One, two, three, four, five. We want Mosley, dead or alive."

The hall was filled to capacity. The Reds declared themselves as the British flag and local District Colours were paraded down the aisle by a Colour party of ex-Servicemen wearing their medals and decorations, to take up position below the platform. The spectacle of the marching on of the "Union Jack", generally to the roll of drums, invariably drove the Reds into paroxysms of rage. They would stand up in their seats and howl their hate, at the same time shaking their clenched fists at that emblem of Britain's former greatness.

This pantomime served one very useful purpose; it showed the organisers of the meeting the strength and whereabouts of the trouble-seekers, and it afforded them the opportunity to post tough and reliable stewards unobtrusively round those areas where outbreaks of noise and violence could be expected. The gallery if there was one, and the rear of the hall were the favoured spots for the hooligans enlisted in the service of Karl Marx to gather.

What was noticeable was the way that the local Red intellectuals and leaders, those who were using the roughs in the interests of communism, had selected seats for themselves near the exits so that they could make a quick get-away if things looked unhealthy.

It had been the responsibility of the officer in charge of stewards to ascertain that none of his men were carrying weapons; he would detail a couple of subordinate officers to search the Blackshirts reporting for duty at public meetings, "Frisk", I think, is the word used in police and criminal circles for this form of inspection.

As the stewards were volunteers who risked possible serious injury for no more material reward than a pint of tea and a plate of food before being dismissed, most of us found this duty distasteful, and were relieved when after a time it was discontinued. The frisking of Blackshirts by their own officers had been allowed to lapse by the time of this Nottingham meeting; but I cannot recall a single instance either then or of any member of British Union having been found carrying a weapon of any description.

The storm of abuse that greeted the "Union Jack" that night in Nottingham was exceptional in its vehemence and duration. At last it abated; then Mosley walked alone on to the platform, which was the signal for it to break out again, but this time with even greater fury.

He stood motionless waiting until the yells and jeers would subside sufficiently to allow him to make a start. Then the baying having at length died down he spoke of the folly of driving Italy into a position where she would have to resort to arms for the sake of her very existence. He pointed out the suicidal stupidity of provoking war against a friendly people, particularly at a time when Britain's own defences were in a deplorable state, thanks to the neglect of the late Labour Government and of the contemporary Government of Stanley Baldwin.

Every mention of Anthony Eden as the leading protagonist of sanctions and war drew a roar of applause from those parts of the hall where the Reds were congregated. So Mosley invited the prosperous Tory types occupying the front seats to turn round, and study the kind of persons who were applauding a Conservative foreign Minister with such enthusiasm.

Presently the uproar rendered Mosley's voice inaudible, despite loudspeakers. A senior Blackshirt officer went up to the man who was making most noise, and from whom the other Reds seemed to be taking their cue, and asked him politely, as per the prescribed drill, either to sit down and shut up, or to leave the hall.

The approach of the Blackshirt steward was the signal for the interrupter's friends to leap to their feet, fold up their collapsible iron chairs, and to commence to lay about with those handy weapons.

We Marched with Mosley

A squad of stewards, tough lads from Merseyside, who had been standing in readiness, flung themselves on the Reds, and with fists versus flailing chairs started to clear the rear of the hall. It was a hot scrimmage, but muscles toughened in ships' stokeholes, in heaving in wet hawsers, and in lumping cargoes on the dockside, prevailed. Genuine members of the audience who had come to learn what Mosley had to offer, scrambled out of the way and took refuge in the wooden dressing cubicles that line the side aisles.

A military-looking gentleman of middle age who leaned over the railing of the gallery, beaming delightedly on the turmoil beneath, was identified as the Chief Constable of Nottingham. He appeared far from distressed at the treatment he saw being meted out to some of the worst elements of his city. Doubtless he recognised many of the hoodlums, and being aware of the antecedents of many of them, was unable to dissemble his joy at seeing them getting their just desserts, and being bundled one after the other out of the building. When it became apparent that victory was going to the Blackshirts, there was a panic rush for the exits by people who so far had been quietly seated. They were the Left Wing intellectuals leaving the hall voluntarily, fearful lest they too should be recognised and slung out headlong with that absence of gentleness that had marked the departure of their more militant comrades.

Order restored, those who had taken sanctuary in the cubicles, emerged and resumed their seats. Mosley had taken up the threads of his interrupted discourse, and a doctor newly qualified was busy patching up the injured in a space at the back of the hall beneath the platform, when suddenly bricks, stones, and broken bottles, collectively known as "Irish confetti", showered in from outside and fell among the audience. They had been hurled in through side doors that had been opened wide on account of the stuffy atmosphere.

A three-quarter brick landed at the feet of the young doctor as he attended a victim. He gazed down at it in mute astonishment, then stared round, exclaiming, "I never knew that such people really existed."

I explained to him that Nottingham was not unique in possessing citizens who belonged to that stratum of society known as "the submerged tenth", and that it was from this submerged tenth that the Reds recruited their street-fighters and terrorists.

The "Mind Britain's Business" campaign to prevent war against Italy saw the emergence of British Union from a position of relative unimportance in national affairs, to one of sufficient political impact to influence a considerable section of the public. The Old Gang while professing to ignore, or to treat these blackshirted interlopers with the contempt they considered they deserved, were in reality acutely conscious of the lengthening shadow that was being thrown across the sham battlefield of democratic party politics, by these new intruders.

There was a stiffening of what had been nicknamed the "Jelly Front against Fascism". Questions, often imbecile, but generally apprehensive, were being asked in both Houses of Parliament.

When some young Blackshirts in Gloucestershire, who were also aviation enthusiasts, joined a local flying club, there were immediate protests against "Mosley's private flying corps." A small fleet of powerful black vans purchased for the conveyance of stewards and equipment to and from meetings, with wire-mesh over the windows to protect passengers from "Irish confetti", were at once dubbed by the press "armoured cars".

The Earl of Kinnoul who had inveighed against these vehicles in the House of Lords, did not avail himself of Mosley's offer to be seated in one, while small arms were loosed off at it; so that he could ascertain for himself the density of the armour. To the fascists who rode in them these vans became known as "agony wagons"; nor with their bleak and chilly interiors, their draughts and austere seating, were they misnamed.

Their story was interesting. They had been built by Messrs. Armstrong, Siddley for the Soviet Government of Russia for the use of the secret police, the dreaded O.G.P.U.; but the celebrated trial and subsequent conviction for espionage of Monkhouse and other British engineers in Russia had led to the cancellation of the order. The vans thus became 'frustrated exports', in the present inimitable terminology of the Board of Trade; so British Union snapped them up comparatively cheaply.

They were strong, reliable vehicles, and served the Movement well and for a different purpose from that for which they had doubtless been intended. In the service of the O.G.P.U. they would almost certainly have been used for the rounding up of the victims of Stalin's purges, and their conveyance to the Lubianka Prison for execution as "Trotskyists, saboteurs, counter-revolutionaries, deviationists and wreckers".

More public halls were refused to Mosley and to other British Union spokesmen; at the same time objections were being raised in a number of places to the holding of open-air rallies and meetings. In many instances these bans applied only to British Union. The Reds and the Pinks were permitted to hold their anti-fascist indignation meetings in public places and buildings denied to those they condemned as the destroyers of freedom. Secure in their knowledge that they had powerful friends behind them, the Reds increased their violence.

Political creeds as well as religious thrive on persecution, therefore the Movement now made some of its most significant progress. In the days of Lord Rothermere's backing recruits had flocked in, and financial aid had been generous. Money was never again to be as accessible as in those balmy days; but in general the quality of those who then enrolled had not been of the highest.

The men and women who now joined the Movement came in with their eyes opened, and were under no illusions as to what was in store for them. They enrolled mainly for the preservation of peace, and in the conviction that peace could best be maintained by national unity and strength, and not by internal dissension and weakness. The exhibition of empty threats followed by humiliating retreat, which was how the Baldwin Government "stood up to" Mussolini, persuaded a number of people jealous of their country's good name, to go over to Mosley's cause.

11 - Mind Britain's Business

The fascist recruits who came in during 1935 and 1936 knew that in joining a revolutionary movement they were saying goodbye to comfort and safety. They realised that henceforth they would be liable to victimisation at work or in business, there would be loss of friends, even disrupted home life, and always the risk of grave physical injury. From this time until the implementation of Defence Regulation 18B in May, 1940, the quality of those who enrolled in British Union reached its best. The tone of the Movement never stood higher.

As Mosley explained to Beverley Nichols: "We have advanced as a religious movement. People have joined us, not as they would a political party, but as they would join a church. And that is the spirit in which we have accepted them. We have said to them, 'By joining us you will get nothing... except victimisation... Do you still want to come?'

"When a man says "yes" to these questions, he is a man I can trust. Ten men like that are stronger than ten thousand who automatically vote at the elections for a Member who they think is more likely to pander to their interests. The men like that will be heard and listened to, long after the ten thousand who shout them down have been forgotten. And I have not ten men... but thousands."[31]

British Union was to experience more set-backs; but these were mainly financial, which hardened rather than weakened resolve. From the time of the Abyssinian War until Winston Churchill became Prime Minister in 1940, was the period in the history of the Movement to which survivors can look back with the greatest pride. Gone were the days when District Officers in their rawness and inexperience compromised themselves, and involved British Union in all manner of scrapes and difficulties; when District Treasurers absconded all too frequently with funds, and when District Headquarters had often been no more than social centres, clubs where beer and cups of tea flowed, rather than offices for political administration.

---

31   *News of England*, by Beverley Nichols, pub. Jonathan Cape.

Oswald Mosley inspects members of British Union 1935.

Gone too was the easy optimism of the early days, that "1914 spirit" as it has been described; it had been replaced by determination and stern resolve. All could see that they were in for a long, hard and hazardous struggle. There was no timetable for victory now; only the knowledge that unless Mosley prevailed, the sun would set on Britain and on her imperial glory. The Hard Left with gratuitous "liberal" assistance was weakening Britain and destroying the spirit that had built the British Empire. The mastermind behind this plan of deliberate self-destruction was that of the Red International who operated directly through the Communist Party of Great Britain, and indirectly but even more effectively through its innumerable stooge organisations, such as the International Peace Campaign, the National Peace Council, the Council of Action for Peace and Reconstruction, British Youth Peace Assembly, London Federation of Peace Councils, China Campaign Committee, Abyssinia Association, and the New Times and Ethiopian League, and always including the Left Book Club. This was the time of which George Orwell wrote in his 'Inside The Whale' that "for about three years, in fact, the central stream of English Literature was more or less under communist control".

The Hard Left worked openly and unashamedly for these ends; the "liberal" blindly and stupidly in the professed interests of peace and of solidarity against "fascism, hunger, and war", and other equally meaningless catch-cries designed to ensnare the kind, unthinking, and emotional British masses.

The Right was too subservient to the great financial interests, and at the same time too inert, to come to grips with anything. Its policy described by Mosley as "bluster, and run away" in international affairs, with drift and stagnation at home, seemed to be the most of which it was capable.

This was that shameful period in Britain's history, when she espoused not only all the wrong causes and all the wrong persons, but also sold the lot.

For those who may think that I am being unjust to those who persuaded our country to adopt those policies, I beg them to recall not only Haile Selassie, but Doctor Negrin, Senores Azana and Largo Caballero, Doctor Kurt Schuschnigg, Doctor Benes and M. Jan Masaryk, Colonel Beck, Field Marshal Smigly-Ryds, and King Carol of Rumania. Those are some of the heads of states whom Britain, or persons of high political standing in Britain, urged to embark on policies to follow courses of action that all ended in ruin and disaster.

It was a stinking and putrescent period, on which posterity will look back with incredulity and contempt. On the one hand there was lethargy and rot; on the other, the Red cancer spreading wide and deep, using the sentiments of pity, love of fair play, and abhorrence of war as the channels for its propaganda.

While Tories, Liberals and Socialists blathered and dithered, only the Fascists and Communists knew where they were going.

12 - Red Opposition

For British Union, 1936 had been a year of increasing progress with bigger meetings and rallies, and more impressive propaganda marches. The Movement was not allowed to get away peaceably with its success. The opposition, from the lethargic Right to the volatile Left with its intellectuals adept in name-calling and in coining slogans, with its stone-throwing street-fighters, and razor–wielding gangsters, was alarmed at the lengthening columns of Blackshirts on the march through England. Those faceless beings who marshalled these same opponents, were yet more alarmed at the manner in which the public, in ever-increasing numbers, gathered to hear Mosley.

So great was the general interest that, except in small country towns, Mosley now almost invariably spoke to concourses of thousands and tens of thousands. A. Raven Thomson, A.K. Chesterton, William Joyce, John Beckett, and Clement Bruning, commanded big audiences wherever they spoke. All five were first class public speakers; but as orator and debater Joyce eclipsed them.

These successes provoked the Reds to yet more determined efforts to disrupt our meetings. Agitators, specialists in fomenting trouble and organising riots, and roughs to whom violence was a pleasure, were moved about the country, frequently in furniture vans, to inflame opinion against Mosley, and at the same time to endeavour to intimidate his followers with their savage methods.

The Reds as members of an international organisation which had made a study of rioting and street-fighting "from China to Peru" had printed text books on the subject, going into precise detail how to prepare and organise riots, and how the counter-measures of the police should themselves be countered. One example will suffice; the communist manual which came into my hands stated categorically that the most effective way to discourage the police was to throw vitriol over them as they emerged from their riot vans, and were still bunched together.

An open-air meeting on Corporation Field, Hull, addressed by Mosley, was the occasion of what could have been a fatality, when a bullet penetrated his car window.

At this meeting the violence was unusually severe, and the communist tactics callous and culpable in the extreme. They formed a squad of young children, mostly under ten years of age, to stand immediately in front of the platform and there beat tins cans, and create pandemonium; while the Red United Fighting Front stood far back, lost to sight in the crowd.

The moment Mosley mounted the rostrum, in this instance a hired coal-lorry, the Reds opened up at long range, a barrage of bricks, stones, broken bottles, and pieces of scrap metal, most of which fell short among the crowd, or on the children placed there by the communists. One small girl zestfully beating a tin, received a three-quarter brick wrapped in newspaper full in the face; she dropped without a sound, her features a bloody pulp.

At almost the same moment the reporter for a Hull newspaper, busy with pencil and pad alongside the platform, suddenly put his hands to his face, made a spasmodic half-turn, then without a cry sank to the ground.

Blackshirts and onlookers collapsed beneath the furious fusillade which continued without let-up for some moments. Finding things going their way, bolder members of the Red Front came forward and bombarded the platform from closer range. This was probably the roughest, toughest meeting we ever held.

It was not only in the North that we met violent opposition. On Sunday 4th October, 1936, we planned a great march through East London. We had gained mass support nowhere so rapidly nor with less doubts than in the entirely working-class area of what is known as the East End. On this Sunday it had been intended to march from Cable Street to four meetings to be addressed by Mosley in Bethnal Green, Bow, Limehouse and Shoreditch, places where sympathy for British Union was strongest, as was later shown in the London County Council Elections of 1937.

The Reds and their friends, the fellow-travellers, feeling that the tide was turning against them, decided to resort to still sterner measures to stem the fascist advance. They made up their minds that Mosley's proposed march and meetings should not be allowed to take place, at whatever price. They laid their plans long beforehand.

There was a prominent member of the underworld named Jack Comer, alias Jack Spot, self-styled "King of Soho", whose reminiscences appeared in the '*Sunday Chronicle*' (11.1.1955), in which he wrote of his preparations to fix the Mosley men when they appeared in Cable Street. He recalled how:

"On the day before the procession was due, I went to an old cabinet-maker in Aldgate, and asked him to make me a weapon... the old cabinet-maker did a beautiful job. He made me a short, turned sofa-leg and filled the top, the wider end, with lead. I slipped this into a paper carrier-bag."

As the Blackshirts began to arrive at the rendezvous in small batches and parties, most of them having travelled by bus or by Underground, they were set upon by Jack Spot's friends, felled with similar clubs and other weapons, kicked when they were down, and quickly converted into hospital cases.

One of the first to reach Cable Street with a few companions had been "Tommy" Moran, a popular British Union speaker, a fearless fellow from out of the Royal Navy, and a former cruiser-weight boxing champion of the Fleet. Moran's friends soon lay sprawled in the street, uninterested in what was happening nearby, where the ex-sailor with his back to a wall, was putting up a terrific fight against half a dozen or more men who were attacking him simultaneously.

Headline from *The Blackshirt* highlighting the Newcastle violence.

His assailants closed in on him; but one after the other he sent them reeling back with clean boxing blows; until he too at last was knocked down by a blow on the head from a chair-leg wrapped round with barbed wire.

A newsreel cameraman happened to have his apparatus in an upstairs window ready to film the start of the Blackshirt march, when Moran made his epic resistance immediately in front of his lens. The camera caught the entire incident, which was soon being shown as a news feature in cinemas throughout the country.

From the point of view of the Movement's opponents this news item was the worst possible propaganda. The spectacle of one unarmed man battling against impossible odds – I think the camera showed nine men attacking him – inspired cinema audiences to applaud. That would never do. Fascists had to be shown as low-type thugs and bullies who with coshes and knuckle-dusters beat up poor harmless old Jewish shopkeepers. Therefore the film, despite being a genuine scoop, had to be withdrawn in a hurry.

As the reds had built barricades across the proposed route, and were calling their defiance at the police and Blackshirts from behind them, the Chief Commissioner of Police, Sir Philip Game, forbade the march for fear of serious bloodshed.

While the banning of the march by the police at the very last moment was a palpable surrender to the threat of mob violence, it is possible at the same time to sympathise a little with the Commissioner in his dilemma, and to understand some of the reasons that prompted him. The Reds would have seen to it that the Blackshirt march was turned into a bloodbath and an orgy of destruction of property; as it was, when the police moved up to remove the barricades they were assailed with fury. They were showered with missiles from behind the barriers, and at the same time heavier objects were dropped on them from upstairs windows. Many police constables were injured, and later several police horses which had had broken bottles thrust into their muzzles, had to be destroyed.

The Cable Street riot became headline news; it remained the main topic of conversation for days, and in the Commons the Home secretary was bombarded with questions. The consensus of opinion as expressed by the spokesman for the Establishment was that although it was the communists and not the Fascists who had run amok and wounded policemen, the former had only done so because they had been provoked by the Blackshirts. [32] The fact that Mosley had wanted to march in orderly procession with his followers through those parts of London where he was a popular figure, and his British Union esteemed, was labelled gross provocation. Of course what his enemies feared was that today's popular figure would be tomorrow's hero.

Exactly one week after the Cable Street affray, there was trouble in Liverpool. Mosley had been advertised to speak in the Boxing

---

32 "The first results of the demonstration and violence were much the same as after the Olympia meeting in 1934; there was an immediate stimulus to recruitment for both fascists and communists and Special Branch estimated the significant, if transient, boost to fascist membership in East London to be around 2,000." *Fascism in Britain* by R. Thurlow, p.111.

Stadium, and the Lancashire Blackshirts had arranged to march behind their drums from the Liverpool Headquarters in Mount Pleasant to the Stadium.

The Communists who were not only powerful on Merseyside, but had the teeming and willing underworld of that wide, densely populated area to draw on, were determined that neither the Blackshirts should march, nor Mosley speak. They received assistance from other reds, delivered in furniture vans from as far away as London, hoping to emulate their Cable Street success.

However, the Liverpool City police who are accustomed to dealing with some of the roughest and most vicious inhabitants of any city in Britain, were determined that as official permission for the march had been given, and the Stadium booked in the normal lawful manner, neither should be prevented by mob intervention from taking place.

One or two British Union members were attacked on their way to Mount Pleasant, the assembly point, where Captain Wright, National Inspector for Lancashire, had a milk bottle broken over his head. Otherwise the muster and the march started with a minimum of bother; but as the column of marching Blackshirts swung round the corner by the Adelphi Hotel into Lime Street, it was confronted by a vast, yelling and savage crowd. It seemed as if the human dregs of all Merseyside were concentrated there in hate-filled opposition.

It may be supposed that carried away by my own antipathy to those communists who opposed Mosley's Movement on the streets of Britain, I have exaggerated the unprepossessing feature of many of them, and have endowed them with a degree of viciousness of both outward appearance and inward proclivity that they could not have really possessed. It would be well-nigh impossible for anyone who has not seen and heard mobs crazed with hatred, and lusting to express that hatred in physical form, to imagine the hideous and deprived features of many of the "submerged tenth" of our population.

The march to the Stadium was an intimidating experience. As the Blackshirts came into view, drums beating and colours flying a howl of fury went up from the Reds and missiles flew through the air. Henceforth the term "Red menace" became even more loaded with meaning for those Lancashire Blackshirts. That night the Stadium was packed, despite the continued efforts of the massed Reds to prevent the public approaching the building. Again the police had to fight to keep open lanes for ticket holders and others to get to the meeting. The meeting was quiet, except for the applause which was thunderous; outside, the police pushed the rabble steadily back. The mob as is customary on Merseyside, then vented its thwarted spite on shop windows, and until the early hours of next morning, howled and rioted and looted and generally ran amok, long after the last Blackshirt had gone home and was asleep in his bed.

Next day's newspapers had little or nothing to say about the orgy of destruction and plundering, nor about the orderly and successful meeting; but what some papers did stress was the righteous indignation of thousands of worthy Liverpolitans, at the effrontery of the Fascists who had presumed to march through their streets.

So completely distorted was the picture presented in the press, that it was to be wondered at that the Blackshirts did not find themselves standing indicted for rioting and looting.

13 - The Public Order Act

"He (Mosley) is one of the weakest individuals in British politics." - Herbert Morrison

All the foregoing rows, riots and rumpuses received the full attention of the press, sometimes with banner headlines, but seldom with unvarnished truth. The nearest approach to anything favourable to the Blackshirts was on those rare occasions when a newspaper would have to compare their conduct with that of the Reds, and be compelled to admit that the fascists showed respect for law and order. As a general rule anything that would have been favourable to the Mosleyites was played down or ignored; conversely all that was detrimental was proportionately magnified.

As the disturbances at British Union meetings occurred more often and with greater violence, there was indignation in Parliament, where questions concerning Mosley and his Movement became increasingly frequent and more charged with venom. All Parties seemed for once to have found something political on which to agree; they were unanimous concerning the Blackshirt menace, and rallied together in defence of their sacred cow, financial democracy.

There must have been Members of Parliament whose own strong anti-communist views should have guaranteed some sympathy for the only political party uncompromisingly opposed to red treason and Pink subversion; but in the prevailing mood of the Commons, most members of which, like their constituents, had their opinions ready-made for them by their favourite newspapers, none dared to declare himself in agreement with any point of fascist policy or belief. With one or two honourable exceptions the Members of the Right lacked the courage of their convictions.

13 - The Public Order Act

There was countrywide agitation. In the newspapers there were letters, feature articles and editorials; over the wireless there were the broadcast opinions of pets of the Establishment, and of the B.B.C.'s own spokesmen. There were leading questions in Parliament, and diatribes from politicians of the Left; while those of the Right for the most part remained silent.

It was obvious to those who could read the portents that legislation against British Union was on its way.

Soon Parliament was bubbling with excitement and in anticipation, as members, those of Labour in particular, vied with one another in their denunciations of Mosley and his followers, and in demanding their suppression.

Herbert Morrison's contribution to the debate leading to the passing of the Public Order Act, is worth recording. With his famous quiff dancing on his brow in time with his gestures of indignation, he stood up in the Commons and fired a broadside into Mosley, that surely should have wrecked the latter's political chances for ever. With head flung back he roundly denounced the Blackshirt leader, proclaiming: "This is a man of straw, a weak man, of no substance, no staying power, no virility in being able to stick to his guns... He is one of the weakest individuals in British politics." [33]

He had been stung into this attack by a Conservative Member, Lovat-Fraser, one of the few who would not compromise with truth, and who had angered him by speaking up for Mosley and describing him as a man of "remarkable and outstanding talents". Morrison could not sit in silence, and let him get away with heresy like that.

In view of Morrison's assessment of Mosley's character, it was surprising that when four years later he became Home Secretary and Mosley's gaoler, he should have troubled to keep so worthless and feeble a creature under lock and key for years.

---

33 *Hansard* Vol. 317

While the proposed Public Order bill was being debated in the House of Commons, there were revelations of the unhappy conditions prevailing in certain industrial parliamentary divisions before the advent of the Blackshirts. Commander Bower, Tory Member for Cleveland, spoke up, saying:

"I am very greatly concerned about the organised hooliganism and complete denial of free speech... I mean fully-organised, deliberate hooliganism, rowdyism, intimidation, violence, obscene abuse, and in some cases personal violence inflicted upon members of my party." [34]

Alone among the national daily newspapers, 'The Morning Post' made favourable reference to the Blackshirts, when "Sentinel" wrote in his column (10th October 1936): "They are loyal to King and Country. They never assault the police and , except when attacked by hooligans, do not resort to the gentle laying on of hands... it is difficult to understand why the leaders of the so-called Labour Party condone the lawlessness of an East End mob, while furiously demanding the suppression of a handful of law-abiding fascists."

The Bill produced by Sir John Simon, Home Secretary, while purporting to safeguard the peace of the realm, was aimed solely at Mosley's Movement.

As Bernard Shaw shrewdly remarked with his usual perspicacity, "English parliamentarians are concerned deeply for the rights of free speech and free assembly only until the appearance on the political scene of an opponent who looks as if he might beat them at their own game. Whereat, and not for once suspecting themselves of hypocrisy, they set out to destroy that opponent by denying him those same rights they had proclaimed with such vigour."

Nor did their brazen effrontery end there, for even as they proscribed our propaganda methods they prated of freedom.

---

34 *Ibid*

The Public Order Act of 1936 prohibited the setting up of any political party on "quasi-military" lines. It forbade the wearing of political uniform; therefore out went the black shirt, likewise badges of rank, and out with these went the semi-military organisation and administration methods.

Actually these prohibitions affected the Movement less adversely than the sponsor of the Bill had hoped, or we members of British Union feared. The uniform by now had fulfilled its main purpose. When it had been a novelty, it had drawn attention to, and thus advertised the Movement. Such advertisement was no longer necessary.

By this time the bonds of brotherhood and unity which the black shirt had so greatly helped to build had become cemented through mutually suffered attack, oppression and misrepresentation. The uniform was no longer necessary as visible token of membership of our devoted band.

All Blackshirts were brothers; no Act of parliament could deprive them of those enduring sentiments of comradeship and concord.

The loss of the black shirts was most felt sentimentally, for the British fascists had become deeply attached to that erstwhile controversial garment, which had been gathering increasing respect in its four years of existence. Many showed bloodstains, honourable marks of how that respect had been hardily earned.

As for the interdiction of "quasi-military organisation", District headquarters no longer quite so resembled Army orderly rooms. District Officers now labelled District Leaders, ceased to acknowledge smacking salutes from zealous subordinates. The difference was in outward form only; the spirit, the ardour, and the sense of discipline remained unchanged.

The Act introduced greater and lasting changes in other directions. The maintenance of law and order at open-air meetings in public places became the exclusive duty of the police. The convenors of such meetings no longer required their own stewards, as theoretically the constabulary would protect the platform and restrain disrupters; in actual practice this has all too often meant that at the first sign of rowdiness the police would close the meeting, which of course was the exact result that those who organised the counter-demonstration had set out to obtain.

Concerning public meetings held indoors the Act was vague, ambiguous, and equivocal, no doubt intentionally. Those who called the meeting were supposed to provide a sufficient number of stewards to marshal and control the public; but in the event of persistent interruption or disorder, and the refusal of the interrupters to keep silent or to leave, the Chairman was directed to call on the police, presumably stationed in the street outside the hall, to eject the trouble-makers.

Again in actual practice it does not always work like that. Apparently if the meeting has been called by a "reputable body" such as the Conservative Association, the stewards seem to be able to manhandle interrupters with impunity. There was a post-war incident when, following the cries and protests of members of the League of Empire Loyalists at the Conservative annual conference in Blackpool, one year stewards fell upon the shouting Loyalists, punched and pummelled them, and finally threw them out battered and crumpled, without the police having been called in, and so far as is known, without official or legal reaction to what were severe bodily assaults.

Imagine the countrywide outcry had those stewards been Mosleyites, and the interrupters Pinks or Reds.

The Public Order Act of 1936, which was passed with the blessings of all parties at Westminster, was aimed at British Union alone. Many years later when there was talk of it being invoked by the Government to curtail the activities of the Campaigners for Nuclear Disarmament, there was flaming indignation from organisations such as the Council for Civil Liberties, and those newspapers of the left which had previously extolled the Bill when Mosley and his followers were the victims.

13 - The Public Order Act

It had been a splendid example of balanced lawmaking when used against Blackshirts, but it became legislative tyranny when directed at the likes of Canon Collins and the Reverend Michael Scott.

14 - "Stand By The King"

"I have found it impossible to carry the heavy burden of responsibility and discharge my duties as King as I would wish to do without the help and support of the woman I love." - Edward VIII, in his Abdication broadcast.

The year 1936 was one of continual crises, with troubles coming to a head here, there and everywhere. There had been the Italo-Abyssinian fracas with the threat of sanctions drawing Britain into war with a people with whom she had never before quarrelled; and there had been General Franco's patriotic revolt in Spain against communist murder and outrage, fostered by Liberal/Socialist weakness and corruption.

In France, Leon Blum had formed his Popular Front Government, which beneath its Liberal/Radical cloak was responsive to communist influence and initiative, and was industriously and systematically corrupting and weakening that country, and dividing it as at no time since the Franco-Prussian war.

To the consternation of the League-lovers, Germany and Japan ratified their Anti-Comintern Pact, in which they were to be joined shortly by Italy smarting from the strictures administered at Geneva by Eden and Litvinoff.

The line-up for the Second World War was being clearly demarcated. This was that fateful year to which Hitler referred as "the turning point of an age".

In Britain, Stanley Baldwin was still Prime Minister, but his stock was falling. That typical, solid, middle-class Englishman who in his baggy clothes and with his perpetual pipe had appeared so dependable, now admitted to the House of

Commons on 12th November, "with appalling frankness," that he had won the General Election of the previous year with a manifesto that was largely false. So misleading was that publication, said Mosley, that had it been the prospectus of a commercial undertaking, it would have landed its authors in the dock at the Old Bailey.

Over-awed by the Peace Pledge Union with its eleven million signatures, and acutely aware of the voting power of all those tens of thousands of deluded persons who were swept off their feet by a mass emotional gush had applauded George Lansbury's amazing outburst at Fulham, "Honest Stan" had not dared to proclaim the pressing need for Britain to catch up on her long-neglected defences.

Consequently, in order to cash in on the prevailing sentiment he had promised the Peace Society at the London Guildhall on 1st October, 1935, that he would not rearm, and at the General Election had issued a statement full of pious protestations of peace. When in November 1936, events forced him to own up to his tricks, there was disgust and loss of confidence in the apparently worthy and eminently respectable-looking, literary-minded iron-master who was also Prime Minister.

Early in the year King George V died, and was mourned by all for the good, dutiful fellow he was. British Union shared the general grief, and recalled how in the previous year during their Silver Jubilee, the King and Queen had driven in semi-State past the Black House, gay with emblems of loyalty, and had smilingly acknowledged the cheers and salutes of the Blackshirts who had lined the pavements to greet them.

On 20th January, the gay and charming Prince of Wales, the country's darling since his service with the Army in France, was proclaimed King Edward VIII. The Movement rejoiced, for it felt that with a member of the war generation, a kindred spirit, on the throne, there would be a close understanding of the hopes and aspirations of British Union.

As Prince of Wales the new King had actively interested himself on behalf of the ex-Servicemen, his old comrades in arms, whom through the rigour of a long campaign he had come to love and understand. Since the war he had visited the "distressed areas", and had seen with compassion the mass misery of the unemployed. The under-privileged saw in him their champion; on him they had pinned high hopes.

Mosley and his followers who had striven so hard and so long on behalf of the imposed-upon workless masses welcomed him, not only as a popular ruler, but within the confining limits of constitutional monarchy, as an ally.

"Teddy", as he was affectionately known to those tens of thousands who looked on him as their hero, was indiscreet enough to alarm the Establishment. He had visited the forlorn valleys of South Wales, where he beheld pithead gear that turned no more, and had seen blast furnaces that had been declared redundant, and in order that their owners might be compensated, had been rendered useless forever by dynamite.

"Whoever ordered their destruction, assumed a terrible responsibility," the new King is said to have remarked to the Chief Constable of Glamorganshire. In reply to a further question as to the identity of the owners, he was informed that they were Messrs. Richard Thomas and Baldwin. The story of that conversation and of the ensuing incident was narrated to me by the late "Tommy" Moran, a celebrated British Union character, who was present in person on that occasion.

Edward VIII had been expected to address some words of comfort and hope to the hundreds of ex-miners and former furnace workers who had gathered. He stood looking down on them from the side of a slagheap; they stood a little below, looking up at him in silence. No one spoke. It was one of those rare moments when the communion of minds make words unnecessary. They stood in silent mutual sympathy... impetuous, warm-hearted young ruler, and the poorest, most destitute of his subjects.

Edward VIII. visit to Glamorgan, South Wales in 1936

Deeply moved, he turned to the small party of local officials and notabilities accompanying him, saying in a tone of fixed determination: "Something must be done!" Something was done; but not that which he had visualised. That remark helped lose him his throne.

As Prince of Wales he had been a sociable and merry lad. He loved field sports, particularly riding to hounds and steeple-chasing; and he loved parties. The names of many ladies both gay and serious had been linked with him. Now at last he had met one whom he wished to marry; but she was American and had been previously married. The press of probably every country in the world except Britain had followed the romance step by step. In the United States the most trivial items concerning the couple were headline news.

In Britain that amorphous entity, the Establishment was well aware of the amatory inclinations of the monarch; but it had suppressed the story or any suggestion of it, not without considerable unease. "They" were becoming increasingly apprehensive about a king who was not only embarrassingly unconventional, but had developed a too-acute social conscience, and might one day become really awkward.

On 26th November, 1936, Stanley Baldwin told his colleagues of the cabinet that King Edward VIII sought necessary legislative action to enable him to marry Mrs. Simpson, an American citizen.

There the matter rested still a cabinet secret and very hush-hush for a week, until Doctor Blunt, Bishop of Bradford, unable to keep throttle closed one moment longer, opened his safety valve and let the land resound to the shriek of his released dismay, that the King of England contemplated marriage to an American woman with a previous husband still alive.

The facts that the lady's reputation was without blemish, and that she looked well-bred and charming, meant nothing at all to the middle-aged and ageing middle-class gentlemen of cabinet, or to the middle-aged and ageing bishops. To them she was someone as unsuitable as she was incomprehensible. Reared in the atmosphere of Victorian Puritanism and rigid social rules, they were incapable of understanding the outlook of a young man hastened to an early maturity through four years active service on the western Front, and who in retaliation for youthful years spent in an environment of destruction and carnage, had kicked up his heels gaily with the "bright young things" in the 1920s.

By the 1930s, the prince was applying himself conscientiously to his arduous duties. He had freshness, frankness, and boundless charm, and was probably at that time the most popular person in the world. He became Britain's ambassador at large, and of goodwill. He travelled on official business everywhere, made friends everywhere, and almost wore himself out. He returned very nearly a wreck from one of his world tours.

He had entered his reign with every intention to rule constitutionally, but equally determined to press for reforms on behalf of the workless and the destitute. He understood the dreadful responsibilities of his exalted office; he did not flinch from them, but he knew that he would need beside him daily the presence of the woman he loved, to help and to sustain him. He did not ask his Government to make his wife Queen of England, but he sought the legislation to allow him to marry lawfully the lady of his choice.

For the subsequent tribulations of prince and people, the bishops must take a large share of responsibility. They showed a prejudice and a narrow Puritanism more in keeping with the doctrines of John Calvin, rather than permit themselves to be influenced by the precept of Archbishop Cranmer, who encouraged Henry VIII to substitute Anne Boleyn for Catherine of Aragon as his wedded wife. The bishops seemed to have forgotten that the Church of England had been founded on connivance at divorce.

The apparent indiscretion of the Bishop of Bradford took the country by surprise. Everyone excepting the few who read the foreign press, was staggered. The first general reaction was one of pleasure that the King should at last have made his choice. There was a little disappointment in some quarters that he should have preferred a foreigner; but as the pleasing features of Mrs Simpson became known through the many portrait photographs quickly published, they won sympathy and admiration.

There was less congratulations as the doubts expressed by the bishops and the Cabinet became known. Soon it was being asked widely how could the King of England who was also titular head of the Church of England, be permitted to marry a divorced woman, even if the innocent party, when that Church is opposed to the marriage of divorced persons.

Those bishops who were such sticklers for the literal observance of the tenets of the faith, were perfectly sincere in their opposition to the marriage; but their objections were a godsend to those sections of the Establishment who feared that the new King would be likely to become the innovator of unwelcome changes. There was talk of an ultimatum. If Edward VIII insisted as he did, on his right to marry Mrs. Simpson, he must forfeit his crown. If he wished to remain on his throne, he would have to renounce the lady.

His subjects began to take sides. Against the King were Baldwin and the bishops. For him were Beaverbrook, Churchill and Mosley.

Told by Baldwin that, as a divorced woman, Mrs. Simpson would not be acceptable as queen consort, Edward tried to arrange a morganatic marriage instead. When even this proved impossible, Edward decided to renounce the throne – which he did on December 10th 1936.

Throughout the growing crisis, the BUF organised a great nationwide campaign in support of Edward, under the slogan of "Stand By the King", and this slogan was painted on literally thousands of walls all over the country. There were large demonstrations by BUF members and other "Octavians" in the West End of London and outside Buckingham Palace.

On the Sunday following the Abdication, Cosmo Lang, Archbishop of Canterbury, gave a broadcast talk on the radio which lacked Christian charity, to put it mildly. This talk was widely resented and criticised, even by those who thought that Edward should go. Lang's friends described him as a pious man devoid of rancour, and in every way worthy of his holy office; but to most listeners on that occasion his words seemed calculatedly cruel. His castigation of the ex-King drew upon himself the equally cruel but not undeserved quip, that Edward had left his realm "for the sake of auld Lang swine".

Thus ended in a few months the reign on which the highest hopes had been placed. The most loved prince of any land in modern times was sent into exile without his subjects being given the opportunity to express their views on the matter.

When Hitler, a dictator, desired to introduce far-reaching constitutional changes, he had held a referendum of the German people; but when Baldwin, a self-proclaimed democrat, wished

Edward VIII and Wallis Simpson meet Adolf Hitler 1937

to be rid of a much loved but potentially awkward monarch, he cast him off without attempting to consult the wishes of his people.

To this day there are people in Britain who delude themselves that their country is still a democracy. It was a London club friend of Sir Philip Gibbs who declared: "Democracy has no power over its own fate; there is no such thing as democracy. It is at the mercy of those on top."[35]

---

35   *Ordeal in England*, by Philip Gibbs, p.126, pub. Right Book Club.

15 - The London County Council Elections

The New Year, that of 1937, saw us Blackshirts going about our duties attired as other men, our political allegiance proclaimed only by a small "flash and circle" chromium badge worn on the lapel.

Rallies, marches and meetings were held as before the passing of the Public Order Act. Our weekly newspaper, '*Action*', was sold on the streets by members as previously, except that the vendors were in plain clothes; and door to door canvassing went on without official interference.

This year British Union made its debut at the polls to test the strength of its electoral support in those parts where sympathy was most apparent. It was agreed also that it would be advantageous for those members who had been given theoretical training in electioneering, to obtain practical experience.

British Union candidates contested the Boroughs of Bethnal Green, Shoreditch, and Limehouse in the London County Council Municipal Elections. Raven Thomson, at that time Director of Policy, and E.G. Clarke, "Mick" to his friends, who was the Movement's full-time organiser in East London, put up for Bethnal Green. Anne Brock-Griggs, Chief Women's Organiser, and Wegg-Prosser, a well-known London member, stood for Limehouse. In Shoreditch the candidates were William Joyce, Director of Propaganda, and Bill Bailey, an East End character.

In those days householders only were qualified to vote in local government elections. In East London where family ties are strong and the consequent overcrowding an accepted fact, the preponderance of people entitled to vote on the L.C.C. Register were middle-aged. This should have put British Union candidates at a disadvantage, as to outward appearance the Movement's following was composed largely of younger persons, those who shared the parental roof and had no vote.

Under any circumstances the results of these first attempts at the polls would have been astounding; but with the voting restricted mainly to the older and more staid elements, the outcome was a shock of pleasurable surprise to supporters, and a shock of rather less joy to discerning opponents.

In Bethnal Green, Raven Thomson and Mick Clarke polled 23% of all votes cast. In Limehouse, Mrs Brock-Griggs and Wegg-Prosser polled 19%, and in Shoreditch, Joyce and Bailey achieved 14%. Great was the rejoicing throughout the Movement when these quite remarkable achievements were made known.

The press disparaged these results and jubilated at the defeat of the fascists; but one or two newspapers did print the apprehensive views of their political commentators, who being trained and experienced observers, realised the significance of what British Union had achieved.

It was doubtless with these election results in mind that the late Hannen Swaffer, a leading Left Wing journalist, writing in the 'World's Press News' (5.8.1943), in an article entitled 'Saved by the War', stated: "But for the war we might today have been a Fascist country."

There were other repercussions from the Movement's intervention in the L.C.C. Elections of 1937, and from the increased self-assurance gained thereby, and subsequently displayed by some East London Blackshirts.

Thanks to the Public Order Act, members of British Union, now indistinguishable from other Londoners, put in an appearance at the public meetings called by the Labour Party. Contrary to their own published orders, but recalling the past treatment of their own speakers from Labour supporters and their Red friends, they now gave the Labourites strong doses of their own medicine.

They went in numbers to East End Labour meetings, where they hooted, jeered, and created such uproar that Herbert Morrison, Leader of the L.C.C. since 1934, took fright, refused to stand again for South Hackney, and took himself to the safety and greater respectability of East Lewisham. Likewise Clement Atlee, after having represented Limehouse in Parliament since 1922, found the changed political climate so uncongenial, that at the next General Election he transferred himself to West Walthamstow. These flights from East London constituencies by two top ranking Labour leaders were heartening portents.

The wartime evacuation, the bombing, and then the post-war resettlement elsewhere of thousands of East End families, has scattered the Mosleyites of East London over the metropolitan area, and out into the Home Counties. Nevertheless, so acute were the memories of these two leading figures of the Labour Party of the ascendency of British Union in what had been their old strongholds, that at the first General Election to be held since 1935, they crept away to less turbulent constituencies until that day when they were able to accept the sanctuary of the House of Lords.

Another financial crisis smote the Movement in May 1937. The flow of funds into the British Union account dwindled and nearly dried up. Pressures from various concealed sources had been brought to bear on some of the largest financial backers, so that for their own financial safety and solvency they had had to withdraw their support. Other persons who had been contributing to the Movement, but who lacking political discernment had become discouraged at what they considered the absence of concrete or spectacular success, and led to believe from the popular press that the L.C.C. Elections' results demonstrated the final rejection of British fascism, they too discontinued their contributions.

Faced with what at the time must have seemed not far from complete financial disaster, Mosley was left with no choice but to reduce expenditure ruthlessly. It was no occasion for sentiment or compassion; nearly all the paid staff – 101 out of 140 – had to go. All the subordinate full-time organisers and propagandists were dismissed; and with the exceptions of John Garnett and myself, all the National Inspectors were paid off.

It spoke volumes for the kind of men recruited to the staff during the past two or three years that they faced their dismissals like the gallant fellows they were, and went off to look for other jobs at a time when "other jobs" were well nigh non-existent; yet they remained unshaken in their loyalty.

The offices of the National Headquarters in Great Smith Street, Westminster, were reduced to one third of their former size; the offices of the Northern Headquarters in Corporation Street, Manchester, were closed altogether.

The financial set-back and the sudden drastic reductions and changes sent a wave of shock throughout the Movement. Among those given their notices of dismissal as paid employees of British Union were William Joyce, Director of Propaganda, and John Beckett, Editor of *Action*. These two important officers took badly the termination of their salaried appointments. They brooded, they confabulated, and finally they acted.

Joyce visited a South Coast town where lived a wealthy old gentleman who in the past had contributed handsomely to British Union, and who at the same time was a personal admirer of Joyce for the brilliance of his mind, the distinction of his oratory, and his physical courage. What transpired at this meeting is not known; but Joyce returned to town with a substantial cheque.

Next he and Beckett hired a hall and called a meeting, at which they announced their intention of forming another party, a variation of the New Movement to be known as the "National Socialist League", under their dual leadership. The meeting was well attended by loyal Mosleyites, who for the most part had come either out of curiosity, or in order to spy.

Next morning there was a veritable procession of horrified or disgusted Blackshirts to the offices in Great Smith Street to expose the treasonable transactions of Joyce and Beckett.

Mosley's reaction was to order the expulsion from British Union of the two founders of the National Socialist League, and of any other of his followers who may have accompanied them. At the same time, he remarked that the new organisation would make a useful refuse bin for his own dissidents, cranks and extremists.

The only fascist of any worth who went over to the "N.S.L." was John McNab, an Oxford graduate, a close friend and a great admirer of William Joyce, who followed him from personal loyalty and affection.

Most Blackshirts were distressed that two comrades, who were also important officers and who had been admired and respected, could behave with such petulance. A few people may have been deeply disturbed; but those with more experience of the world prophesied that no organisation could last for long under the dual control of a pair of men as personally ambitious as Beckett, and as touchy and as self-opinionated as Joyce. This forecast proved remarkably accurate. Meanwhile little sleep was lost by those who administered British Union over the formation of what was dubbed the "Joyce-Beckett Faction".

John Beckett, a native of Cheshire and an ex-Serviceman, was one of the few officers of British Union who was also an experienced politician. He had been in the Labour Party, and during the 1920s had represented in Parliament both Peckham and Gateshead. His most publicised performance in the House of Commons had been when he had walked off with the Mace, in order to draw attention to the time-wasting procedure of that assembly. He made his gesture with rather more éclat than had Fenner-Brockway, who had once similarly enlivened parliamentary proceedings. Beckett, a strongly built and muscular man had picked up "that bauble" with ease; but Fenner-Brockway, a long, thin, gangling person, had sagged at the knees and seemed as if about to fold up beneath its massive weight, which had somewhat spoiled the bold effect of his *coup de théâtre*.

Beckett, a clever and an able man, who held the mentality of the masses in contempt, and who was well versed in serving up what his reader wanted, had been editing '*Action*' with success, and adding to his own reputation. The fact that he had been suddenly confronted with the notice of the termination of his paid services had come as a shock to his self esteem, and a blow to his standard of living. He felt injured and affronted, hence his angry attitude. If Beckett was a man of talent, Joyce possessed greater. He was of Irish origin, American by accident of birth, but had been brought up in the British Isles. He professed always a deep and abiding love for England; those of us who knew him, and deplored his subsequent actions, never doubted the sincerity of his affectionate regard for this country.

If he had chosen law, he would almost certainly have become a famous Counsel, as he was a master of rhetoric, and a scintillating debater, the speed and clarity of whose mind was amazing. However, he had turned to politics and from Conservatism, had progressed to the new idea, of which he became a leading apostle in Britain. With his rash courage and scathing tongue he soon made a name for himself. His admirers had even been speaking of him as heir-presumptive to the leadership of British Union, which view was doubtless shared by Joyce himself.

His anti-Semitism was as flagrant as it was genuine. Nor were his embittered attacks on the Jews difficult to understand, when one realised the origin of the hideous facial scar that he carried. This badly healed wound was a legacy of the days when he had spoken from Conservative platforms in East London. He told how at a meeting broken up by Reds, mostly Jews and aliens, he had been seized, held down in the road, a razor inserted in his mouth then drawn up towards his ear. This had left him with a frightful cicatrice and an aversion to Jews. Actually his rabid verbal attacks on the Jews were harmful to British Union; as for instance the occasion when he addressed an open-air meeting in the centre of Leeds on a Sunday afternoon. He was galloping his hobby-horse as hard as it would go, when a middle-aged, prosperous looking Yorkshireman in the audience turned to some senior Blackshirts, exclaiming in disgust: "I had come here especially to hear what your Party thought it could do to help the wool trade; but all I have had to listen to is a lot of silly clap-trap about Jews."

In stature Joyce was tiny, almost a dwarf. One could forget this as he stood alone on the platform and spoke passionately and convincingly, yet effortlessly in his flawless English; but Joyce himself could never forget his diminutive size. What he lacked in inches he endeavoured to compensate himself by his aggressiveness, his unconcealed contempt for anyone who dared to disagree, and by his flaunting arrogance.

Hector McKechnie, Organiser of National Meetings, had a revealing tale concerning Joyce, who had been booked to take a meeting in some large town in the Midlands, for which McKechnie had made the usual advance publicity arrangements with posters, press notices, and handbills. The morning after the meeting, Joyce came hurrying into McKechnie's office brandishing one of the latter; bursting with indignation he cried: "Look at this. Read it. 'Speaker, W. Joyce.' Have you ever heard of W. Shakespeare or of J. Christ? Why do you have to choose to advertise me as W. Joyce and not William Joyce?"

Joyce had many estimable qualities and great ability; but all were impaired by his over-riding conceit and insolence. Many years later, Mosley talking over old times with me, said reflectively: "Francis Bacon writing on dwarfs depicted Joyce to perfection." Someone else described him long ago as an "over-educated schoolmaster," and that observation too was not far off the beam as an assessment of one side of his gifted, complicated self.

The revelation that Mosley no longer regarded him as an absolutely key man, and that he could dispense with his full time, paid services, came like a slap in the face. Wrongly interpreting his dismissal as a slight on his capability and on the value of his work for the Movement, Joyce went off in high dudgeon.

16 – *Another Step Forward*

1937 to 1939 were probably the happiest in the annals of British Union. The increase in morale and strength could be both felt and seen. Externally, while there was malice and hatred from many quarters, there was growing respect, even admiration from others. Despite these signs of incipient success, most fascists knew better now than to predict a quick journey to power; nevertheless their confidence was soaring, and they felt assured that ultimately Mosley would win.

Membership swelled, local finances became stable and healthy, and there was increasing demand for '*Action*', now edited with just as much revolutionary zeal but more dignity by Raven Thomson, who having private means was able to undertake this highly important task at little charge to the Party.

Senior local officers began to assume many of the former administrative functions of National Headquarters. This was a tremendous step forward.

Everywhere the Movement was becoming more firmly established. The teething troubles were over. The four hundred District formations of British Union discovered that they could walk alone, and without the helping hands of salaried full-time Staff Officers.

In London where almost every hall of any size or importance was denied to Mosley, most of the propaganda was conducted on the streets. Even the public parks, controlled by the London County Council under the leadership of Herbert Morrison, were forbidden to him. In a few instances when the parks themselves were not denied, loudspeakers were banned; which in effect banned Mosley, whose audiences had grown so vast that without amplification his voice, powerful as it is, would have reached only a fraction of the crowd.

Since the Reds had rioted in Cable Street, the Blackshirts as they still thought of themselves, even if there was an interdiction of their favoured haberdashery, had not been allowed to march through East London. So marches were held from the Victoria Embankment, or from Millbank, to Bermondsey, to Ridley Road, Dalston, or to Trafalgar Square; but when the ban on loudspeakers was applied to Trafalgar Square, it became useless to attempt to hold rallies there. It did not escape our notice that when a combination of Left-Wingers aspired to save Spain with their larynxes, they were permitted to do so in Trafalgar Square with all the most powerful mechanical aids, and with no interference from any official source.

The Blackshirt marches held at regular intervals through the London streets became increasingly spectacular occasions; for with the mounting membership the numbers of marchers increased by thousands. To encourage the long column were several bands, drum and trumpet, drum and bugle, and drum and pipe; heading the women's contingent was their own drum corps. In the centre of the parade were the massed standards. The red, white and blue of the Union jacks, and the black and gold of the Districts' insignia, with their escort of ex-Servicemen with breasts agleam with campaign medals and decorations. The Press could never make up its mind what kind of men followed Mosley. One week we would be described as some species of ape men; then a week or two later we would find that some popular anti-fascist scribe would be writing us off as a collection of "weedy clerks".

Every little set-back for the Movement would be seized upon with joy by the newspaper hacks, and would be pronounced each one in turn as "the death-knell of fascism in Britain". Shortly there would be another huge demonstration of strength on the streets by British Union that would release torrents of inky abuse, and demands for yet more rigorous repression of Mosley, from those journalists who had proclaimed but yesterday the imminent demise of the New Idea. Actually the members of the British Union derived considerable amusement from the descriptions of themselves and of their comrades, and the accounts of their activities, as they appeared in the popular newspapers and in some of the weekly reviews. In a meeting at Doncaster at about this time Mosley denounced the British press as "probably the most lying and prostituted press in the world".

It is doubtful if ever a political leader or a political party in Britain have received such generally dishonourable treatment as have Mosley and his Movement. The ceaseless denigration, misrepresentation and bare-faced lying by the newspapers, the B.B.C., and by public men, contrived to poison men's minds, so that otherwise reasonable and open-minded citizens were incapable of assimilating anything in the least degree favourable to British fascism.

Many members of British Union at some time or another met with an experience similar to that of Doreen Bell, one of the Movement's youngest, most able and convincing public speakers.

Miss Bell, travelling by train in ordinary clothes, for it was after the Public Order Act, found herself in a compartment with a non-conformist minister. They got into conversation, and then to discuss the sad state of Britain, the sufferings of the unemployed, and the poor general outlook. From that, Miss Bell came to propound the remedies; she gave the clergyman the broad outlines of Mosley's policy for breaking the power of finance, and for the restoration of agriculture, textiles, coal, steel and shipping. She told him also how the slums should be swept away, and the people re-housed through a great nationwide effort.

Her listener glowed with approval, and expressed his total agreement; until Miss Bell, rising to leave the train at her destination, said with her usual frankness: "Those are the policies advocated by Oswald Mosley and British Union." The clergyman was so shocked that, forgetful of what he was saying, he blurted out: "If I had known that, I would never have agreed with anything that you have told me."

In the summer of 1937 King George VI and his Queen were crowned. Whatever damage had been done to the Throne by the Abdication was forgotten. Britain and the Empire rejoiced at the start of the new reign. Even the '*Daily Worker*' had to advise its readers not to let their sour faces spoil the festivities.

All loyal Britons wished long life and happiness to the former shy and retiring Duke of York, who had been called on so suddenly to assume the awful responsibility of sovereign. It was with reluctance but in compliance with his sense of duty that he took up his brother's burden. George VI became one of the most conscientious and hard-working monarchs to have graced the British throne.

The burden that was placed on him when he accepted the crown became in time too onerous. He was worked to death by the palace officials, and by his own unflagging conscience on behalf of us, his people, who must take some share of responsibility for his decease, completely worn out before his time.

During 1937 Mosley spoke in Leeds, Sheffield, York, Huddersfield and Doncaster without incident and almost without interruption. His policies for the wool, coal, and steel industries filled his Yorkshire halls with ready listeners.

Red opposition was little in evidence. Memory of the ability of the Blackshirts to obtain hearings for their speakers was still fresh. Also the Spanish Civil War was occupying most of the attention of the Left; certainly it was absorbing the energies of the Communist Party, which was busy recruiting for the International Brigade, howling for "Arms for Spain", begging for "Milk for Spain", and arranging for the transit to this country of a number of unfortunate little Spanish and Basque children to be used as political bait and pawns.

Throughout a succession of British Union meetings in Yorkshire, the best the Reds could do to oppose them was to muster a knot of pathetic, broken-down, under-nourished, middle-aged men and women to stand in threadbare clothes and leaking shoes on a raw, damp winter's evening outside a hall in Doncaster, drearily chanting again and again:

"One, two, three, who are we?
We are the working-class.
Down with the upper-class!"

It was a spectacle of pathos and hopelessness.

On Sunday, 18th July, 1937, Mosley spoke to an audience of some twenty-five thousand persons on Southampton Common. There were no more than about a couple of hundred Reds present, many of whom were instantly recognised as old enemies of the Movement from the East End of London. With adequate police arrangements such a limited number of trouble-makers could have been controlled easily; but there were no more than twenty-five uniformed police present, and in several instances their conduct was questionable.

There was considerable stone-throwing, with the police doing nothing to stop it. Mosley, who had been hit in the face by a stone, drew the attention of his audience to what was happening, and pointed to one man who was throwing stones at him from beside a complacent policeman. Finding himself the object of unwelcome interest, the constable rather sheepishly ordered the stone-thrower away, who having moved a few yards, resumed his interrupted missile practice.

It was reported in the next issue of '*Action*' that Vice-Admiral G.B. Powell, District Leader of Portsmouth, and Mr. Bailey, District Treasurer of Southampton – "men no longer young, withstood the assaults of the Reds with great gallantry and gave good accounts of themselves." The courage of those two elderly Blackshirt officers won the outspoken admiration of many bystanders.

When after the meeting a party of fascists boarded a tram-car to take them back into the town, hooligans stoned it until most of its windows had been smashed; nor did the hooligans appear to be inhibited by the fact that the tram contained besides Blackshirts, members of the public, including women and children.

The quite inadequate police precautions may have been deliberate; as the news that a Mosley meeting had been wrecked would have been a humiliation, which both the newspapers and the B.B.C. would have rubbed in with vigour. On the other hand the local police may have felt themselves in the dark as to their powers under the new Public Order Act, so that they hesitated to commit themselves.

Southampton has always been a tough place from British Union viewpoint; but the quality of its local membership was the best. It had to be in order to survive.

A prominent local Blackshirt was "Tommy" Thomas, a former engineer officer of the old White Star Line, who selling '*Action*' alone one evening in the centre of town, was set upon simultaneously by two roughs. The elderly man threw each headlong, the one after the other. With one opponent lying winded in the road, the other half stunned in the gutter, he received the congratulations of the many eye-witnesses.

Anti-fascist violence was not confined entirely to the cities and bigger towns. Towards the end of August, 1937, as he sat in his study one Saturday night after dark, probably preparing next day's sermon, the Reverend H.E.B. Nye was startled by the sudden crash of breaking glass. Window after window of the isolated Lincolnshire rectory were being shattered by stones hurtling into the lighted rooms from out of the darkness on the lawn. The attack stopped when the rector turned loose his dogs, which ran barking a challenge across the grass and into a shrubbery.

The police were summoned, and found a quantity of stones on the lawn yet to be thrown, and evidence that the attackers were at least six in number. The Lincolnshire Constabulary were of the opinion that the assailants were other than local for the Rector was both popular and respected, and that their object had been to intimidate the Reverend Nye, whose favourable impressions formed during a holiday in Germany had been published in '*Action*'.

On Sunday, 3rd October, 1937, there was a Blackshirt march from Parliament Square to a meeting to be addressed by Mosley in Southwark Park Road, Bermondsey. On this occasion the attacks on the police by the Reds were both vicious and sustained; there were many casualties. The conduct of the police was described by '*Action*' as "magnificent". The meeting had been arranged to be held on the south side of the Thames rather than in the British Union strongholds of East London, so as not to provoke the Jewish populace of the East End. Nevertheless, next day's issue of the '*Daily Mail*' (4.10.1937), reported:

"Many of the demonstrators... appeared to be foreigners. Large numbers of men of swarthy complexion... were marching in small bands encouraging others to smash the police cordons."

Elsewhere that same newspaper published:

"One hundred and eleven arrests were made after squads of mounted police had carried out repeated baton charges on Communist counter-demonstrations during the Blackshirt march through South-East London yesterday... Extra police drafted into the area were stoned from roof tops. About thirty people were injured, including several women."

There was an attempt to launch a driverless car from a side street to plough through the ranks of the marching fascists; but some agile person scrambled in and stopped it in time.

The day following the march was a busy one for the magistrates. Said Mr. Bernard Campion, Stipendiary Magistrate as he viewed the succession of distinctly non-Anglo-Saxon features and gesticulating hands in the dock before him:

"It is extraordinary how many of the population of Stepney and Whitechapel seemed to have chosen Bermondsey for a Sunday afternoon walk."

Some time later, during the proceedings, he observed: "I can see there was some organisation at work deliberately trying to cause disorder. Whether it was right for this march to have been held is not for me to say; but when I am faced with such organised and deliberate attempts at violence, then it is my job to enforce law and put down disorder. Don't thank me, thank those people who sent you and your misguided friends to agitate... Twenty-one days, without the option."

One week later the 'Sunday Express' (10.10.1937) reported:

"Scotland Yard is convinced that much of the recent trouble in the east end has been stirred up by foreigners, and that the task of keeping an eye on the aliens' activities has become too big."

That same autumn there were questions in Parliament (21.10.1937) concerning allegations that funds for British Union were coming from abroad. Sir John Simon, Home Secretary regretted his inability to give specific details, but stated that his informants had let him know that Mosley's Movement was receiving financial aid from foreign sources.

Mosley promptly repudiated Sir John's assertion, and challenged him to produce "one single shred of evidence". Nor was any confirmation of the accusation forthcoming then or at any other time since.

The most irrefutable confirmation of Mosley's denial that this Movement had ever been subsidised from Italy or Germany was the statement made by Richard Stokes, M.P., in the House of Commons on 10th December, 1940:

"In connection with the British Union, I must say a word about the chief protagonist of that organisation, Sir Oswald Mosley. I think it should be said, although I am not a sympathiser in any way with their point of view or their activities. He appeared before the Advisory Committee, and the Committee invited his solicitors to help them in discovering whether or not any foreign money was coming into the organisation of the British Union. After a most exhaustive search, in which all the banks joined, the committee and solicitors had to admit that no foreign money of any kind whatsoever was coming into that organisation."

It is hardly surprising that few people should be aware of the finding of the Advisory Committee headed by Mr. Norman Birkett, K,C,, later Lord Birkett, or of Stoke's exposure in Parliament of yet another anti-fascist canard, as the newspapers were remarkably reticent.

In one of the several "unsympathetic" studies of British fascism published in recent years is an account of how money, in the shape of bundles of foreign notes packed in cardboard shoe-boxes, reached BUF headquarters from the Italian Embassy. Mosley's comment to me on this item of "history" was, "A most unlikely story. Grandi was scrupulously correct, and would never have lent himself to a transaction of that sort".

As for some correspondence between Count Grandi and his Roman Foreign office "discovered after the war, in which the ambassador was alleged to have reported that financial support of Mosley was a waste of money. This, said Mosley, was in all probability a product of one of the "forgery factories of Europe", which had been hard at work since the end of the war manufacturing all sorts of evidence. One of these "factories" had even produced his marriage lines from the record of the burgomaster's office of a town in Germany he had never visited.

In November 1937, British union received a blow that was really felt. The Executive Committee of the National Association of Wholesale Newsagents, with neither warning nor explanation, suddenly refused to handle further issues of '*Action*' – despite it having the largest circulation of any political weekly. This illuminating example of the freedom of the press in Britain was the most effective suppression possible of the Movement's newspaper, for until this it had been on sale and display at almost every newsagents' shop in the country. Thereafter members of the public were able only to obtain copies either posted direct from the publishers, or through local branches of British Union. No reason was given for this arbitrary ban. Neither apology nor excuse offered, only a peremptory refusal to discuss the matter.

Thus did the Establishment manifest its power.

17 – Dangerous Incident At Walton

On Sunday, 10th October, 1937, Mosley was scheduled to address an open-air meeting on some waste ground adjoining Queen's Drive, Walton, a suburb of Liverpool. Trouble was expected as the tough and vicious Liverpool reds were openly boasting that they would never let the Leader of British Union speak anywhere in public in Merseyside.

When Hector McKechnie, who at that time organised Mosley's meetings, and I called on the Chief Constable of Liverpool to discuss arrangements, that officer qualified the recital of such of his plans as he saw fit to make known, with the observation: "That is, of course, providing that Sir Oswald is allowed to speak."

This caused McKechnie and myself to exchange looks of question and doubt. McKechnie was inclined to interpret it as a veiled hint that the Reds might get the upper hand, possibly only for a short space of time. I thought that the Chief Constable was warning us that in the event of the crowd, or a proportion of the crowd, becoming ugly he would close the meeting.

It was a clear bright autumn afternoon when the Liverpool Blackshirts, indistinguishable from their fellow Liverpolitans except for their small buttonhole badges, collected round their large loudspeaker van, then the most powerful in the country. By the time the public-address equipment had been tested and proved, a very large crowd numbering several thousands was assembled, with but a handful of uniformed police.

The concourse was generally well-behaved and orderly while waiting for the meeting to open; but now and then, some stones would be propelled from out of the depth of the crowd in the direction of the vehicle, which was also the platform. This desultory bombardment was no more than had been anticipated; but when Arthur Greenhagh, one of the Movement's registered speakers in the Lancashire area, mounted the roof of the van to stand behind the microphone, there was an instant fusillade of missiles.

Greenhalgh was a middle-aged man who had been invalidated out of the royal Navy after having distinguished himself at the Dardanelles, for which he had received a citation. His solitary figure outlined against the sky made an inviting target; the Reds could not resist it. Showers of stones and other missiles converged on him from all sides. He was hit repeatedly, but continued to speak without falter until a half-brick hurled with force struck him on the shoulder, smashing his collar-bone.

He lowered himself to the ground, was strapped up by the ambulance people, then returned to the van top to continue his discourse, although his own officers endeavoured to dissuade him. For his gallantry on this occasion he was later granted one of the Movement's rarely bestowed awards.

The great crowd that witnessed the stoning of Greenhalgh obviously disapproved the conduct of the reds, but remained quiet. Meanwhile the police, such few of them as were in evidence, pressed the Mosleyites into a tight compass round the loudspeaker van, at the same time pushing back the spectators. Their obvious intention was to keep the Blackshirts and the reds apart; but in actual fact it meant that the fascists became defenceless and delectable targets for the stone-throwers to practise on from out of the safety of the crowd.

Plain-clothes police officers mingling with the audience pounced on one or two young louts in the act of throwing stones; but police in and out of uniform were far too few in number.

Mosley arrived almost unnoticed, smiled greetings to one or two old friends standing nearby, then after a word to the mechanic in charge of the public-address equipment, swung himself up on to the platform. He stood silent for a moment beside the microphone in characteristic attitude, estimating the numbers and attitudes of the assembly.

The instant the Reds realised who it was on the platform, they yelled their hate and pelted him with stones. Mosley stood erect, a grim smile on his face, waiting for a pause in the deafening, frenzied row beating against him.

Suddenly he lurched, swayed, looked as if about to fall headlong, partially recovered, then slowly sagged down to his knees, and finally collapsed. A shout of exultation went up from the Reds, to be followed immediately by a loud gasp or groan from the thousands of ordinary citizens.

Two St. John's ambulance-men hurried up the ladder to his side. As they knelt beside him attempting to staunch the flow of blood from a deep wound in his temple, they too were stoned; they and the unconscious man were struck repeatedly.

Mosley still unconscious was lifted to the ground, then driven to Walton Hospital, where the full gravity of his injury was ascertained. He had had a very close call. The frontal bone had been penetrated; had the blow been only a fraction further back it would have been fatal. In actual fact the blow that he had received could have killed many another man.

The wounding of Mosley was the signal for rather more energetic action by the police. The doors of a nearby Council yard were thrown back, revealing five or six mounted policemen and their sleek chargers. The horses were urged into a hand-canter towards the crowd, which cheered with enthusiasm, hoping to see retribution come to the stone-throwers; but the hooligans merely standing still and looking inoffensive, rendered themselves unidentifiable. This unimpressive action was described in the newspapers as a "mounted police charge".

Superintendent Burgess of the Liverpool C.I.D. himself arrested a youth named Melander, caught, he alleged, in the act of stoning Mosley. Burgess, who had been standing in the crowd directly behind Melander, claimed he had seen the missile leave the young man's hand, and from where he stood had been able to follow its flight until the moment it struck Mosley's head, whereat he had made a grab at the thrower, and held him.

It was the fault of the new Public Order Act that one of the finest police forces in Britain which exactly one year before, on the occasion of Mosley's meeting in the Liverpool Stadium, had acted so commendably, should have failed utterly at Walton to prevent bloodshed and outrage, or to uphold free speech. The Walton incident was a poor police operation, for which the Government was largely responsible, possibly in more ways than one. The small number of uniformed police present when mob violence had been expected, was highly suspicious.

Mosley's temperate habits and sane living hastened his recovery, so that he was kept in hospital for less than ten days. The circumstances and gravity of his wound broke temporarily the campaign of silence by the press; the boycott was lifted for a time, and he became big news. Reporters and correspondents were calling constantly at Walton Hospital, or were telephoning for progress reports; when he was finally discharged, head still in bandages, he was beset in the hospital entrance hall by a pushing, shoving pack of press reporters and photographers.

Melander, the youth whom Superintendent Burgess had arrested, was being charged by the police with having inflicted grievous bodily harm on Mosley. He made his first brief appearance in the Police Court in Dale Street, but was remanded until the police had completed their evidence.

A week or two later he made his second appearance in the Courts, with Mosley now sufficiently recovered, Greenhalgh and myself were subpoenaed as witnesses. Mrs. "Bessie" Braddock, Labour Member for Liverpool Exchange, was in Court following proceedings intently, while Mr. Sydney Silverman, Labour Member for Nelson and Colne, who is also a lawyer, appeared on behalf of the accused.

Mosley was cross-examined by Silverman with the most punctilious politeness on both sides. This was a great disappointment to the many policemen who had crowded into that particular courtroom in the hopes of enjoying a pyrotechnic display of the first magnitude, as there were few more ferocious denunciators of fascism than the Member for Nelson and Colne, who was now able to confront Lucifer himself in the safety of a law-court.

Outside in the corridor a detective was heard lamenting the peaceful exchange between witness-box and the body of the Court, and remarking that now he would be able to accept the parable of the lion lying down with the lamb.

This time Melander was remanded to the Assizes; a few weeks later he appeared before the judge at the Strangeways Assize Courts, Manchester, where Mosley, Greenhalgh and myself again had to stand as witnesses. Burgess stuck to his story that he had clearly seen the stone leave the young man's hand, and had followed with his eye until the moment it struck Mosley. The accused admitted throwing stones, but denied his marksmanship.

In his address to the jury the judge emphasised the well nigh impossibility of identifying one stone in its flight amid a shower of missiles converging on the same target. Therefore when the jury returned, it was with a verdict of "Not Guilty". Mosley's whispered comment to myself was that no other verdict could have been properly arrived at.

18 - The Ruin Of Lancashire

All this time most of Europe and much of the world continued in deep depression. Alone among the great industrial nations Germany had tackled seriously the problem of slump and unemployment, and was winning through. Across the Atlantic, President Roosevelt's "New Deal" was under way, and at least was giving hope to the millions of Americans caught up in the avalanche of financial disaster.

In Britain where there was little slacking of the "economic blizzard", the decline of Lancashire and her cotton industry worsened. The truth was that Lancashire was becoming a derelict county. She was dying. Her pulse, the throb of a thousand mills, beat fainter and fainter. Her skies, once shadowed by the smoke of countless tall chimneys, were almost clear again; her rivers, polluted for more than a century, flowed once more with unaccustomed clearness.

In her ports and cities and her numerous mill towns despondent men and women, apathetic and listless from a diet of tea with skimmed milk, bread and "marge", and chips, stood in interminable queues outside the Labour Exchange to draw their dole or Public Assistance money. Other times some tended their allotments, others raked over slag and cinder heaps in search of anything combustible, but most idled in the dreary streets until driven indoors by the raw, bleak, damp climate, when they brooded over empty grates.

There were pictures that I came to know only too well in my work for the Movement in the North of England.

"On Change" in Manchester and Liverpool, the brokers, the mill owners, and merchants were asking one another whether this was the end of "King Cotton". Growing numbers of the most

165

affluent sections of the industry, deciding that the answer was in the affirmative, were cutting their losses and getting out while they could.

Realising that the established political parties offered nothing in the way of help nor hope, numbers of Lancastrians of all degrees and social levels were now prepared to listen to Mosley, who alone had a practical answer to Lancashire's particular problem.

Everyone in the cotton trade understood that their ruin was being brought about by the huge textile factories recently established in India, Japan and China, financed largely by British capital, and equipped not only with British machinery but with more up-to-date plant than many impoverished Lancashire mill owners could afford to install in their own mills.

In 1917, Lancashire had been able to boast 61 million spindles, but by 1937, the year under review, the total had been reduced to 37½ millions. In that same time looms had dwindled from 808,796 to 461,209, a drop of 43 percent. The number of operatives had fallen from 712,000 to 445,000 persons of both sexes, of whom 140,000 were totally unemployed while countless thousands of those officially listed as still at work were on short time. The Cotton Trade organisations estimated that Lancashire's loss amounted to five thousand million (5,000,000,000) yards of cloth, and that almost all this loss was due to the competition of the coolie-manned mills of Asia.

In 1937 a skilled worker in an Indian cotton mill received the equivalent of one shilling and five pence half-penny a day for a working week of fifty-four hours. This worked out roughly at eight shillings for a forty-eight hour week. What chance did Lancashire stand in competition with cloth produced at such rates?

It is perhaps worth mentioning that the leading cotton magnates of Bombay were the Sassoons, a family of Jewish multi-millionaires originating from Baghdad, one of whom, Sir Philip Sassoon, had held ministerial posts in this country and was persona gratissima with the Establishment during the 1920s and 1930s.

While it was perhaps an unavoidable misfortune that Lancashire should have to meet this coolie competition in foreign markets, there was no justifiable reason that she should meet it within the British Empire, but it was worse than scandalous that the British home market should be open to all-comers.

The iniquitous and indefensible Congo Basin Treaty which a British Government had been so blind, stupid or subverted by financial interests to accept and sign, had thrown open to the traders of the world the British possessions in Central and east Africa. Inevitably this meant that the goods produced by the half-starved Asiatic coolies monopolised the African market, and British goods were virtually excluded. This suited perfectly those great banking houses of London and New York, which were the financial fairy godmothers of the Asiatic mills.

Distressing as was the spectacle of Britain's African colonies being run for the benefit of the exploiters of the Orient, it was yet more painful to see Britain herself flooded with coolie-manufactures on behalf of those same financial interests.

It was truly shocking to come into a depressed and neglected mill town with its silent mills and smokeless stacks, its people shabby and under-nourished, to pass down a shopping street with its many empty premises, shutters up and peeling paintwork, then to come on one of the derelict shops open again.

The shop I have in mind was now festooned with placards proclaiming: "Isidor Glass. The Cheapest Man in Town!" Mr. Glass's window and his shelves inside were crammed with cotton shirts, socks, ties, handkerchiefs, overalls and women's underwear, manufactured in Japan and selling at prices so infinitely low that even the long unemployed Lancashire cotton-workers could afford to make replacements to their diminished wardrobes. This in actual fact epitomised the triumph of international finance over British industry.

The Labour Party had no remedy for cotton, except to nationalise the industry. The socialist pamphlet on the subject devoted seventeen of its twenty-two pages in explaining how the cotton trade operated; it offered nothing constructive other than vague generalisations about exploring new markets and other shibboleths almost meaningless, so dear to socialist planners.

The Conservatives urged "rationalisation", a word much in vogue then; this was defeatism. Rationalisation meant the scrapping of millions of spindles and much other machinery, the sacking of many workers, and some compensation for the mill owners for the number of spindles and looms they had thrown out and broken up. The bosses would get a little of their money back, but the workers nothing.

Mosley's policy was clear, simple, and like his policy for agriculture, ruthless. He would denounce the Congo Basin Treaty, and exclude from Britain and from the huge Colonial Empire all cloth from the coolie-operated mills of the Orient. The Government of India would be required to compel the Indian mill owners to improve considerably the pay, hours and conditions of their employees. At the same time the further industrialisation of India would be restricted, and the Indian peasantry encouraged to become farmers with improved skills and techniques, and living standards, rather than remain the victims of poverty to be herded into the dreadful urban settlements and shanty towns clustered round the mills.

Concerning British textiles and the self-governing Dominions, Mosley's policy was – "Britain will buy from those who buy from Britain." In ratio to the purchase by the Dominions of British manufacturers, prominent among which would be cloth, made-up cotton goods and clothing, so would Britain buy from them their primary products. These straightforward and practical plans to restore Lancashire to prosperity promptly and permanently, were accepted readily by many persons in all sections of the cotton trade. In consequence this became a period of great progress for the Movement throughout the county.

Henceforth, whenever Mosley addressed a public meeting in a cotton town, he could be assured of a crowded hall; whence people had to be turned away, generally in their hundreds.

One such occasion was his meeting in the King George's Hall, Blackburn, on a lovely spring evening when it seemed a shame to be indoors. He told his audience of some two thousand or more persons, mainly unemployed and near-destitute cotton workers, how Lancashire had come to have lost three-quarters of its pre-war export trade. He explained what steps he proposed to take to remedy that disaster.

He was acclaimed loudly, but what was truly indicative of the sympathy and support of his listeners was the collection taken during the interval at the end of the speech and immediately prior to question time. The collecting boxes returned by the stewards were almost as heavy as lead; when opened they disgorged hundreds upon hundreds of pennies, not the pennies of the workers of which the Labour Party had used to boast, but of greater significance, the pennies of the workless.

The 'Northern Daily Telegraph', published in Blackburn, in its issue of 9th May, 1938, the day following that impressive meeting, devoted six inches of column space to what Sir John Grey had said at the opening of the Liberal Spring Fair in Burnley, another six inches to the utterances of R.A. Cross, M.P., to a few dozen members of the Rossendale Junior Unionist Association, and forty-eight lines to the verbal bashing that the Bishop of Blackburn had administered from his pulpit to Hitler and Mussolini.

Mosley, whose audience would have outnumbered several times the combined listeners to the two politicians and the Bishop's congregation, was not granted one line of print. He and his two thousand acclaimers might never have existed. Such was the freedom of the press in the 1930s.

Blackburn was one of the larger cotton towns where the local British Union formation was exceptionally active under the virile leadership of Bill Sumner, a battered but extremely intelligent former corporal of cavalry, and ex-Regular, whose rasping voice frequently could be heard proclaiming Mosley's message across the granite sets of the bleak and draughty market-place.

Once when his platform was not far from that of an open-air Labour Party Rally, Sumner stopped speaking and looked long and searchingly at the respectable old windbags who, with their voices, were busy saving democracy in Spain. When one of the Labour spokesmen paused for breath, Sumner intervened.

"Look at them!" he cried, in his harsh, grating voice. "Take a look at your working-class leaders, with their bowler hats, their black suits and their big bellies. Working-class revolutionary leaders! Pah! What sort of a revolution do you think they would be likely to lead?" he jeered.

There was derisive laughter from members of the crowd round the Labour platform, as well as from Sumner's own audience. The poor old worthies of the local Labour Party who were doubtless also deacons of chapels, accustomed to long uninterrupted harangues and with no gift for repartee, stood open-mouthed in self-conscious silence. "I felt real sorry for them," said one of Sumner's own supporters later. While Bill Sumner, the District Leader of Blackburn, was a tough, broken-nosed ex-trooper, who was trying to rear a large family on the meagre allowance of the Public Assistance Board, his Women's District Leader at that time was the daughter of a well-known Lancashire land or mill-owning family. She was a young girl straight from the schoolroom, who had joined British Union under the compulsion of a strong social conscience. The District Treasurer was a fresh-faced, upstanding young trade unionist, a carpenter of the name of Jack Birtwistle. The District members were mainly mill workers and mechanics, most of whom were jobless; but there was also a sprinkling of small shopkeepers and business people.

Apart from his public meetings, Mosley addressed gatherings of businessmen invited to meet him at luncheons served in the banqueting rooms of hotels and restaurants. Reece's Restaurant in Liverpool, and the Victoria Hotel in Manchester, were but two of the venues for these gatherings. These were intended to have been events of limited duration so as to allow the guests to get back to their offices; but it was not unusual to see Mosley still surrounded by eager questioners and listeners as tea-time approached.

British Union activities in 1937, which had been a strenuous year, culminated in a rally in the Free Trade Hall, Manchester, shortly before Christmas. This was the biggest and most important indoor meeting of the year, which normally would have been held in London, but all the major halls of the capital were denied to Mosley.

Because of the ban in London a contingent of London members of the Movement, availing themselves of a cheap Sunday railway excursion, came down to participate in the rally. Delighted as they would have been at any other time to welcome their companions from the South, the local officers who had been organising the occasion were not so pleased, as the Free Trade Hall with seating for only about three thousand could have been filled two or three times by local people.

The Movement in south-east Lancashire had reached such a strength that new problems arose. It was no longer possible to accommodate in any one building available in the area all the members, friends and enquirers who sought to see and hear Mosley.

If Blackshirts and sympathisers were to monopolise all seats, as they did, Mosley spoke only to the converted; he would have infused them with renewed faith and confidence, but the excluded enquirers would remain lost to the Cause. On the other hand, to have admitted the seekers and waverers at the price of shutting out the believers, would have been a disappointment to those hundreds of hard-working and devoted fascists to whom a great and enthusiastic rally addressed by their Leader was both a reward and an incentive.

This time the doors had to be closed long before the advertised hour, while the police endeavoured to persuade to go home the thousands of persons gathered in Peter Street and behind the hall. It was vexing to look out into the street to see a great orderly queue extending down to Deansgate, and another thick file of humanity encompassing the block of buildings, and to have to explain to them that there was no possibility of admittance.

19 - The Britain First Peace Campaign

Anthony Eden's departure from the Foreign Office in February 1938 brought as much relief to us members of the British Union as it dismayed his admirers of the Left. His withdrawal from the Government gave Chamberlain and his more pacifist-minded colleagues a better chance to negotiate with the two dictators.

Although the British and French Lefts had stormed and raged over the Anschluss, there had been little danger of going to war on that issue. Therefore we followers of Mosley were no more concerned over what had taken place than to express our pleasure and relief that at last poor, poverty-stricken Austria was about to enjoy some of the prosperity that Hitler's statecraft and Schacht's economics[36] had brought to Germany, and especially that this great change could have been achieved peacefully, and without bloodshed.

By July, the Left however were quite ready to wage war for Czechoslovakia. This belligerence of the Labour Party was more than some socialists could stomach. One of those to resign from the Party on this issue was the Labour peer, Lord Sanderson, who was reported in the '*Daily Telegraph*', 9.3.1938, as having stated: "I cannot work for a party whose foreign policy involves so much hatred of other Powers... and whose attainment of office I would regard as a menace to the peace of the world."

It was to avoid war on the pretext of protecting Czechoslovakia, that on 9th July, 1938, Mosley initiated his "Britain First" campaign. British Union staged meetings, rallies and protest

---

36   Schacht, the "financial wizard", re-established a stable currency after the post-war runaway inflation, for which he was made Governor of the Reichsbank. He took part in the London Economic Conference of 1933, and was made Minister of Economics in 1934, in which capacity he made barter deals and mobilized finances to create credit within the nation, putting the banks under strict government control.

marches throughout Britain, wherever there were sizeable enough branches to warrant such demonstrations.

When one of Mosley's peace meetings was advertised to be held in Stratford on Sunday, 24th July, following a march from East Ham, the local branch of the Communist Party opened a fund, days in advance of the fascist procession, to defray the fines of those of their friends likely to fall foul of the police. It was hoped that the Home Secretary took note of this revealing prognostication.

As time went on and the Czechoslovakian crisis became yet more acute, the Movement stepped up its appeal for a sane and statesmanlike approach to the problem. During this decisive stage of the crisis Mosley addressed great public meetings throughout the London area, speaking among other places in Ealing, Shoreditch, Marylebone and Kentish Town. It was estimated that during those hectic days, at least half a million Londoners must have heard his message from his own lips.

During this period two million anti-war leaflets were distributed by British Union, concerning which there were allegations of discrimination by the authorities against the Movement on at least one occasion. The particular instance cited was when leaflet distributors were hustled away by the police from the vicinity of Westminster, in many cases after having had their names and addresses taken, while communists paraded unhindered up and down Whitehall bearing posters inscribed "Chamberlain Must Go!" and "Save Czechoslovakia!"

Immediately following the Munich Agreement, when Chamberlain had seemed to have saved Europe from war, there was an unexpected hitch that threatened to bring down his structure for peace. What had happened was that the Czechoslovakian Government of Hodza after having accepted the proposals for the transfer of Sudetenland to Germany, finding itself unpopular with the Czech populace, who like most newly-emancipated people, suffered from delusions of grandeur, and tended to xenophobia, resigned.

The Hodza Government was replaced by a pro-communist and pro-Russian military dictatorship under General Girovy. The affair was no more than a flash in the pan; but it gave renewed hope, if only momentarily, to those tens of thousands of persons in this country who had been unwittingly absorbing the "Moscow line" daily from the *'News Chronicle'* and *'Daily Herald'*, and who therefore hoped to see Hitler thwarted at this eleventh hour.

Again the situation was strained and tense. The atmosphere was sombre when British Union announced its intention to hold a demonstration for peace on the last Sunday of September, with a public meeting in Hammersmith following a protest march from Westminster. This was to have been not only the climax of the "Britain First" campaign, but British Union's sixth anniversary rally.

The Chief Commissioner of Police, Sir Philip Game, forbade the march, but consented to the meeting to be held in Stanlake Road. The *'Daily Worker'* cried jubilantly that it was on account of the earnest representations from Clement Attlee and Arthur Greenwood to the Home Secretary that the great planned demonstration through the streets was forbidden.

The meeting that was held in Hammersmith was attended by thousands jammed tight from one end of Stanlake Road to the other. Almost everyone was wearing a small replica of the Union Jack. Mosley's rhetoric reached new heights; surrounded by a sea of friends and followers, he called:

"Here tonight we are assembled to tell the Government and Parties and Parliament that Britain demands peace. They forbid us to demonstrate for peace; but they permit the Labour Party to demonstrate for war...

What do they ask us to fight for? Not for Britain... We have fought for Britain before; and if Britain were attacked, we would fight for Britain again... But say the Labour Leaders and the financial press, 'We British people have got to fight so as to stop one lot of Germans joining up with another lot of Germans, in order to subject those three and a half million Germans in

Sudetenland to the tyranny of the Czech majority, and at the same time to deny the principles of self-determination about which Labour has preached ever since the last war.

Chamberlain made a journey to Germany last week, which at the time I said was an act of courage and of commonsense... The press said an agreement was reached. The British Government, the French Government, the German Government, and even the Czech Government agreed that the three and a half million Germans in Czechoslovakia should be allowed to return to Germany.

Now, what has happened? Something has got busy. What is it? Why are we again threatened with war? Why is the Labour Party screaming for war?"

Mosley ended his speech with the words: "We give ourselves to England. We stand for peace!"

The sequel was as amazing as it was unpremeditated; the thousands of persons jammed together in that street, even as they sang together the national anthem with tremendous feeling as men and women inspired, turned spontaneously and began to progress in the direction of Westminster. They became a solid mass of humanity animated by one purpose, that Government and Parliament should see and hear for themselves what thousands upon thousands of their fellow countrymen thought of the drive to war at the behest of international socialists on behalf of international usurers.

First the human flow extended across the carriageway and both pavements, halting the traffic, and ever growing in size as spectators on learning what it was about, attached themselves, scores at a time. Then, although no one had purposely attempted to marshal the mass, it coalesced of its own accord into a great orderly procession of all types and classes of men and women united in their desire to preserve peace. They took up, and were chanting in unison the apt slogan:

"Nineteen-Fourteen Echo: We Will Not Fight For Czecho!"

When this people's protest march, for such it had evolved into, after having traversed in reverse the banned route, approached Whitehall and Parliament Square, it was to find all further progress barred by massive police reserves, which had been rushed in to seal off the area.

By the winter of 1938 the Royal Albert Hall, Olympia, and the Seymour Hall were successfully refused to British Union owing to increased pressure to ban Mosley. The latest public meeting-place to be added to the list of refusals was the Queen's Hall, which while available to the Labour Party, the Left Book Club, and the Friends of Soviet Russia, was denied to Mosley on, said the letting agents, the personal instruction of the directors.

Therefore, as in 1937, the grande finale of the year's indoor meetings was that held in the Free Trade Hall, Manchester. The march that was to have preceded the meeting was banned by Chief Constable Maxwell, probably on the instruction of the Manchester Watch Committee; but the meeting itself was one of the most enthusiastic ever held. Again thousands of disappointed persons had to be turned away from doors closed long before the advertised time.

The enthusiasm reached new heights; and when at the close of the meeting, and after the public had departed, the local active Blackshirts gathered below the platform to be addressed privately by their leader, there seemed to be nearly as many persons present as during the public meeting. His followers cheered, shouted in unison and stamped until Mosley reappeared from his room back-stage. When their repeated roars of delight had died down sufficiently to allow him to speak, he gave them some brief words of encouragement. Looking down with affection at their flushed and excited faces he said soberly:

"I know that most of you would willingly give your lives for our cause; but I wonder how many will endure for it."

Turning to me on the platform beside him, in a lowered voice he added: "For that is much the harder thing."

About this same time, a handful of Members of Parliament increasingly aware that the probity of the press was not all that that same press proclaimed it to be, raised the matter in the Commons. Hansard, 15.2.1939, quoted Lieut.-Colonel Moore-Brabazon, Conservative Member for Wallasey, as saying:

"Oswald Mosley, although he is the leader of a political party, is not mentioned at all. That must be because some form of arrangement and conspiracy exists within the press. If that is so, we have not a free press, and that state of affairs should be altered."

Earl Winterton, Conservative Member for Worthing, Father of the House of Commons, in this same debate asked:

"Why is it that the leader of a certain movement with which no one is in agreement in this House, I think, addresses meetings which I understand are fully attended and crowded, but who never has a report of his speeches in any of the London or provincial press... Speaking as an old Member of this House... I wonder what the explanation is. I wonder further, whether the questions asked by the Hon. Member and by me will be reported in the press, and whether there will be any answer to it in the press."

'*The Times*', '*The Daily Telegraph*', and '*The Manchester Guardian*' did actually report, although unobtrusively enough, the questions and observations of those two distinguished parliamentarians, but refrained from offering any explanation or making a direct reply. The great popular newspapers on the other hand ignored the debate in the same way as they ignored the existence of Oswald Mosley and his Movement.

It was left to the '*Aeroplane*', 29.3.1939, in the hands of men who "thought in terms of the future", to come out boldly:

"One may dislike Sir Oswald Mosley. But a press which ignores meetings at which audiences amount to many, many, thousands at a time, and are moved to great enthusiasm, cannot profess to be a representative press... the great danger of such suppression of truth and suggestion of falsehood, is that we may be driven into a war in which we are not concerned, and in the interests of alien political movements and international finance."

20 - The Empire Betrayed

When he realised the terrible implications of Chamberlain's Polish Pact – a suicide pact as he termed it – Mosley addressed his followers with more than usual fire and fervour.

"Out for Britain!" he exhorted us. "Dire is her need. The Parties come out for war in their master's quarrel. They serve the vilest tyranny with which a nation can be cursed. That tyranny is the money-power which decrees war.

In their blood feud the merchants of usury command death. Humbly their political jackals hurry to do their bidding. The Parties are unanimous... all of them... Tory, Liberal, Labour, and Communist, are all together at last. Not in the service of Britain... our country they have never served. Not in defence of Britain; but in defence of Poland, and the investments of the City of London in foul industrial conditions, where Poles are sweated for a weekly wage of ten shillings."

May Day, 1939, we celebrated on Sunday, 7th May, with the greatest show of strength British Union had yet made. A march from Westminster to Hackney was preceded by an inspection of members, who standing shoulder to shoulder in three ranks facing the carriageway and the river, extended in unbroken lines along the Embankment from Westminster to Hungerford Bridge.

As the column of Blackshirts, longer by far than at any previous demonstration, made its way to the meeting place, there was never a trace of opposition. The thousands who watched from the pavements, either did so in pensive silence or with encouraging cries and gestures.

When at the meeting place Mosley called for a show of hands of those in favour of war for Poland, two hands only (one had to respect the courage of their owners) appeared above the packed thousands of faces.

"Britons fight for Britain only," was his theme that fine sunny afternoon. He went on to declaim:

"The British people can stand alone and can if necessary meet the challenge of any nation on earth, provided that their system is modern, and that they are inspired again by their own great spirit... The call of Britain, in her defence, they would ever answer; but they would not have their people betrayed by the call to war of the vile interests of finance, seeking power to preserve their own corruption."

He ended with the words:

"Let not our generation be dismissed with the contempt of posterity, that history might write, 'Like dumb cattle they were driven to the slaughter, because they had not the manhood, the wit, and the will to live in peace and greatness."

The drive to war continued relentlessly. The protesting voices of the few who understood fully, or only partly, what was happening, were inaudible in the combined thunder of press, radio and Parliament. Cardinal Hinsley told the Catholic Truth Society:

"I wish that I could muzzle the press... and shut the cinemas. If we could stop all publicity for a fortnight or a month, there would be I think some hope for peace."

The forces of anti-Christ were for the time all-powerful and triumphant; as those were the forces that controlled and directed all propaganda, the calm, warning voice of the Cardinal went unheeded. British Union made yet more strenuous efforts to reach the people, but almost every hall in London and most of those in the provinces were denied us. The press and the B.B.C. completely boycotted us; we might never have existed. The wholesale newsagents maintained their refusal to handle '*Action*'; and many advertising companies and agencies would not arrange publicity on behalf of the organisation, even if prepaid.

It was frustrating; but due to the self-sacrifice and increased activities of members of the Movement on the streets, where they handed out leaflets, paraded with posters, sold copies of '*Action*', and held street-corner meetings, new members were recruited, sympathy won, and interest aroused.

Repeatedly Mosley drew attention to those financial interests in Poland, which Britain's young manhood would soon be called upon to defend. At the same time he exposed the kind of industrial conditions that those self-same interests maintained in that country. '*Action*', 6.5.1939, reported: "Poland is in pawn to the great International Financial interests. British, French, and American finance predominate in Poland. All its major industries are run with foreign capital."

This same newspaper article also stated that excluding Russia, Poland possessed the most backward and disgraceful industrial conditions in Europe. Long ago in his meeting in Barnsley in the south Yorkshire coalfields, Mosley made known that the average weekly wage of a Polish collier was in the neighbourhood of ten shillings, and that the largest and most opulent office blocks in Warsaw were those of the foreign finance companies with industrial stakes in Poland.

Rumania, too, yet one more country which Britain was by now pledged to defend, was another paradise for international money-lenders, where the wages of a skilled industrial worker varied from forty to fifty shillings a month, and those of a peasant approximated twenty shillings a month. The '*Daily Telegraph*', 2.3.1938, admitted that "Jews still control about 80% of its commerce". Everywhere were the same sordid obligations to be paid with British blood.

Loans by British Government to Poland now totalled some £60,000,000. Rumania had been graciously pleased to accept an offer of £12,000,000 at the very time that Australia's request for a modest £5,000,000 was turned down. New Zealand, too, who had sought a loan was rebuffed; in the words of the 'Sydney Bulletin', all that she got was the "cold shoulder". At this same time, loyal neglected Newfoundland now completely broke, had the bailiffs in. It was inopportune that while Britain was handing out vast sums of money to Poland, Rumania, Turkey and Greece, so that those backward countries could purchase arms wherewith to defend the coal mines, oil fields, and industrial plants within their territories but owned by the usurers of London, Paris and New York, the report of the De La Warr Committee should have been published.

For two and a half years this Committee of the Economic Advisory Council had been investigating the conditions prevailing throughout the Colonial Empire with its five hundred million inhabitants. It had found widespread malnutrition, leading to increasing maternal and infantile mortality, and through physical and mental debility to progressive inefficiency in every aspect of work and life.

It was a document as depressing as it was damning. It continued: "Deterioration is taking place... Health and vitality are on a lower level than that which ruled a generation ago. The effect of malnutrition is cumulative, and the natives are becoming progressively unable to cultivate their land and thus maintain even the meagre diet they now have."

All these evils the Committee ascribed to the abysmally low economic level prevailing throughout the British Colonial Empire. From Hong Kong came the horrible plain statement of fact that: "Twenty-five of the next hundred children to be born in Hong Kong will never have a first birthday."

This dreadful indictment, for that was what the report of the De La Warr Committee amounted to, shocked Mosley into publishing his view. He wrote:

"The Colonial empire was founded by men of courage and vision, who devoted their arduous lives to putting down slavery and oppression. Those Empire-builders must surely turn in their graves as there arises on the scenes of their labours a new system of slavery and oppression, more subtle but no less ruthless than the old. And Democracy gives this system its blessing, while it prepares for a European War in the name of Liberty."

A few days later he wrote again on the same theme: "We are not Tories who regard the Empire as a lucrative field for exploitation. Neither are the Socialists who regard it as a thing unclean, to be discarded at the earliest possible moment. We believe it is a sacred trust laid upon us and on our children after us, a trust which can be honoured only by just government and the development of its immense resources for the benefits of all its inhabitants, whether white or coloured."

Again, it was too late; already the rot was too deep. They were the internationalists of both sorts who were destroying the British Empire. Those most responsible were the "pink pedagogues", those Left Wing school teachers who had riddled the British educational system, and indoctrinated a large proportion of an entire generation so that they scorned their heritage, ignored their responsibilities, but leaned to some nebulous and flabby socialist world state of their own imagination, vaguely inspired by Karl Marx.

This flaccid philosophy of resignation also had permeated large sections of the so-called ruling class, those who had not already surrendered themselves to the other internationalists, the international bankers. The abasement of patriotism fostered in many schools resulted in hundreds of thousands of persons knowing nothing of their imperial heritage, and caring less. Those teachers of the Left sowed their seed so well that "imperialist" is now as dirty a word as "fascist".

Between them the two kinds of internationalists, those of financial exploitation and those of petty rancour, have succeeded in making an end to that Empire conceived by Sir Walter

Raleigh, and born that day in May, 1607, when the first sod was dug on the banks of the James River to take the first post cut in the Virginian woods to start the building of Jamestown and the plantation of Virginia.

Exactly as foreseen by Sir Francis Bacon, who had likened the foundation of Jamestown to the sowing of the proverbial mustard seed, and who had visions of the venture started there, growing and spreading until it embraced much of the earth, the Empire that was born that day expanded until it covered one quarter of the solid surface of the globe, and in the words of its own post held "dominion over palm and pine".

It was in pursuit of this same vision of imperial splendour that, two and three-quarters centuries later, Cecil Rhodes entered Oriel, Oxford, Raleigh's old college, there to ponder his plans to expand the Empire in Africa. At Oxford, Rhodes had his ambitions further kindled by the exhortations of Ruskin, who addressing his pupils, would adjure them: [37]

"All that I ask of you is to have a fixed purpose of some kind for your country and yourselves... Will you, youths of England, make your country again a royal throne of kings, a sceptred isle, for all the world a source of light, a centre of peace... This is what England must do, or perish; she must found colonies as far and as fast as she is able... seizing every piece of fruitful waste ground she can set foot on, and there teaching her colonists that their chief virtue is to be fidelity to their country."

Those defamers of the British Empire lie when they say that it was all grabbed in greed and lust for gold. True, much of it was acquired in pursuit of commercial enterprises; but the high principled instructions issued by the Virginia Company of London to its pioneers, how they were to behave in general, and how to comport themselves towards the indigenous red Indians in particular, were the precursory formulae for subsequent colonial venturers to practise on the native populations.

---

37   *Cecil Rhodes*, pp.43-44, by André Maurois, pub. Collins.

That there were regrettable lapses from that standard, no one can deny. There was nothing very high-principled about the Guinea slave trade with its appalling "middle passage"; nor was the wiping out of the aborigines of Van Diemansland anything but brutal. The opium trade, too, was an out-and-out disgrace to Britain. But there were infinitely more numerous examples of empire-building in furtherance of high ideals, as when the Colonial Office of Victorian time sent officers to the African lakes and neighbouring territories ahead of trade, and in instances ahead of missionaries even, in order to put down raiding and slave-trading.

There was never a band of more devoted men than those officers of the old colonial Service. Apart from being something of a superman, Edgar Wallace's "Sanders of the River" was very much a prototype of a pre-1914 West African District Officer. The reminiscences of C.A.W. Monckton of the New Guinea Constabulary, contained in three fascinating volumes, give an illuminating account of selfless Empire-making in a savage land.

Youngsters between the two World Wars devoured such books, and were thrilled and inspired by them. Nowadays, such works moulder unread in library vaults, while the young seek their inspiration in the biographies of New Orleans jazzmen, and follow with fascination the improbable homicidal and sexual encounters of James Bond.

There must be many humble coolies, peasants and villagers in Asia and Africa now a prey to the despotism of a half-trained, inexperienced and often corrupt native bureaucracy, and who subjected without redress to the heartless exploitations of their own unprincipled capitalists, regret the departed sahibs, tuans and bwanas.

As if in confirmation of which conjecture a lady from Uganda, Betty Kagwa, asked if people[38] "really had any idea what life in many countries that have obtained independence is like." She went on to state: "In my own country of Uganda to criticise

---

38   *Daily Telegraph*, 31.8.1970.

the President, or indeed any Minister or institution of the State, is likely to lead to imprisonment. In many of these countries relations and fellow tribesmen of those in power live in the lap of luxury, but the man in the street lives in perpetual fear of doing or saying the wrong thing and ending up in prison, or worse. Ask a poor man in the bush whether he receives a more impartial and sympathetic ear to his problems nowadays from a minister than formerly from 'Bwana D.C., and the answer might well surprise..."

The sorry and insidious victory of the Left Wingers has been so complete that in this country today almost no one, except a few old men in pubs and clubs who in the pride of their young manhood had served the Empire, regrets the passing of the world's greatest dominion, which from its heroic beginning to its ignominious end had existed gloriously for over three and a half centuries.

The Empire of Rome in its decline had had its long twilight; but the passing of the British Empire has been as swift as the passage of daylight to dark in the torrid zones. It was as recently as 1898 that Sir Joseph Chamberlain surveying that domain "on which the sun never sets" had proudly proclaimed that Britain's imperial greatness was still only in its infancy.

When a few weeks after the publication of the findings of the De La Warr Committee, Neville Chamberlain at last declared war on Germany, to the exultation and relief of all those persons who had long been goading him, he destined to destruction not only the mightiest territorial possession the world has seen, but one of its noblest conceptions, the Pax Britannia.

The Second World War in which the leaders of Britain's two great allies, Russia and the United States, pledged themselves to use their alliance to destroy Britain's Empire, hastened its end. Nevertheless the war only speeded up and made certain of its dissolution, as it was already being destroyed from within by the deliberate malice and subversion of the Left, and by the blind, fatuous lethargy of the Right.

21 - Earl's Court

It was during the summer of 1939, with the possibility of war becoming a probability, that British Union reached its peak of strength, significance and influence.

After the denial to Mosley of every major hall in London, it was found that the great Exhibition Hall at Earl's Court could be made available. This vast place was at once booked for a rally and public meeting to be held on the evening of Sunday, 16th July.

It was currently believed that Earl's Court, at that time the largest hall in the world, had escaped the general prohibition, because those "faceless" men responsible for the ban had not thought of the building in connection with political rallies, nor had they believed that Mosley would attempt to hold a public exhibition of the strength of his following on such a scale. This was by far the most ambitious concentration of strength tried by the Movement in its seven years of existence. It turned out to be not only British union's mightiest demonstration, but the largest political meeting to have been held indoors not in Britain but in the world.

Thirty thousand people gathered in the largest hall on Earth, to listen to the man whose name was not allowed to be mentioned in the British press, who was not permitted to utter a word over the B.B.C., and whose published writings the wholesale newsagents refused to handle, but whose audience on that summer's evening was the greatest concourse ever to have been brought together beneath one roof.

Mosley's listeners came from far and near. I found myself beside a man who had motored up from Plymouth, who though in mufti turned out to be an admiral of the Royal Navy. Parties

"Britain First" Peace Rally, Earl's Court, London. July 1939.

and individuals came from as far as Edinburgh and Dundee. In London, the London Passenger Transport Board put on special through-trains on the Underground to bring in the thousands of members and friends from East London. The organisers of the rally put on all the pageantry and colour they could devise. The massed standards of the Districts of Britain were paraded down the centre aisle to the crash of drums, then were crowded together in vivid ramparts of colour on either side of the platform.

Then at last to the shrill fanfare of red-tabarded trumpets displaying the flash and circle emblem of the Movement, Mosley appeared escorted by his three senior officers. Head erect, stern-faced he strode down the length of the hall with his Director General, Neil Francis Hawkins on his right, his Assistant Director General (Administration), Bryan Donovan, on his left, and his Organiser of meetings, Hector McKechnie, bringing up the rear.

The sustained cheering that greeted him drowned completely the drums and trumpets that were playing him in. The tumult of his welcome, a seeming never-ending roar, followed him as he climbed to where he was to speak from a lofty rostrum, not unlike the Whitehall Cenotaph.

Above his head hung an immense flag bearing the flash and circle, above which was suspended an even larger "Union Jack" said to be the largest in Britain. Immediately below him, on either side, were the hundreds of sets of standards, making a brave display of red and black and gold, and gleaming metal. Each member of the massed Colour Parties and escorts was a be-medalled veteran of the First World War, showing between them almost every naval and military decoration and campaign medal that could have been worn by former British Servicemen.

Alone on his lofty rostrum Mosley stood in silence for several long minutes before his wildly cheering, waving and saluting followers would let him speak. At last he began:

"Fellow Britons, tonight the British people are here, and tonight from this great audience will be heard the voice of the British people, telling Parliament, telling Parties and Government something it is time that they should hear."

He concluded what was probably his greatest achievement in grand oratory, with a burning call to patriotism:

"This heritage of England, by our struggle and our sacrifice, we shall give again to our children. And, with that sacred gift we tell them that they come from stock of men who went out from this small island in frail craft across storm-tossed seas to take in their brave hands the greatest empire that man has ever seen; in which tomorrow our people shall create the highest civilisation that man has ever known.

So we take by our hand these our children, to whom our struggle shall give back our England; with them we dedicate ourselves again to the memory of those who have gone before us... to the dead heroes of Britain, in sacred union we say: 'Like you, we give ourselves to England... across the ages that divide us... across the glories that unite us... we gaze into your eyes, and we give to you this holy vow... we shall be true today... tomorrow... and forever... England lives!"

Later, when the public and the press men had left, he spoke privately to his active followers, his devoted Blackshirts, thousands upon thousands of them crowded into the arena. He thanked them for all they had done to make the demonstration the success it had been.

"Thank you, my comrades, in struggle," he said to them in a voice quieter and softer than usual. I need say no more of an evening that will not only live for ever in our memory, but one day will live in British history. Splendid organisation was combined with devoted service that sustains no other force in Britain. Above all, and beyond all, was the spirit of our Movement in you, my companions. Such things once born, can never die, and in the final struggle can never know defeat."

The significance of Earl's Court was too immense, too portentous to be totally ignored by the press. As an item of news it was relegated to inferior position, but the columnists and commentators had perforce to remark on it.

Cassandra of the 'Daily Mirror', 17.7.1939, wrote: "There is no doubt that numerically the adherents to Fascism are increasing. To have filled Earl's Court, which I believe is the world's largest meeting hall, is a considerable achievement.

Each reverse of the National Government helps fascism. Mr Chamberlain's tragic hesitancy brings recruits to Mosley's creed. This strange young man with his violent remedies and his uncompromising courage may yet serve to rock the smug conservatism that acts like a drug on our political life. If so, he deserves a place in history."

William Hickey of the 'Daily Express' felt impelled to write in like vein: "You may think what you like of Sir Oswald Mosley's politics; but the fact that the estimates of his Earl's Court meeting on a Sunday evening in summer go up to 20,000 is impressive... The meeting becomes a political occasion."

'*The Times*' reported: "The hall was estimated to hold some 30,000 people, and it was fairly well filled."

The '*Manchester Guardian*' printed: "An audience of probably more than 20,000 people assembled at Earl's Court... to hear Sir Oswald Mosley... An overwhelming majority of those present were his followers... The speech itself was a remarkable effort."

It was in connection with the Earl's Court demonstration that the British Union published an appeal for help, both active and financial. As it synthesises the spirit and aspirations of our Movement in its greatest days immediately before the Second World War, it is reproduced here in full:

"We appeal to all Britons, who love their country and who are proud of the great heritage of British Empire, to do their part to save Britain from sinking to the level of a third rate power. Britain can be great again, and her people can achieve through modern science and opportunity a happiness and prosperity never previously known, but it is useless to hide from ourselves the fact that since 1918 our Empire has shown all the signs of disintegration and our people are threatened with gathering disaster.

Mosley, realising this fact founded the 'British Union', a Movement without class or social barrier, dedicated to the supreme idea of placing Britain again in her rightful place among the nations. He asks all to help and to give their services or some part of their income to the great cause. Mosley is giving both.

Enrol as an active member, or if your personal affairs prohibit you from openly acknowledging your support of this Movement of the British people, join us as an inactive member, but remember nothing can be achieved without sacrifice. Don't leave it to others, it is for Britain... DO IT NOW"

22 - The Phoney War

On 4th September, 1939, the day after the Declaration of War, there were raids by the Royal Air Force on German battleships in the Schillig Roads, Wilhelmshaven, and at Brunsbuttel where the Kiel Canal joins the North sea, believed to be at the instigation of Winston Churchill who had been installed as First Lord of the Admiralty the previous day, and was eager to get in his first blow against the Nazis.

Fifteen Blenheims from Nos. 107, 110 and 139 Squadrons took off for Wilhelmshaven and fourteen Wellingtons from Nos. 9 and 149 Squadrons made for Brunsbuttel on what was Britain's first act of open hostility; but the odds were against them, the weather bad with visibility almost nil, the German anti-aircraft defences highly efficient, some of the bombs dropped proving to be 'duds'. The five Blenheims of 139 Squadron were lucky: they were unable to locate the target and returned without loss. 110 Squadron lost one Blenheim attacking the pocket battleship Admiral Scheer, but 107 Squadron were less fortunate – they lost four out of their five aircraft in the attack.

Of the Wellingtons from No. 3 Group, the majority failed to reach the target and turned back, one of them believed to have bombed the town of Egsberg in neutral Denmark some 110 miles away, killing and wounding a number of inhabitants.

The remainder, two sections of three from No. 9 Squadron made the target, sighting a battleship and five cruisers steaming at high speed due west and made an unsuccessful attack. One was believed to be shot down by anti-aircraft fire and a second by an attacking force of Me 109's scrambled from their Nordal 11/JG77 base, its kill claimed by Pilot Sergeant Alfred Held in what the Luftwaffe suggested was their first victory in the War against the RAF.

Later, in the First Casualty List of the War, appeared the names of Aircraftmen 2nd Class and Volunteer Air Gunners K.G. Day and G.T. Brocking, both members of British Union, killled in action in Wellington L4275. The body of 20 year old Day was picked up ten days later by a cargo steamer near the Elbe Lightships and buried two days later with full military honours at Cuxhaven Cemetery. An unconfirmed report suggested that Goering was present at the ceremony. Young Day's body was reburied at Becklingen War Cemetery, Soltau, Germany after the war, but the body of his 22 year old comrade Brocking was never found, his name now inscribed on the Air Force Memorial at Runnymede, just one of the 20,547 World War II Allied airmen with no known graves.

Historically embarrassing it may be, but the first name on the first casualty list of the war was that of a Mosley Blackshirt – Ken Day. It is believed that another airman in that operation was also a Blackshirt, returning severely wounded; he recovered only to be arrested during the summer of 1940, and locked up under Defence Regulation 18B while still on sick leave. Some time later the sea washed up on the east coast of England the body of another young airman. Sodden with water but safely buttoned in a breast pocket was his paid-up British Union membership card.

Was it entirely by chance that squadrons selected for the very first and almost suicidal air operation were those containing a high proportion of Oswald Mosley's young men? Is it possible that the decision to use those particular squadrons an act of cynicism? It must have been glaringly apparent to the powers-that-be that the Services contained many Blackshirts. Open-air rallies addressed by Mosley were attended by uniformed members of all three Services; one impromptu procession contained several R.A.F pilots conspicuous in their long flying-boots in the foremost ranks.

More names appeared in further casualty lists. On 16th November, 1939, Leicester District mourned a keen and energetic member in Lieutenant Albert Edward White, R.N.V.R., "missing presumed lost", with H.M.S. Northern Rover.

During the first week of December, Leslie Runicles, an active member of the Movement in West London, was officially listed as having gone down with H.M.S. Rawlpindi, sunk after "a very gallant action against great odds". Some weeks later the International Red Cross reported that Runicles was one of the handful of survivors of the sinking. He had been picked up out of the sea, and was a prisoner of war in Germany.

Another Blackshirt member to distinguish himself during 1939 was Thomas Ward of South Shields, First Officer of S.S. Oakgrove, who was awarded the order of the British Empire for devotion to duty when his vessel was attacked by two enemy planes, receiving five direct hits by bombs, and the decks swept by machine-gun fire.

In view of later developments, it is interesting to recall that 'Action', 19.10.1939, printed an article by General Fuller on the strategic aspects of the war, in which he warned that if the war continued long enough, Britain would be likely to suffer bombardment from the Continent by rocket. From the surprise that was evinced later when the "V2's" began to fall, it would seem that the General's prophecy had been disregarded in official quarters.

After the expected mass air raids failed to take place, a curious air of complacency took over in Britain, which even the Battle of the River Plate on December 13 did not disturb. Britain's politicians were confident that the economic blockade would rapidly deprive Germany of essential supplies and all they had to do was to sit back and wait for her to collapse.

The Phoney War period provided an excellent opportunity of securing a negotiated peace. The BUF therefore embarked on a nationwide campaign of public meetings in favour of an honourable, negotiated peace, and these meetings not only proved to be among the most enthusiastic we ever held but brought us new members of every possible type, including pacifists. All of them were drawn to the only substantial organised body opposed to the premeditated mass destruction.

Motorcycle and Car racing legend Fay Taylor

One of those to enrol in British Union at this time was Miss Fay Taylour, the racing motorist who had been described not long before, by the '*News Chronicle*', as Britain's finest woman driver.

Fay Taylour came into the Movement in somewhat unusual circumstances, as detailed in a letter from herself and addressed to "The Secretary, British Union," in which she described how a detective from Scotland Yard called to inform her: "It had been reported that I expressed disagreement with the Government's war policy. I told him that it was perfectly true, and that I could see no reason whatever for us going to war, and every reason why we should not.

He then asked me if I was a member of your Organisation, and I replied that I was not; but it seems from his inference that Peace not War is your policy, so I feel I must become a member at once. Will you kindly enrol me?

Yours faithfully

Fay Taylour."

Another woman racing driver to come into the Movement at this time and for the same reason, was Mrs. Douglas Duff, the widow of a young officer of the 9th Lancers. She held her air pilot's licence, and she had travelled in Tibet without the permission of the Government of India; but more remarkable was her Able Seaman's Discharge in sail, in square rig, too.

She had made several trips in Gustav Erikson's wind-jammers under the Finnish flag to Australia, and back with grain. About the only thing she had not done at sea had been to live "before the mast"; instead, she had been given a bit of a cubby-hole to herself in a deck-house amidship.

There had been one occasion at sea when an unwise jocular taunt from Captain Erikson led to her placing his best uniform cap on the button of the main top-gallant mast, the last twelve feet or so of which was a bare pole. Then to Erikson's alarm, she reached the deck again by sliding down one of the top-gallant stays, instead of making the normal descent by the ratlines.

Although she must have been exceptionally tough and strong, she was no strapping Amazon. She had other attributes besides those of good looks and physical courage and endurance. She had a gift for dashing off spontaneous satirical verse, guaranteed to induce severe irritation in those "Very Important Persons" at whom it was aimed.

That first autumn of the war, the Movement gathered quite a little galaxy of racing motorists. Another who joined us then was W.G. Barlow, a member of a well-known Lancashire family, who had flown as a pilot of the Royal Flying Corps. He was a quiet, reserved man; but his shyness masked a staunch and sterling character. In most things that he did he was motivated by a deep sense of duty: he was also a very determined man, particularly where some matter of principle was at stake.

He and his wife had bought a copy of 'Action' from a street seller in London, not out of interest but for fun, so that they could enjoy "a good laugh", as he admitted later. They had been amazed to find that the contents of that newspaper tallied so closely with their own views, that they lost no time in getting to National Headquarters in Great Smith Street, S.W.1 to present themselves for enrolment.

In order to endow the war with the aura of a crusade, and thus inspire some enthusiasm, the Government put up a profusion of posters proclaiming: "Freedom is in Peril; Defend it with all your Might!"

Some persons in high places appeared to have broad and accommodating views concerning the term "Freedom", because two days before the Declaration of War, plain clothes officers of the Special Branch acting on the orders of the Home Secretary, Sir John Anderson, later Lord Waverley, took into custody G. Thomas who was British Union prospective parliamentary candidate for Wood Green.

This proved to be of great significance, for it led to the BUF's modest collaboration with other anti-war groups and provided the Government with an excuse to silence all opposition, a few months later.

After two months in prison, Thomas was restored to his family with neither apology nor explanation, but in poor physical condition as the first twenty-five days of his incarceration had been spent in a cell without daylight. This cell, little better than an oubliette, was filthy and verminous. When he protested that there were bed-bugs, he was told that he had time enough in which to catch them.

Later he was transferred to another cell into which daylight entered: but he complained that, for seven weeks, his bed sheets were not changed once.

Thomas was not allowed to see anyone, not even his wife; nor was he allowed to communicate with his lawyer. Twice he was hauled before an "Advisory Committee", set up by the Home Secretary; following his second appearance before this body, he was released as summarily as previously he had been apprehended. Before he was turned loose he was informed officially that under the new Defence Regulations that came into force at the outbreak of the war, there could be no redress.

When news of this outrage reached Mosley, he expressed his disgust in an article in 'Action': "Some may have thought it an exaggeration to state that this Government has swept away elementary rights which Britons have enjoyed from the days of the Petition of Rights and the Habeas Corpus Act. Some may have thought it still more an exaggeration to state that British Government in the year 1939, has not only receded to some of the methods of the Star Chamber, but had borrowed from 18th century France the system of lettre de cachet, by which a government on the order of a Minister, could consign a victim without trial to the Bastille."

As the War dragged on, and Britain's position became increasingly desperate, with agonising shortages of outstandingly first class and experienced military leaders, General Fuller was not recalled to the service of his country.

Lieutenant-General Sir Giffard Martel, an old Tank Corps pioneer who was further to distinguish himself in the Royal Armoured Corps in the Second World War, who was also a friend and admirer of Fuller, urged the authorities to make use of that gifted brain, one of the two best military brains possibly in the world, which still reposed beneath a bowler hat.

Martel represented that Fuller should be called on to plan the development and future use of the Royal Armoured Corps. He wrote subsequently:[39] "I, therefore, proposed that Major-General J.F.C. Fuller should be brought back from retirement and charged with this work ... It was very unfortunate that more work was not done in this direction, and that the valuable services of General Fuller were never used."

---

39   *An Out-Spoken Soldier*, pp. 172-3, by Lieut.-General Sir Giffard Martell,

The reason that one of the two greatest living authorities on armoured fighting vehicles and on strategy and tactics attuned to the scientific attainments of the times,was that in the eyes of those politicians whose war it was, the General was damned by his association with Mosley.

Early in the war, a voice was heard over the German wireless, the *Deutschland Sender*, foretelling in precise and flawless English all manner of unpleasant things soon to befall this country. After some little doubt and hesitancy, the voice was identified as that of William Joyce, now about to become better known as "Lord Haw-Haw". This was a somewhat inappropriate nickname, as whatever Joyce's failings, they did not include an affected diction. He was, in truth, a highly gifted and polished orator.

The press made much of the fact that Joyce had been at one time a member and then a senior officer of British Union. It was hoped to discredit the Movement by associating it in the public eye with someone now universally regarded as a traitor. These aspersions did not work out with the hoped for results, as Joyce's act of disloyalty to Britain was nowhere more roundly denounced than among those who had at one time held him in esteem.

We of British Union, when taunted with past association with William Joyce, were quick to retort that whereas our organisation had expelled him formally from its ranks years before the war, the Conservative Party, which had made use of his talents long before he became a fascist, had failed to dismiss him when he went over to their political enemies at home.

Now that Joyce has long expiated his treason, it is possible to write of him with neither heat nor bias. As I have explained elsewhere, he was spirited and able, but physically small; he was also cocksure, aggressive and vain which so often are the outstanding characteristics of under-sized persons. I believe that in his own vehement way he loved Britain, and thought sincerely to serve her true interests, even by working against her with her enemies.

In his quarrel with the Government of Great Britain, and with that whole set-up that we now know as the "Establishment", he took sides with his King's enemies, which was treason and for which he was found guilty, condemned and hanged.

I feel sure that Joyce was so certain of the righteousness of his stand, that he believed himself a martyr for a cause and the victim of that hypothetical Judaic-Masonic-International-Financial plot, against which he had so consistently inveighed.

Almost his last words were: "I am proud to die for my ideals, and I am sorry for those sons of Britain who have died without knowing why."

That he had physical courage, he had demonstrated many times in the past; he never displayed it better than as he walked to the scaffold. His moral strength at his trial and after came from the sincerity of his belief.

William Joyce was no villain. He had been arrogant and misguided. Vanity was the greatest contributing factor to his undoing; but in his last hours as he awaited his executioner's summons, he shed all vestiges of his former insolence and conceit. His approaching death lent him courage, humility and dignity.

In June 1964, a statue was set up in Thetford in honour of Tom Paine, a native of that ancient borough. Not a few Thetfordians objected to this exaltation of a former fellow townsman who was so enamoured of Revolutionary France with whom his country was at war, that he chose not only to live there, but to become the Deputy for the Pas de Calais during actual hostilities. However, most inhabitants of present day Thetford seem content to have Tom Paine, seven feet high in gilded bronze, for ever commanding their attention in dumb gesture.

I submit that the extent of Tom Paine's treason eclipsed that of William Joyce, who did no more to help the enemy than to address the people of Britain over the German broadcasting system, whereas Paine assisted at the councils of his country's enemies. A statue to the memory of William Joyce would be not only unwelcome now, but still likely to be unacceptable a hundred years hence: nevertheless in years to come, opinion as to the flagrancy of Joyce's conduct undoubtedly will be modified.

Cyril Connolly in his review in '*The Sunday Times*', 1.11.1964, of J.A. Cole's book,[40] wrote:

"One cannot read this book without being reminded of the stench of hypocrisy which underlies these judicial executions. No other renegade broadcasters were hanged. If he had not cast his news so well, might he not be living today?"

There had been at least one other candidate for the appointment in Berlin secured by Joyce. But whereas the successful candidate ended on the scaffold, the unsuccessful applicant joined the Royal Air Force, eventually to become, I believe, a chair-borne squadron leader who passed the war years in comfort, untroubled by Defence Regulation 18B.

---

40 *Lord Haw-Haw and William Joyce*, by J.A. Cole, pub. Faber.

23 – Swan Song Of British Fascism

In January 1940, Hitler waved his olive branch again; when he made another attempt to avert calamity, and appealed the Allies to consider his proposals for a peace settlement. '*The Times*', 31.1.1940, reported him as saying:

"The German people do not feel any hate against France or Britain. The German people only want to live in friendship with these two peoples. The German people have no claim... nor want to take anything from these peoples."

Chamberlain replied obliquely to this new "peace offensive" in a speech at the Dorchester Hotel, as reported in the '*Manchester Guardian*', 1.2.1940, when he said among other things that the purpose of the Allies was to fight on ... until we put an end to that vicious policy of economic nationalism."

This did not sound in the least in keeping with a sacred cause, but completely in accordance with those very war aims of which Mosley was accusing the British Government.

Again, the strange fatality of history! How ironic that it should be the son of the late Joseph Chamberlain, that almost fanatical advocate of economic nationalism, who should now endanger, and be instrumental in bringing down in eventual ruin the British Empire, in order to protect the preserves of these usurers who regarded the entire globe as their rightful field for exploitation.

In March, Mosley again made clear his attitude to the war, when he reaffirmed: "We want peace, and do our utmost to persuade the British people to declare their will for peace." At the same time, he emphasised once more: "We are determined by every means in our power to ensure that the life and safety of Britain shall be preserved by proper defences until peace can be made."

He likened his stand to that of that great statesman and patriot, William Pitt, then the Earl of Chatham, who speaking in 1777 in opposition to the War of American Independence, a war that he considered unnecessary, had thundered:

"It is a shameful truth that not only the power and strength of this country are wasting away and expiring, but her well-earned glories, her true honours and substantial dignity, are sacrificed... In a just and necessary war to maintain the rights and honour of my country, I would strip the shirt from my back to support it. But a war such as this, unjust in principle, impracticable in its means, and ruinous in its consequences, I would not contribute a single effort nor a single shilling."

Still, Mosley and his followers strove desperately to persuade the great mass of people, who in their hearts longed for peace, to bestir themselves to attain it. But the Government with all the resources of mass propaganda at their disposal were able to shepherd the reluctant multitude, with little difficulty, in any required direction.

There were moments of encouragement, as when early in 1940, Mosley on being invited to address the Accrington Discussion Group, one of the oldest and best-known debating societies in Lancashire, was unable to find a single speaker in a packed house prepared to declare himself in favour of the war. Several local Labour leaders and Trade Union officials debated with him on points of policy, but not one would stand up to defend the war, or to say that it ought to be continued.

On 27th January, 1940, Churchill addressed a noisy meeting with frequent interruptions, in the Manchester Free Trade Hall. He informed his audience, "Herr Hitler has already lost his best chance."

One heckler, Bernard Talbot, a one-eyed, one armed ex-serviceman, who was also a member of British Union, was plucked from his seat, hustled to a small room behind the stage, and there beaten by a group of stewards with the buckle ends of their belts, until he collapsed into insensibility. A reporter of the weekly review, 'Truth', who had looked in through the door, wrote to his paper that he had been "horrified and sickened" at what he saw being done to the very badly disabled serviceman. He took note also that Talbot's assailants were Jews; which confirmed the victim's own story.

His speech that evening so rudely interrupted by unbelievers, was one of the more memorable feats of Churchillian oratory. In his peroration, he cried:

"Come then, let us to the task, to the battle, and the toil; each to our station; fill the Armies; rule the Air; pour out munitions; strangle the "U"-boats; sweep the mines; plough the land; build the ships; guard the streets; succour the wounded; uplift the downcast; and honour the brave.

Let us go forward together in all parts of the Empire, in all parts of this Island. There is not a week, nor a day, nor an hour to be lost."

One week later, 4th February, Mosley replied to Churchill and his exhortations in that same great hall, which as usual when he had been advertised to speak, was filled to capacity long beforehand. He found himself addressing a cheering and applauding mass rally of his own friends and followers, whom he told amid no scenes of violence or noisy opposition:

"Churchill implies that directly he gets the chance, he is going to attack somewhere or somehow... In other words Churchill wants to take the offensive. Saturated in the strategy of the last war, and unable to grasp the new facts of modern science, he wants at any cost to attack... In fact, it may well be that the quickest way to lose a modern war is to undertake an orthodox and old fashioned offensive.

Yet Churchill evidently lives for the day when hundreds of thousands of young Englishmen are to be thrown somewhere against the defences of the other side, in a quarrel, which is no concern of the British people. He may not know just where or how, but he is living for the day when he can order the attack.

He asked why the Germans did not attack, and implied that the reason was cowardice. That statement will appear as silly in the eyes of most ex-Servicemen, who fought the Germans in the last war, as his statement that Hitler Germany is weaker than Kaiser Germany will appear absurd in the eyes of anyone who has studied modern Europe... In fact, if Mr. Churchill could still learn as well as talk, it might occur to him that the one thing an intelligent adversary desires in present conditions, is to be attacked. A brief study of the facts of modern science, and of the psychology of the other side, might save Mr. Churchill from repeating his errors of the last war on a scale which might bring a major disaster to the British Empire."

Encouraged by the demand for 'Action', by the eagerness of the public to accept and purchase peace pamphlets, and by the applause he drew when he spoke to massed audiences on the subject of a peace settlement now, before the bombs began to fall on London and Berlin and before the armies met and locked in battle, Mosley decided to contest parliamentary by-elections.

Thus it was that during the first five months of 1940, we came to fight three such by-elections. In each case the candidate was a veteran of the First World War, but that did not prevent each candidate forfeiting his deposit.

The Movement fared badly in these, our first attempts to enter Parliament. In Silvertown where the candidate was the hardy but genial speaker, and idol of the Movement since his epic display of pluck and prowess in the Cable Street riot, Tommy Moran, ex-R.A.F. and ex-R.N.V.R., and former naval cruiser-weight boxing champion, the result was not bad but shocking. Moran polled no more than 151 votes, against Labour's 14,343 and the Communist's 966.

Intervention in Silvertown was a mistake and a humiliation. It should never have been contested, nor should the other two seats;

for all three were constituencies where British Union had either no organisation and but few contacts or weak, inexperienced and generally immature formations.

In Silvertown where Labour had been entrenched since the days of Keir Hardy, and the Reds had flourished for twenty years, Moran's opponents put out the story that a vote for Moran was a vote for Hitler.

In North-East Leeds, Sidney Allen, who had served in the 5th Battalion, the West Yorkshire Regiment, from September 1914, until December 1918, with four years active service on the Western Front, was labelled "Hitler's Agent", and polled 722 votes. This was rather better than Moran, and could have been better still if the Post Office had not taken a week or more to deliver Allen's printed election addresses. British Union did have a small following in North-East Leeds; but it was very far from being a "fascist stronghold"

In Middleton and Prestwich, where the candidate was Frederick Haslam, a former Lancashire Fusillier, who had won the Military Medal on the Somme, and later had been commissioned, the by-election coincided with Hitler's onslaught in the west. The British Expeditionary Force was in the direst peril, and already there was talk of invasion. Men had ceased to think politically, unless it was to look for someone or some party on which to vent their dismay. In this particular Lancashire constituency where there was a healthy and robust young District formation, the Movement's activities had been confined practically to one corner of the parliamentary division, Prestwich, which to all intents was a residential suburb of Manchester. British Union had only a meagre handful of members and contacts.

An open-air meeting at Chadderton during the Middleton and Prestwich election campaign was the one and only occasion between the outbreak of war and the suppression of British Union by Parliament, making use of the wartime Defence Regulations, when any violence was offered to Mosley or to any of his speakers. The calm acceptance of our attitude to the war by the thousands of people in London and the provinces, who stood and listened without any show of hostility or even impatience, is a matter for serious reflection; especially when the fevered campaign then being waged by the press, Parliament and B.B.C. against British Union is taken into consideration.

At Chadderton stones were thrown, and the loudspeaker broken. Mosley, who was speaking on behalf of Haslam, his party's candidate, was struck by a stone. He leapt down from the platform to deal personally with the man whom he had seen throw it. A knot of hooligans immediately converged on him, but got little satisfaction from the encounter; for, as they found, Mosley had lost neither his old boxing skill nor the vigour of his punches.

When one recalls Lloyd George's experiences of the Boer War, and those of Ramsey MacDonald in the First World War, when the lives of both peace-seekers had been endangered by infuriated and patriotically-exalted mobs, it is not without significance that except for the isolated incident at Chadderton, Mosley's audiences and those of other British Union speakers, listened in attentive and generally sympathetic silence.

That year we celebrated May Day on Sunday, 5th May, in brilliant sunshine. There had been seventeen subsidiary meetings, addressed by our speakers, held on various pitches throughout East London during the day. Then at 7 p.m. Mosley spoke to an audience of tens of thousands "packed almost to suffocation point" in Victoria Park Square, Bethnal Green, where our Movement's colours and standards were paraded for what was to be the last time.

In picturesque and amusing metaphor, he compared the position of this country, and of his Movement's attitude to the situation, to that of some hypothetical man's old mother who, taking up her umbrella, and armed with no more than that and her shrill tongue, sets forth to the "local" to give the toughs assembled a piece of her mind.

As he reminded his listeners, any normal and affectionate son would do his utmost to dissuade his unwise parent from embarking on so rash an enterprise; but if she persisted and for her headstrong action, got knocked down and kicked, then any dutiful son would wade in to her assistance.

"That," he explained, "is exactly how we of British Union feel toward our mother-country in this present circumstance which is as dangerous as it is unnecessary. That, also, is exactly how we are prepared to stand by our motherland if and when retribution for her folly comes."

He concluded one of the most rousing speeches he had ever made, with an impassioned appeal to all those present, to: "Come and join us, and help build the Britain of our dreams." Finally he called on his audience to vote for peace by a show of hands. Instantly a "forest of arms" shot up. Only three persons could be found to vote against the resolution.

'*Action*' reported: "After a mighty rendering of the National Anthem, it was some minutes before the audience would allow Mosley to leave... Thus ended the greatest day that British Union had yet witnessed...."

24 - England's Finest (?) Hour

"I will be hanged if some eternal villain
Some busy and insinuating rogue,
Some cogging cozening slave, to get some office
Have not devised this slander."

Othello, Act 4, Scene 2 William Shakespeare

When the German Army reached the cliff tops of the Pas de Calais, and the invasion of Britain would seem surely to be the next item on Hitler's agenda after the mopping up of the scattered armies of France and of the remnants of the British Expeditionary Force (BEF), the British Government called for a defence force recruited from local civilians, preferably ex-Servicemen, to co-operate with the military in defence of the kingdom.

These auxiliaries to the Army were to be known as the "Local Defence Volunteers"; they were more generally referred to as the "L.D.V.s".

At that time I was living in Canterbury, where I had come from the North shortly before the war to help organise that parliamentary constituency for Lady Pearson, who was to contest it on behalf of British Union in the General Election due that autumn. The outbreak of war ruled out any idea of a General Election; but I remained in Canterbury, engaged in war work, and in my spare time looked after the District like any other voluntary, unpaid officer of the Movement.

When the call went out for Local Defence Volunteers, I presented myself for enrolment within an hour or two of the opening of recruiting. Next morning, a Sunday, the Canterbury L.D.V. were ordered to assemble near the centre of the town; where we were hastily detailed into Companies according to which parish or ward we lived in. Officers were appointed, and we fell in with our respective Companies.

From the top of the down where we had been posted, the flames of blazing Dunkirk were visible, glowing, flickering, dying down, then flaring into the night sky. The warm spring night, scented with hawthorn and the blossom of unseen orchards, trembled to distant gunfire, and was shaken now and then by the sudden reverberating boom of an exploding ammunition dump or fuel store.

At intervals blackened-out passenger trains sped northwards and westwards from the coastal towns of the south-east, carrying to distant improvised camps and reception centres, exhausted soldiers, most of whom were without arms or equipment. Packed in like cattle bound for market, they slept in all improbable attitudes as the sea water dried slowly out of their clothing, and the realisation that they were safe back in England soaked even more slowly in. This is that period of our "rough island story", described by Churchill as "their finest hour..." a claim which is open to dispute.

For some of the nation, it was undoubtedly their finest hour. The fighter pilots of the Royal Air Force, many of whom were ardent followers of Mosley, excelled in daring and in gallant sacrifice. Others like the fishermen, longshoremen, and yachtsmen who manned the little ships on their perilous passages in and out of Dunkirk across the North Sea, proved their traditional heroism and devotion.

Churchill, too, the more desperate the hour, the greater flared the fires of his wrath, the more determined his decision to keep fighting, and the more dramatic his utterances; but the Government as a whole gave way to unworthy panic.

From their deeds and from their declarations one would have thought that the members of the Government really believed what was being printed in the newspapers; in which case they were falling victims of their own propaganda, for it was the

Ministry of Information that was letting out the official news to press and radio in such agonised accents.

Taking their cue from Duff Cooper's Ministry of Information, national and local authorities, and most of the press, exhibited unwarrantable fear at the very moment when they should have set examples in cool thinking and calm nerves. With, (as they thought), the certainty of invasion at hand, the powers-that-be issued a host of contradictory orders.

The civil population was told to defend its homes, villages and towns, with improvised weapons and sullen resistance. They were instructed how to make petrol bombs out of milk bottles; these were called "Molotov cocktails" and had been evolved during the Spanish Civil War. They were bidden to pepper the Germans with shotguns, nor to despise the archaic pike. They were to throw up road obstructions, and to barricade their streets. Every man was expected to go down fighting; and it was hoped that many women would emulate their sacrifice. Churchill, I think it was, coined the grim phrase, "Take one with you, when you go."

To encourage the ladies of the land to fight á outrance they were told that all those of Anglo-Saxon type, of good physique and still in possession of their reproductive powers would be set aside for stud purposes for the raising of Nordic supermen. The chosen sires would of course be detailed from the ranks of Hitler's S.S. My wife was informed of this treat in store by a spokesman at an officially sponsored Civil Defence meeting. She would have been amused, but for the fact that most of the audience seemed to accept it as gospel; propaganda had conditioned the public into acceptance of almost any lie so long as it appeared to emanate from an official source, or was printed in the press.

Even as one authority exhorted civilians to die fighting, never mind how hopelessly, another official body told them still more emphatically to "stay put", to stop at home, keep indoors and leave the roads clear for the rapid movement and deployment of troops. Someone, at least, had taken to heart the lesson of the impassable, refugee-congested roads of northern France.

With so much precipitate and ill-considered haste, countless mistakes were made. For some time no one knew clearly what was expected of him. A number of would-be Vaubans [41] got busy, and were responsible for wrongly sited strong points, machine-gun nests that faced the wrong way, and ridiculous obstructions on the highways. Old scores were paid with interest, when locally unpopular residents had their garden walls demolished so as to open up hypothetical fields of fire.

Church bells were silenced, and were to be used only to raise the alarm when invasion came, just as the fiery beacons of 1588 had warned England of the approach of the Spanish Armada.

Among the frenzied preparations was a hurried erasing of the place names from signposts, milestones, railway stations and tradesmen's vans. Local memorials including those of the last war, were defaced in the hope of confusing the German paratroops who, presumably, would be arriving without maps or references.

One outstanding feature of this time of confusion, initiated by some of the political leaders, and taken up with enthusiasm by their dupes throughout the land, was the "Fifth Column" scare.

As cowards when scared, in order to distract attention from their own inadequacies, are liable to lash out at anyone or anything incapable of retaliation, so did the frightened politicians of 1940 seek to cover their shortcomings by doughty deeds on the Home Front. Press, Parliament, most Ministers, and all Government spokesmen, by making Mosley's Movement their scapegoat, were able at the same time to pay off old scores with interest and without fear of reprisal.

It was reported that in Norway, Vidkun Quisling, leader of the New Movement in its Nordic and racialist form, had welcomed the Germans as his Nordic brothers, and as the liberators of the

---

41   Marshal of France (1633-1707), one of the greatest military engineers, particularly of defence works, in European history. R.R.B.

land that he loved from the thraldom of the financial democrats. Yet Bernard Ash[42] writes that Quisling's followers played little part in the conquest of Norway; and Ralph Hewins in a letter to the '*Daily Telegraph*' 19.5.66, states that "not one Quisling has yet been convicted of helping the invader".

In actual fact, probably the heftiest blow in defence of Norway was that struck by a member of Quisling's National Samling party, when Lieutenant A. Bonsak,[43] an elderly gunner, who personally trained and fired each gun of a shore battery commanding a stretch of Oslo fjord, sank the heavy cruiser, Blucher, flagship of the German invasion armada. When at the end of the war the run-away Government, consisting in the main of Reds and near-Reds, returned to settle accounts, the old soldier's epic part in the defence of his country was overlooked, instead he was imprisoned for his membership of the N.S., stripped of his pension, and finally allowed to die in poverty.

In 1940, Anton Mussert's men, too, were being universally condemned for the betrayal of Holland; but as A.J.P. Taylor has since revealed, Dutch National Socialist traitors were non-existent.

The only European country with an active Fifth Column appears to have been Belgium, where the traitors would seem not to have been Leon Degrelle's Rexists, but extreme Left Wing railwaymen who, suddenly waking up to the fact that the Germans had recently become the allies of their own, (the railwaymen's), Russian comrades, came out on strike, disrupted mobilisation and the movement of troops, and hastened their country's surrender.

The term "Fifth Column" had originated during the Spanish Civil War when General Mola, hurrying to capture Madrid in 1936, announced at a news conference that he had four columns of Nationalists converging on the capital, and lying low in the

---

42   Norway 1940, p.28

43   *Quisling: Prophet Without Honour,* pp. 210-211.

city, biding their time, a fifth column of Nationalist supporters. From this term, but now somewhat twisted from its original meaning, derived the appellation "Fifth Columnist" to denote anyone who sympathised with the enemy to the extent of being willing or able actively to help him.

Ultimately, Fifth Columnist came to signify a man prepared to betray his country in time of war. There may be shades and degrees of treason; but the fellow who commits it, whatever justification he may feel, is undeniably a traitor in deed. In the meaning ascribed to the epithet in 1940, Fifth columnist was rightly synonymous with traitor.

At that time the expression became one of the most over-charged and overworked figures of speech introduced to the English language. The public in the grip of war-psychosis gulped down the daily doses of Government concocted absurdities, without pausing to consider the unreason for most of them.

The menace of the Fifth Column, and ways to combat it, became favoured themes of the Ministry of Information, to be plugged by the press with the added innuendo that every member of British Union was a potential "Quisling", as the Fifth Columnists were now known, who would not only welcome the Nazis, but would gladly serve them.

This plugging of the theme "traitors in our midst" was responsible for people letting their imaginations run away with them. The 'Daily Mirror' was probably the most inventive as well as the most strident witch-hunter. One of that journal's more imaginative scribes sent in a story, which duly appeared in its pages, describing the arrest of one country land-owner who was also a retired colonel, who had been caught in the act of flashing signals to German aircraft. The old traitor, who sounded like Colonel Blimp himself, was portrayed as defiant and unrepentant as he was hustled away, presumably to face a firing squad.

Unfortunately, in the interests of security, the name of the miscreant and of the scene of his treachery had to be withheld! If newspaper readers could swallow that balderdash without protest, they must have allowed themselves to be conditioned into zombies.

I was called more than once to the telephone to have the word "Quisling" hissed into my ear, generally in a feminine voice. The caller would then hang up, doubtless happy in the conviction that she had done her patriotic stint for the day.

It was while these alarms were being fanned deliberately to white-heat that I met, on official business at the Royal Army Service Corps Supply Office in Canterbury, a Colonel Gabriel, R.A.S.C. I never made any secret of my political affiliation, and so in the course of conversation mentioned that I was a member of British Union.

"Then," said the colonel, "you cannot possibly know what I know about that organisation. Are you aware that the local fascist leader, here in Canterbury, has a safe-conduct signed personally by Hitler, instructing the German military authorities that when they occupy Canterbury, they are to spare this man and his household?"

"Are you quite sure of your facts?" I asked. "I received that information from an absolutely reliable source," he replied. The smile which I could not repress cut him short. He looked more than a little embarrassed when I explained that I was the "local fascist leader". It might seem incredible today that a man of his years and standing should accept and retail such senseless gossip; but in the atmosphere created by the officially inspired panic that summer, nothing was too outrageous nor too ridiculous to be believed.

E.S. Turner wrote in his witty and scholarly study:[44] "The worst aspect of the Fifth column scare, was that it bred informers of the wrong type. Men and women who disapproved of their neighbours' habits, associations, politics, reading matter, and addiction to foreign travel, laid information, often anonymously at police stations.

---

44   *The Phoney War on the Home Front*, p.220, by E.S. Turner, pub. Michael Joseph.

The police then used their powers of search, and removed such evidence as seemed to them suspicious... up and down the country police officers returned in triumph to base with such works as Lord Addison's 'A Policy for Agriculture, the Duchess of Atholl's 'Searchlight on Spain', and even John Stuart Mill's 'The Principles of Political Economy'... When Members protested to Parliament about the manner of these searches, they were told that the police were bound to follow up information. The mere fact that a person had a good reputation was no reason for refraining from making enquiries about him. One Member thought that a man whose house was searched should at least have the right to know who had reported him; but in the Britain of 1940 this luxury was not possible."

Among those serving Britain in her hour of need, was a group of dedicated beings recruited by the Ministry of Information for special duty on the Home Front, in a corps to become famous as "Cooper's Snoopers", whose motto should have been:

> "For theirs was to poke and pry,
> And to know the reason why."

They sat in crowded railway carriages listening to conversation; they stood with ears cocked in public houses, aware that in vino veritas; and having rung front doorbells they tried to find out from distracted housewives their views on the food rationing, the evacuation, and on the situation in general.

Then there was that mysterious hush-hush and all-powerful caucus, the Defence Security Executive, which shy and retiring body, better known as the Swinton Committee after its chairman Lord Swinton, previously Philip Cunliffe-Lister, had been expressly appointed by Churchill "to report on suspicious political activities", as stated in the House of Commons by G.R. Strauss M.P. on 30th July. This body reported to the Prime Minister and to no other person; but neither its exact functions nor the extent of its powers were ever made known. In comparison the transactions of the Court of the Star Chamber had been open and above board, and its findings the epitome of justice.

Churchill told Parliament: "I take full responsibility for the control, character and composition of the committee." He deprecated questions in Parliament concerning the Swinton Committee, or reference to it in the press.

"Asked whether he approved of a direction prohibiting newspapers from referring to this committee without special permission, Mr. Churchill said, 'Yes, Sir, the Government think it not in the public interest to have the committee discussed.' He was then asked whether he was aware of considerable public uneasiness in this matter, but did not reply."[45]

When the Prime Minister informed the House that the Swinton Committee contained "one prominent Trade Union leader", he seemed to take it for granted that such a revelation would allay all disquiet. Had he, however, made known the identity of the Trade Union leader of his choice, there might well have been increased anxiety, for Alfred M. Wall had been not only secretary to the London Trades Council but had stood for Parliament as the Communist candidate for Streatham in 1924. In fact he had been a communist for most of his life.

The waves of causeless fright stirred up by the Ministry of Information in their effort to make the nation alive to the gravity of the hour swept across Britain with mounting strength. People having first been invited to tell tales against one another, next were told that it was their public duty to inform the authorities of their neighbours' food-hoarding, their surreptitiously concealed cans of petrol, their ill-fitting black-outs, their pessimistic conversation, and their suspicious comings and goings.

With this officially inspired witch-hunt in fully cry, it was not a long step from telling tales anonymously to inventing charges against unpopular persons, safe in the knowledge that there was no possibility of unpleasant recoil against the inventive-minded "patriots" who had levelled them.

---

45   Idem, p.224

It must have been some gentleman or lady with zeal or spite equalled only by his or her ignorance who had gulled the R.A.S.C. colonel into acceptance of their story concerning Herr Hitler's kindly interest in my welfare.

In this crazed, un-British atmosphere, incredible things happened. A seventeen year old boy, employed as a junior clerk, was sentenced at Walthamstow to one month's imprisonment for having been heard to say, "This dirty, stinking, rotten Government." [46]

In Lincolnshire, [47] at Spilsbury Petty Sessions, the seventy year old rector of Bolingbroke-with Hareby was sentenced to four weeks' imprisonment for ringing his church bells three days before the order banning them came into force. He was held in gaol for twelve days before his sentence was quashed at Lindsay Quarter Sessions, where the court pronounced that the rector ought never to have been prosecuted, and that the magistrate who had sentenced him had not only failed to study the Regulation but had been listening to hearsay evidence.

Government spokesmen had seen to it that fear of treachery had been propagated everywhere. Thousands upon thousands of persons now believed that Mosley's followers were the British "Quislings", ready waiting for the Nazis.

The 'Daily Mirror' had seen fit to include the old hereditary land-owning class as the allies of this hypothetical fascist fifth column. Ernest (Big Boy) Bevin, Churchill's Minister of Labour, who saw most things in terms of the old class war, amplified this charge when he asserted: "It (potential treachery) isn't in the workshop, it is all in the middle class."

It was of these same days of unparalleled military disaster on the Continent, soon to be followed it was believed by the invasion of Britain, that General Fuller wrote in his 'Decisive Battles of the Western World':

46   Idem, p.273

47   Idem, pp.260-261

"In England the wind blew less violently. Although the masses of people, secure behind their sea wall, were not greatly perturbed by the German advance, the Government lost its head, and at the very moment when in order to maintain internal calm, contempt of danger was imperative, the country was thrown into confusion by a host of ill-considered panic measures... And hundreds of loyal people whose only crime was that they considered the war a blunder, were arrested and held in custody for years on end, without charge or trial. It was anything but the finest hour in British history."

Finally it was left to Winston Churchill himself to play the spoil sport, when on 5th November, 1940, he told Parliament, [48] that there had been no such thing as a Fifth Column in Britain. No one was better qualified than Winston to make this announcement as he, the Prime Minister, was the person ultimately responsible for both the Swinton Committee and M.I.5.

Nevertheless, many innocent men remained imprisoned without charge or trial until the end of the war.

---

48   *Hansard*, 5th Series, Vol. 365, column 1245.

25 - Defence Regulation 18B:

"Men must learn now with pity to dispense;
For policy sits above conscience."

Timon of Athens, Act 3, William Shakespeare

The BUF was by no means alone in advocating an honourable, negotiated peace after 3rd September 1939. Many other organisations wanted the war to end before real hostilities began, including the Independent Labour Party, the British People's Party and the Peace Pledge Union.

Even the British Government, after the Fall of France, put out feelers to seek terms. In Washington, Lisbon and Berne British diplomats made appropriately discreet contact with the Germans. Lord Halifax suggested to the War cabinet that a favourable reply should be prepared if Hitler offered peace on fair terms. But Churchill was now Prime Minister. So instead of proposing peace Halifax was given the task of firmly rejecting Hitler's peace offer.

At the beginning of May after the Germans broke through the Ardennes, over-ran the Low Countries and reached the Channel coast, Mosley bade us his followers to do our duty as Britons and resist the foreign invader with the utmost determination.

The response of the Government was to rush a new amendment to defence regulation 18B through Parliament, so that within a matter of hours Mosley was behind bars, where he was followed in the course of the next few days by more than 1,000 of his followers, including myself. It was because of the deteriorating military situation, and the first symptoms of doubt, even fear, in the voices of the spokesmen and officials of the Ministry of Information, that Mosley addressed the following directive to his friends and followers:

"According to the press, stories concerning the invasion of Britain are being circulated... In such an event every member of British Union would be at the disposal of the nation. Every one of us would resist the foreign invader with all that is in us. However rotten the existing government, and however much we detest its policies, we would throw ourselves into the effort of a united nation until the foreign invader was driven from our soil."

From the 10th to the 15th of May, Churchill, apart from his Defence duties, was busy appointing the Ministers to form his new National Coalition Government; he invited seven Labour leaders to fill ministerial vacancies. This was their chance... Clement Attlee became Lord Privy Seal; Arthur Greenwood, Minister without Portfolio; A.V. Alexander, First Lord of the Admiralty; Herbert Morrison Minister of Supply; Ernest Bevan, Minister of Labour and National Service; Hugh Dalton, Minister of Economic Warfare; and William Jowitt, Solicitor-General.

If some of these new and now most bellicose members of the War Cabinet, recruited from the Left, had like Atlee seen active service, been wounded, and had earned good and honourable records in the previous war, others had been conscientious objectors, or had occupied safe jobs. All, however, had been pacifists and "little Englanders" between the wars, and were the men most responsible for the impotence of the B.E.F. now faced seemingly with destruction or surrender. To me and my friends, there was something infinitely disgusting in the spectacle of men who, when young, had stood aside from a struggle for the very survival of their country, now, when over military age, sending others to risk their lives in a war in which no conceivable British interest was served.

The Annual Conference of the Labour Party, which wound up on 18th May, was held in Bournemouth. The guest speaker was that archangel of international socialism, the millionaire Leon Blum from France, whose pep talk on saving socialism delighted the assembled delegates, and had them clapping and cheering. It was entirely fitting that the man more responsible than any for the division, weakness and internal rottenness of France, should be applauded by the leading figures of the British political party primarily responsible for their own country's defencelessness. There was a particularly urgent domestic matter claiming the attention of those attending the Conference – and that was the menace of Mosley. The time had come, they felt, if international socialism was ever to bloom in Britain, then Mosley must be silenced.

Hugh Ross Williamson, author, historian and broadcaster, at that time prospective Labour parliamentary candidate for one of the Dorsetshire constituencies, who was present, recalls: "One of the main subjects of conversation which I heard at unofficial talks was whether or not the Labour leaders had made the arrest and imprisonment of Mosley a condition of their entering the Government. The general feeling was that they had..."

Hugh Ross Williamson was quite sure that the Labour leaders had urged the implementation of Defence Regulation 18B "to pay off old scores against former political opponents... and in some cases to punish anti-Semitism". He wrote: "Few of us, who were involved in the pre-war politics of the Left, can have any doubt, not only that it had been used, but that it was designed for this purpose."

On 22nd May, the second sitting day of Parliament since Labour joined the Government, the Amendment (1A) to Defence regulation 18B was made, in order to enable the arrest and imprisonment of Oswald Mosley.

None of this was revealed at the time; and there never has been an official explanation. At the time many thought that Churchill, angered and resentful at Mosley's scathing attacks on himself for the fiasco of his Norwegian campaign, had retaliated out of spite, and invoked 18B with its new provision to silence and suppress an awkward opponent. Churchill himself wrote subsequently:[49]

"Having been brought up on the Bill of Rights, Habeas Corpus, and trial by jury conceptions, I grieved to become responsible, even with the assent of Parliament, for their breach."

49 1 & 2. *The Second World War*, Vol. 2, p.627

18b detainees escorted by British soldiers Victoria Train Station. 1940

Those who believed Churchill capable of such rancour did him injustice. One has but to read his prolific writings to appreciate that however wrong-headed Churchill the statesman and Churchill the amateur strategist may have been, pettiness and spite were not usually to be included among the varied ingredients that went to make up that complex character.... so gifted, so headstrong, so foolish, once aptly summarised by Attlee as "fifty per cent genius, fifty per cent bloody fool."

Those who have worked with Churchill, been driven mad almost by his impulsiveness, wilfulness, and by the bullying methods he used to attain his ends, pay tribute to his magnanimity both to political opponents at home and to fallen foes abroad. It must be admitted, however, that there were occasions when this generosity was withheld from those of his captains and lieutenants who dared to question the wisdom of his intentions or the practicability of his plans. These he seldom forgave for their contumacy.

His histories, wonderful expositions of English prose as they are, are suspect to many professional historians as being like many modern comestibles, "artificially coloured and flavoured"; but they should be studied to gain an appreciation of the man himself. A politician-cum-writer who can quote his sternest critics, as he does, towers above his fellow parliamentarians, who forever seek excuse or to shift the blame. It would seem therefore that, as the price for entering the National Coalition Government, the Labour leaders, like Salome, demanded a boon. Herod's daughter received as her reward the head of St. John the Baptist; the British Labour Party asked as their recompense for the body of Oswald Mosley to be incarcerated under Defence Regulation 18B, subsection (1A).

Thus it transpired that on the night of the 22nd May, 1940, the House of Commons approved the new clause to the Defence Regulations, which suspended not only Britain's treasured and time-honoured Habeas Corpus, but made the new order a vicious and vindictive piece of retrospective legislation.

A document described as a "Detention Order" was drafted as follows:

"Regulation 18B of the Defence (General) Regulation 1939 having been amended by the insertion after paragraph (1) of the following paragraph:

"(1A) If the Secretary of State has reasonable cause to believe any person to have been or to be active in the furtherance of the objects of any such organisation as in hereinafter mentioned or that it is necessary to exercise control over him, he may make an order against that person directing that he be detained.

"The organisation hereinbefore referred to are any organisations as respects which the Secretary of State is satisfied that either:

The organisation is subject to foreign influence, or (b) The persons in control of the organisation have or have had associations with persons concerned in the government of, or sympathies with the system of government of, any power with which His Majesty is at war. And in either case there is a danger of the utilisation of the organisation for purposes prejudicial to the public safety, the defence of the realm, the maintenance of public order, the efficient prosecution of any war in which His Majesty is engaged, or the maintenance of supplies essential to the life of the country.

"The Secretary of State in pursuance of the powers conferred on him by the above mentioned regulation has made an order that you .... be detained.

"You will have an opportunity of making any representations you wish to the Secretary of State; and you have the right, whether or not you make such representations, to make your objections to an Advisory Committee appointed by the Secretary of State."

Next day, 23rd May, Mosley accompanied by his wife drove from their place at Denham in Buckinghamshire to their flat in Hood House, Dolphin Square, S.W.1., arriving at about 3.30 p.m. As they drew up outside the front entrance, Lady Mosley noticed "five large flat-footed men in plain clothes". She drew her husband's attention to them, exclaiming: "Look, Police!" As Mosley stepped from the car, one of the plain clothes officers came forward and arrested him.

Diana Mosley remembered every detail of that day, and how "We got into the lift with most of the men and went up to the seventh floor and along the corridor to our flat. They showed O.M. the order for his arrest, and said he was going to Brixton. They were perfectly civil.

When they had gone I drove to Denham; on the way I saw posters: 'M.P. Arrested.' This was Ramsay. I don't know why they did not arrest O.M. at Denham. I believe they thought he was coming to London earlier in the day. His main people had been arrested that morning at headquarters in Great Smith Street, but we were unaware of this.

Back at Denham I listened to the news, and O.M.'s arrest was broadcast. My stepdaughter and I were having dinner when we saw the big wooden gate opened and across the lawn streamed a crowd of police, come with a warrant to search the house. I told them that it would take them months to do the job properly, as it was a very old house with endless nooks and crannies and huge tithe barns.

I picked up the telephone in the library and they asked whom I wished to speak to. When I told them it was my mother they did not object, though two or three stayed in the room to listen to the conversation.

She had heard of O.M.'s arrest on the wireless and her first words were: "What is the charge?" "Oh, I replied, there's no charge. Even these people do not suggest that he has done anything that is not absolutely legal." "Disgraceful", said my mother, and I said: "Yes, you're right, it is disgraceful," for the benefit of the listening policemen."

This was how Mosley was arrested under an order, the existence of which he was unaware and the terms of which he had yet to become acquainted. Not just the niceties of English law, but the very premise of English law had been jettisoned by the Government of Great Britain in the panic of the hour.

The law officers of the Crown, or the legal experts at the Home Office, or whoever were responsible for the drafting of the Defence Regulations, introduced a polite new legalistic jargon wherewith to cushion harsh deeds with soft words. Thus the terms "arrest" and "imprisoned" were taboo where 18B was concerned, and in their stead the words "detain" and "detention" were substituted.

This was a distinction of such subtlety that those persons who were apprehended by the police, in some cases with courtesy and apologies, but others roughly and with handcuffs snapped on to their wrists as they were dragged off to ancient and disgusting gaols, were unable to appreciate. After his arrest by officers of the Special Branch, Mosley was conveyed to Brixton Prison, and after the usual formalities, was conducted to 'F' Hall, and locked into cell no 1. It came to light later that this particular wing of Brixton Prison had been condemned as unfit for human habitation, and had remained unoccupied for a long time. It was re-opened for the political prisoners, but without being fumigated or adequately cleaned. It stank and was verminous.

As part of its price the Labour Party would appear to have demanded also the body of Captain A.H.M. Ramsay, M.C., Conservative Member for Midlothian and Peebles. They were the posters proclaiming his arrest that Diana Mosley had noticed on her way back to Denham after her husband's arrest.

Ramsay, an old Etonian and a former officer of the Regular Army, was an agreeable and attractive fellow. He had served with the Coldstream Guards in the First World War from Mons onwards; he had been wounded, and had been awarded the Military Cross. His name stood high on Labour's blacklist as he was an openly declared anti-Semite, and was constantly bringing to public notice not only the corrupt practices of individual Jews, but the manner in which Jewry used its "power of the purse" to influence both public opinion and public transactions in its own favour.

In the climate of thinking created at that time by press, Parliament and the wireless, to be critical of the Jews was tantamount to admiring Hitler, and admiration for any feature of Hitler's policy was as good as wanting Hitler to win, which in itself was almost the same as helping Hitler to win. Therefore the ultra-patriotic Ramsay was easy game for people who reasoned on those lines.

Apart from his openly expressed distrust of Jewry, Ramsay had incurred displeasure in another direction. It had come to his knowledge that Churchill, while still First Lord of the Admiralty, was conducting a covert correspondence with the White House. Under the pseudonym of "Naval Person", Winston Churchill had been writing in secret to President Roosevelt, unknown to his colleagues in the Cabinet, and behind the back of his Prime Minister. Furthermore, he had been using the American diplomatic bag, (in this case the Legation's wireless and top secret code), for the conveyance of his highly irregular correspondence.

This information had been leaked to Ramsay by Tyler Kent, a cypher clerk at the American Embassy, who met Ramsay by arrangement at the apartment of Anna Wolkoff, daughter of Admiral Nicholas Wolkoff, a former officer of the Russian Imperial Navy, and at one time equerry to Czar Nicholas II. Ramsay, deeply shocked at the nature of the messages passing between the First Lord's room and the White house, sought to warn Neville Chamberlain;[50] but before he could approach the Prime Minister in person, there was a change of government which put Churchill in No.10 Downing Street.

Failing to warn Chamberlain in time, Ramsay confided in a friend of mine, the late 'Squire' Surtees of Brooke in Norfolk, (who was also distantly related to him), how he had sought an audience with King George VI, and that he was actually on his way to Buckingham Palace to lay his information before his Sovereign when he was stopped and arrested by officers of the Special Branch. His journey instead of taking him to the Palace, ended in Brixton Gaol.

Churchill seems to have been particularly sensitive about this correspondence and everything connected with it. The papers, nearly 2,000 in number, which came to be known as the "Kent Documents", were not only suppressed by the United States Government; but American government-sponsored historians were prohibited from studying them, and Churchill even threatened with prosecution Professor William Leonard Langer, if he were to make use of them in the official war history he was compiling for the American Government.

It would therefore be reasonable to conclude that the "Kent Documents" are likely to be not only potent and startling, but damaging to the reputations of their authors.

Also gathered up that day under the amended order and gaoled in Brixton was an honoured member of British Union, Major H. De Laessoe, D.S.O., M.C., the son of a senior officer of the

---

50   Revisionism: A Key to Peace, in Rampart Journal, Vol. 2, No.1, p.46.

Indian Civil Service, a veteran of the Matabele and Nashona Wars, the Boer War, with both the Queen's and King's South African medals, and of the First World War. He had served as a trooper in Cecil Rhodes' British South Africa Police, and was one of the earliest white settlers in Central Africa. If my memory serves me right, he was a Fellow of both the Royal Geographical and Royal Empire Societies. Both he and his wife were imprisoned with the Mosleys in Holloway prison.

Arrested at the same time was Captain Robert Gordon Canning, M.C., a retired regular soldier who had served in the First World War with the 10th Hussars, and had been decorated with the Military Cross and Mentioned in Dispatches. He was an old member of B.U.F., and was the Movement's expert on foreign affairs.

In his net at this, his first cast, the Home Secretary, Sir John Anderson, caught also Alexander Raven Thomson, editor of '*Action*', who had served in France in the First World War as an officer of the Royal Engineers; George Sutton, Mosley's secretary, who had been four times wounded while serving with the Royal Field Artillery; Captain U.A. Hick, senior officer of London Districts, a veteran of the Boer War and of the First World War, and known to many as "Captain Hook", as a hand and fore-arm lost in action had been replaced by a steel hook.

Other prisoners of State were Captain B.D.E. Donovan, M.C., Indian Army (Retd.), Assistant Director of British Union, who had led a troop of cavalry in action at the age of seventeen, and was later wounded in France; and 'Bill' Risdon, Chief Election Agent, who had enlisted in the "Black Watch" at the age of seventeen, served throughout the war, and had received wounds.

Hector McKechnie, Organiser of National Meetings was a former pilot in the Royal Air Force, while 'Charlie' Hammond had served from 1914 to 1918 in the Royal Navy, and had sailed Polar Seas with Ernest Shackleton. They, too, were brought "inside".

Also detained on 23rd May, 1940 were Neil Francis-Hawkins, Director General, Leader of Westminster St. George's, all of whom had been under military age during the previous war. Watts had been a regular in the R.A.F, leaving the Reserve in 1936.

All values had been reversed. Mosley and his companions in constraint, patriots who had fought and bled for Britain, and had dedicated their lives to her service, and to the service of her Empire, were locked in prison cells at the behest of men who for years had looked to Russia for their inspiration, had declared themselves ashamed of their country's ancient glories, and had long proclaimed their intention of dissolving the Empire.

That first night of the great round-up the new inmates of His Majesty's Prison, Brixton, probably could have shown more campaign medals and military decorations than the grand total displayed by the members of His Majesty's Government.

26 - Brixton Gaol

"Dressed in a little brief authority,
Most ignorant of what he's most assured."

William Shakespeare.Measure For Measure'
Act 2, Scene 2

On that same 23rd May, 1940, and at about the same time that National Headquarters in Great Smith Street, S.W.1, was being raided, 'Charlie' Watts, District Leader of Westminster Saint Georges, was going through the morning's post at the offices in Albemarle Street off Piccadilly where he was employed, when a call from an office colleague brought him out on to the landing. As he came out through the door he found himself confronted by four large men in bowler hats, who immediately closed in on him.

"Are you Charles Frederick Watts of 66, Clive Road, S.E.21?" asked one of their number, who then introduced himself as Detective Sergeant Smith of the Special Branch. On Watts' affirmation that he was the person they were seeking, the detective sergeant proceeded:[51] "I have an order for your detention under section 18B (1A) of the Defence Regulations, and here is a copy for yourself."

The first reaction to the news of Mosley's arrest, on the part of those tens of thousands of citizens who believed in him, was one of profound shock. On reflection, they felt that the authorities had been stampeded into committing a grave mistake; but so firm is the average Englishman's confidence in British justice and fair-mindedness that they assured themselves that once the matter had been thoroughly looked into, those responsible for authorising the

---

51   *It Has Happened Here,* p.1, C.F. Watts (unpublished/MS)

Prison cell Brixton Prison.

arrest would acknowledge their blunder, and thereon order the immediate release of Mosley and the others, who would be set free with apologies and publicly expressed regret.

After saying goodbye to his business colleagues, some of whom of the opposite sex were near to tears, and all of whom wished him a speedy return, Watts was taken to Brixton prison. His arrival coincided with that of a rather bemused-looking Raven Thomson plucked from his editorial chair. He managed to exchange a few hurried words with another new arrival, George Sutton, Mosley's secretary since 1919, who told him that the headquarter offices had been raided by a large party of both uniformed and Special Branch police, and that many of the staff had been arrested.

Other new arrivals being received into the gaol just then were Captain Ramsay M.P., and John NacNab, both of whom after a somewhat devious political odyssey were leading lights of the British People's Party, which opposed the war on much the same grounds as British Union, and H.T. Mills, (probably detained because of his outspoken views on international finance, expressed in 'The Patriot').

The newcomers were locked into reception cells, each about the size of a telephone kiosk, but even less interesting as they were without windows and were entirely closed in. Here they were left to ruminate for hours. For anyone who suffered from claustrophobia, hours of gazing at a blank wall within inches of one's nose, must have been a distressing experience. One 18B prisoner, an ex-Serviceman who had been buried alive by an exploding shell, found the hours of solitude confined in a tiny space without outlook, nerve-wracking in the extreme.

There they sat for hour after hour, while they pondered the fates of their families deprived of their bread-winners, visualised business failing, and themselves ruined. To most of the prisoners it was incredible that this could have happened to them. Most had anticipated that something of the sort would have been likely to eventuate on the occasion of a Left Wing revolutionary government coming to power; but that a government the members of which bore names as famous as Churchill, Chamberlain, Halifax and Eden, could incarcerate for political reasons loyal British subjects with unblemished records, was unthinkable.

At last, and one by one, they were let out of their hutches, and were conducted each in turn to a bath, and there bidden to wash thoroughly, with particular attention to their scalps. Which exhortation Watts, for one, considered superfluous; when he came to record his memories of his first days at Brixton, he wrote:[52] "... as I found, there were already so many bugs... that a few more would have made no difference."

This compulsory bath for the destruction of vermin, followed by a medical check that was in fact a degrading inspection of the prisoner's person, were humiliating formalities, which however necessary in the case of low criminals of the Bill Sykes species, and of gutter-type hooligans, were not really essential for the reception into a verminous and filthy prison of loyal and honourable gentlemen, many of whom had held His Majesty's Commission, and had been decorated for their gallantry, and against whom no

52 Idem, p.4

charge had been made, or was ever to be preferred.

Churchill, who had owned to having experienced grave uneasiness about this imprisonment of political opponents, had directed that there should be nothing punitive in their detention. Unfortunately for the prisoners, many of the bumbles and bullies at various levels in the Home Office and in H.M. Prison Service had their own interpretation of the term "nothing punitive".

Spurred on by the ferociously vindictive attitude of the press, which now filled its columns with extravagant accusations against British Union, and spread wild tales of espionage and treason, these petty officials felt that in hurting the 18B detainees with pinpricks and unpleasant regulations, they were exalting their own patriotism. They felt, too, that the nation, as exemplified by its press, would uphold their conduct.

After the de-lousing process and medical check, there was an impounding of personal possessions, and an issue of bed linen. Carrying their coarse oatmeal-hued sheets, the prisoners were escorted one at a time across an inner courtyard to a four-storeyed block of two hundred cells, 'F' Hall. Everywhere iron-covered doors had to be unlocked to let them through, and were secured again behind them. Watts followed a blue-uniformed warder up a flight of iron stairs to No. 2 landing; the door of cell No. 38, officially "F2/38", was unlocked, revealing a bare, bleak little room about eleven feet by seven, containing a bed board and lumpy mattress, a chair and a tiny table. In a corner was a wash-stand with a chipped and scarred enamel basin and jug; beneath the wash-stand was a battered and most unpleasant looking chamber-pot. In a heap on the bed were three soiled blankets.

The cell window, composed of twenty panes, one of which was hinged to allow some direct contact with the four winds of heaven, was set so high that it called for a balancing act, with the heaped up furniture, to look out. The view however was not encouraging, as it afforded no more than a view of a small exercise yard.

As Watts stood within the doorway, taking stock of his new lodging, there was a sudden clang, followed by a rasping, grating sound immediately behind him. The warder had shut him in for the night. Worn out by the stresses and anxieties of the day, he undressed, lay down, and pulling the frowsty, smelly blankets round him, was soon asleep.

He was woken by another resounding clang, to find his cell door open and daylight streaming in. It was another day.

Let Charlie Watts tell his own story:[53] "A warder came in, rattling a big bunch of keys on a long chain, and said: 'Any applications?' I said, 'Eh', wondering what the hell he meant. So he explained that if anyone wished to see the Prison Governor or Doctor, application must be made in the morning when the doors are opened. I remarked that the only person I wanted to see was the one responsible for bunging me in the rattle. The answer to that was that the gentleman to whom I referred was not in the prison; to which I replied 'Not yet.'

Satisfied that I had no application to make, he passed on to the next cell, and I could hear the banging of doors, and shouts of 'Any applications?' getting fainter as he moved further along the landing. I got up, washed, dressed, then looking through the door I saw headed by Francis-Hawkins, our illustrious Director General.a line of fellows – Shepherd, Pacey, McKechnie, Beckett and others, all making for the toilet recess next to my cell, carrying their jerries to empty down the w.c. ..."

That first morning Watts found the queue of his esteemed superior officers and other old companions waiting to empty their brimming chamber pots in the recess next door, diverting to behold, but when a few days later 'F' Wing became filled with political prisoners, and the neighbouring water closet, the only one in working order, was unable to meet increased demands and overflowed into his cell, he was less amused.

---

53   Idem, p.8

"The doors were once again locked, but after a few minutes mine was opened quietly, and a big warder asked me if I would mind helping with the breakfast. He was so polite about it that I at once said 'Yes.' A very nice fellow this, named Sherwood, who appeared quite friendly.

I was given a two-gallon can of some bill-sticker's paste which was called porridge; another chap had a similar quantity of anaemic-looking fluid called tea; another had a tray with little pats of margarine; and another carried a basket containing lumps of browny black wholemeal bread.

We formed ourselves into a train, and travelled round the landing dispensing breakfast... starting off at cell No. 39, Raven Thomson's, we worked along to No. 50, then across the landing to No. 1. The door was opened, and out walked O.M. He had arrived after me the previous evening, so this was my first intimation of his arrest."

Watts was delighted to find himself sharing the same prison as his Leader. It was, he says, one of the great moments of his life. Mosley's cheerful and unconcerned smile as he accepted his half pint of porridge, reassured him immensely.

As he continued his breakfast round, Watts was distressed to find in the cell next to Mosley's a non-active member of his own Westminster Saint Georges District. This was Andrew Burn, a senior Civil Servant in the Ministry of Health. As Burn came to his cell door to receive his ration, Watts saw with a feeling of dismay that his face was battered and cut, and that he was obviously still somewhat shocked from what had happened.

"Andy" Burn had been arrested at his desk at the Ministry by some excited Special Branch Officers, who started verbally abusing him the moment they got him into their waiting car. On the drive to Brixton he refused to let himself be drawn by the accusations the detectives hurled at him, but sat between them in silence.

This so infuriated one of their number that he began to lash out with his fist at the impassive prisoner. The plain clothes officer was wearing on a finger of his right hand a massive metal ring of crude and ornate design, knuckle-duster in all but name. It was this ring that had caused the damage to Burn's features, so that on his arrival at the gaol he had to be taken immediately to the prison hospital to have his wounds dressed and stitches inserted.

The Special Branch officers who, Burn maintains, were in a state of hysteria, probably explained his injuries as having been received while resisting arrest.

Charlie Watts returned to his cell to eat his breakfast in unhappy mind, as he compared the considerate treatment meted out to his irrepressible self by Detective Sergeant Smith, with the brutal beating that had been bestowed on the quiet and peaceable Burn. Watts had recruited him into the Movement, and therefore felt partly responsible.

In the middle of the morning the prisoners were let out again for further slop emptying; then they were ordered down the stairs and out into a small courtyard for exercise. Here they walked in pairs, round and round endlessly. The fresh air smelled good; for H.M. Prisons have a compounded effluviant of their own, which is as distinctive as it is stale. The boon of this exercise period was that the detainees had the inestimable privilege of speech with the person next to whom they walked. The file of circumambulating prisoners was watched over by prison warders, now to be known familiarly as "screws", who counted and recounted, and recounted again the heads that passed them. After one hour of exercise they were counted back into 'F' Wing, and locked into their cells until dinner time.

A diet sheet hung on the wall of each cell, but the published bill of fare bore little relationship to what was actually served. Dried beans for instance appeared far more frequently in the mess tins than was indicated in the dietary, while other listed foods that would have helped to enliven meals, never appeared. The food was adequate in quantity; but no one could have attempted to describe it as balanced. What few vegetables that were served, were of very poor quality, being either wilted and stale, or rank overgrown specimens. At its best the fare was coarse and monotonous, at its worst inedible.

Some poor fellows, strangely enough mainly from the lower income groups, found themselves unable to swallow their rations, but continued to reject most of their meals day after day, while they nibbled and pecked at one or two scraps they deemed less loathsome.

From 2 p.m. until 3 p.m. there was exercise again; then the political prisoners were herded back into their cells, but not to be locked in. At this time of day they were allowed to sit inside their doorways within view of one another until 4 p.m., when supper was served. This last meal of the day consisted of bread and margarine, a minute portion of cheese, and a pint of excellent "ship's cocoa", both nutritious and satisfying; although a number of detainees found themselves unable to drink it, making do with the fresh water in the ewers on their wash-stands. When the cell doors clanged to at 4 p.m., they remained shut and locked until 7 a.m. next morning.

This first day's routine was typical of what each succeeding day was to be. The two spells for exercise when restrained conversation was allowed were the high spots of each day. The serving of the three meals and the twice daily emptying of slops were looked forward to as breaks in a tedium that stretched on indefinitely until all sense of time became lost.

Two books from the prison library, one fiction and one non-fiction, were permitted; and one could receive and send two letters each week, but all correspondence was rigorously censored.

Some persons might not consider this routine punitive. It certainly was dismally monotonous and frustrating; it seemed uncommonly like punishment to those who experienced it.

Within a day or two of arrival the detainees were interviewed by the Prison Governor, who as a matter of form checked their names and other particulars, read out the list of each prisoner's personal possessions that had been impounded, and promised to provide facilities for writing an appeal to the Advisory Committee then in process of being set up by the Home Secretary.

Everyone, almost without exception, took advantage of this opportunity to write indignant protests against their arrest and imprisonment, and to express the fury and deep injustice that they felt at the slanders on their characters, and baseless imputations against their loyalty to their King and Country.

In the majority of cases the victim was prohibited communication with his solicitor; where a lawyer was employed by the detainee's relatives and friends to set legal machinery in motion on his behalf, he was generally refused access to the prisoner, and was met by governmental obstruction and stone-walling. Those few lawyers who were able to make personal contact with their clients were horrified not only by the terms under which Regulation 18B operated, but by the physical conditions imposed on its victims. Actually it proved a waste of time and money to employ solicitors, as the new Regulation deprived them of all power to help.

On 31st July, 1940, while in Walton Gaol, William R. Edwards, a senior official of British Union on Merseyside, who was also a local businessman, was prevented meeting his solicitor who had called at the prison to see him on legal business unconnected with his detention. At Ascot during the week ending 10th August, 1940, a lawyer armed with the necessary authorisation from the Home Office for a visit on urgent and important business, was twice refused admittance to his client, Bryan Smith of Sheringham, Norfolk, an ex-Serviceman of the First World War, ex-Chairman of the North Norfolk Conservative Constituency Association and a former Conservative parliamentary candidate for that same Constituency, and a company director with his offices in St. Paul's Churchyard.

Legal help being forbidden, their written appeals to the Home Secretary's Advisory Committee were the only outlets allowed the captives who, according to their disposition, couched their protests in terms of pain, bewilderment, rage or abuse.

Mosley accepted the restrictions and irritations of prison life without fuss. He told Watts and the others who wished to spare him the trivial chores of washing up and pot-emptying: "I may be the Leader outside; but here I am one of the boys, and if the boys can take it, so can I."

Watts wrote:[54] "We were not long in 'F' Wing, before we found that we were not alone at night. Several of us came out in a nasty rash, or what we thought was a rash but in reality were bug bites. I was bitten only once or twice – they didn't seem to like me – but others were eaten alive. I went into O.M.'s cell one morning, just after he had finished washing; I happened to catch sight of his arms as he was in the act of rolling up his sleeves. His arms were covered in bites; by far the worst I had seen. I asked him if he had made any complaint about it. Not he! He would have let himself be eaten alive before complaining.

So I went downstairs to Mr. Corbell, the senior 'screw' in the Hall, called the Desk Officer, because he worked at a desk doing the necessary returns and paperwork, and I asked him to do something about it. Corbell was a very efficient and humane screw, who told me that he would fix it. He had O.M. moved to another cell on the ground floor, and provided with an iron bedstead... This did the trick.

We used to have bug hunts every night... They would be lodged in the cracks in the bed boards and tables. Night after night one could hear hammering from cells all over the Hall. This was caused by the bed boards being knocked against the floor to dislodge the inhabitants, which could then be dealt with.

Complaints were made daily to the Governor and to the Medical Officer. Cells were inspected, and some of them temporarily closed. New bed boards and other furniture were supplied to others, but the bugs were never cleared out.

---

54 Idem, pp. 20-21

One chap caught some, put them in a match-box, applied next morning to see the Governor, and then emptied the contents on the Governor's table. It caused quite a sensation....

In one of my letters home, I alluded to the prison as the 'Brixton Bug-house'. The censor reported this, and I was hauled before the Governor, and severely choked off. He never forgave me, and would remind me of my 'crime' on every possible occasion."

27 – The Government Wields The Big Stick

"Stuffing the ears of men with false reports."

Henry IV, Part 2, Introduction, William Shakespeare

No sooner was Mosley safely out of the way, than a campaign was launched by the newspapers of the Left, and by a number of Labour Members of Parliament, urging that his wife also should be deprived of her freedom.

It was a matter of five weeks after her husband's arrest that Diana Mosley was behind bars too. Shortly after lunch on Saturday, 29th June, at their home in Denham, Buckinghamshire, where she was with the two babies, Alexander, nineteen months, and Max, no more than eleven weeks, and their nurse, the police arrived with a Detention Order issued by the Home Office, authorising her arrest.

She was told that as the youngest child was unweaned, she might take him with her. Thinking that her destination would be the County Gaol at Aylesbury, she accepted; but when a moment or two later it was divulged that she was to be taken to Holloway Prison, she declined the Home Secretary's magnanimous gesture. She would not, she said, willingly take an infant into a London prison when the fury of aerial bombardment was likely to fall on the capital at any time.

When she arrived at that grim penitentiary for erring females and was conducted to a cell, reeking, wet and dirty, with no bed, only a thin mattress lying directly on the foul damp floor, she was thankful indeed that she had arranged for both babies to be taken to their aunt's home in Oxfordshire. Years after, she speaks of the "unbelievable filth, squalor, and horror" of the place.

27 - The Government Wields The Big Stick

The news of his wife's imprisonment took Mosley by surprise. It was something for which he had not been prepared. His own arrest he must have reckoned with, because of the long, vituperative agitation from both sides of the House, and from the popular press, that preceded it; but, he declared in harsh contempt, it had not once entered his head that a British Government could sink so low as to snatch mothers from their babies and young families, and gaol them for no better reason than that they happened to be the wives of inconvenient husbands.

If some people were shocked at this manner of treatment of the wives of outspoken critics of the Establishment, others were delighted. An exultant shout went up from the Left, which no longer content with the successful outcome of its vendetta against the Mosleys, began to agitate for the imprisonment of that poor, sick girl, Unity Mitford, Diana Mosley's younger sister.

The Left, which does not at any time allow its progress to be impeded by a sense of chivalry or any other outmoded nonsense, was ruthless in its persecution of any man or woman young or old, hale or invalid, known to hold views directly opposed to its own; hence the heartless cries for her incarceration. Actually, Unity's health was so precarious that imprisonment of any sort would have killed her. Therefore, the girl, who was slowly dying, was allowed to remain at the Mill Cottage, at Swinbrook in Oxfordshire, in the care of her parents, who were pestered by the press and insultingly offered considerable sums for her story.

There were further calls for her arrest and detention in 1941, when the new Home Secretary, Herbert Morrison, later Lord Morrison of Lambeth, indicated that her physical condition was too poor to permit her imprisonment. This incensed Dr. Edith Summerskill, now baroness Summerskill, who demanded to know why the Honourable Miss Unity Mitford should be the recipient of special privileges. To this expression of Dr. Summerskill's humanity and benevolence, Morrison replied somewhat tartly: "It is not a special privilege for a British citizen to be at liberty." [55]

---

55   Henry Page Croft (later baron Croft) was Churchill's Under-Secretary for war from

From time to time newspapermen tried to invade her privacy; the Left continued to natter about her, but with less and less frequency. This lovely, impulsive, warm-hearted girl gradually faded out of the news, until the announcement of her death in 1948 at the age of thirty-three. Even if her end was the outcome of her act of despair in 1939, she died a martyr for the cause of Anglo-German friendship and European peace.

On Monday, 8th July, the British public was startled by the news, released with the usual triumphant fanfare, of the arrest the previous evening of Admiral Sir Barry E. Domville, K.B.E., C.B., C.M.G., R.N. Retd, a former Director of Naval Intelligence, the son of an admiral, and the possessor of a distinguished naval career.

The Admiral had fallen foul of the Left because for some years he had publicly advocated friendship with Germany, and had furthered this aspiration by founding an organisation for the promotion of the Anglo-German friendship, know as "The Link". This association consisted of mainly elderly, well-meaning, middle-class worthies, some of whom in their youth had attended German universities, others had had musical or other cultural relations with Germany, some had done business with Germany, while yet others had been misguided enough to acquire German wives.

The potential treachery of "The Link" was so fearfully apparent to those politicians of the Left with their habitual astigmatism, that they were able in the then state of hysteria of the Home front, to prevail on the minions of the Establishment to knock off the jolly old sailor and throw him into Brixton gaol. His wife, who had been assisting him, they cast into Holloway prison.

A day or two after Mosley had been taken into custody, my home, at that time a flat on two floors above the Canterbury

---

1940 to 1945. He was responsible for the appointment of the first Army Director of Education and for all the correspondence courses, lectures and classes provided thereafter by the Army Education Corps. In 1942, he became Vice-President of the Army Council. It must have been very embarrassing for him to have a sister who was a leading member of the B.U.F.!

District Headquarters at 6, St. Alphege Lane, Canterbury was raided by the police. My wife happened to be entertaining a friend, who was a talented artist and not interested in politics of any kind. They were having tea together in our upstairs lounge, where I had joined them, when I heard the front door open. I went to investigate, and from the top of the stairs saw the Chief Constable of Canterbury and his senior Inspector, both in uniform, which was unusual, at the head of what seemed a large body of police.

There was just time to put my head round the door, warning: "Here come the Gestapo!" so as to mitigate the shock of having a posse of policemen suddenly erupted into the tea party.

I returned to the landing in time to confront the Chief Constable, who brandishing a paper, announced: "I have a magistrate's warrant authorising the search of these premises. I must warn you, that everyone else found at this address, must accompany us to the Police Station, and if necessary submit to being searched."

I objected to the proposal that a friend of my wife, who was not only a loyal Englishwoman but the wife of a serving soldier, and who was paying what was only a social afternoon call, should be taken to the police station to be compulsorily searched, as if she was some shoplifting or dope-smuggling suspect.

Of course my protest was useless; but I need not have worried about Phyllis D... She was not only tougher than I thought, but possessed a sense of the ridiculous. My wife told me afterwards that the threat of being forcibly searched prompted her to ask with a wide-eyed innocence that she could assume very well:

"Oh, I suppose that means that you will have to search the baby's nappies, too!"

A couple of plain clothes officers took me to the Station in a police car; I was kept there for several hours while being interrogated. My wife, our children, and our guest were brought there also, while the house and its contents were investigated. No one suffered the indignity of being searched, nor could the individual policemen of all ranks have been more polite or considerate.

When they had assured themselves that there was nothing at 6 St. Alphege Lane, nor anything in our replies to their many questions to justify our further detention, they let us go, but it was to transpire that if the local police were assured of our integrity and loyalty, higher placed persons elsewhere did not share their views.

Next day I had a call for help from a sterling local member of British Union, Alfred Smith, an ex-Serviceman, who had enlisted in the Army Service Corps in May, 1915, and who had served throughout the rest of the war. For the past fifteen years he had been the licensee of a public house, the 'King William IV', in Union Street, Canterbury.

"Smithie" who was a married man and the father of a young family, had that morning been notified by his brewers that he and his family must be out of the "King William" within the next few days. He was offered no explanation for this eviction from what was both his home and livelihood. He learnt later that his landlords had been reluctant to subject to such harsh treatment an old and valued tenant who had conducted his business in an exemplary manner, and against whom no previous complaint had been made by either the police or customers. But the brewers were helpless; they were acting under orders from the Home Office to turn out the Smith family at once.

Fortunately, 6 St. Alphege Lane was a comparatively commodious place, so we were able to provide the homeless and dispossessed Smiths with shelter, and with somewhere to house some of their possessions.

Shortly afterwards, on the 3rd June, 1940, Inspector Port of the Canterbury City Police arrested me in my office at the Canterbury Barracks. I was taken by surprise at this development; for I had felt that after the police raid on my home, and the subsequent interrogation, both of which had concluded satisfactorily, I had received my conge. When I remarked on this unexpected turn of events in my own case, the Inspector replied that he was equally surprised and mystified.

"But here," said he, producing a foolscap size sheet of shoddy paper carrying a smudgy and faintly duplicated text, "is the order from the Under Secretary of State for the Home Department, directing that you, Richard Reynell Bellamy, shall be detained."

That night I slept, or tried to sleep, locked in a cell at the police station. Sleep was impossible, because the neighbouring cells contained poor, unfortunate women, refugees and the wives of refugees who had fled to England from Middle European countries to escape Hitler. They had run from the Nazis, only to be rounded up as suspects and potential Nazi agents by the Government of the very country that had offered them asylum.

Their menfolk had been picked up and carried off to unknown destinations a day or two previously; now it was their turn to be taken by the police, and packed off to other unknown destinations. They filled the police station with their protests and lamentations.

Next morning I was informed that I was to be sent under escort, with one other prisoner, to Walton Gaol in Liverpool. My wife had been told of my impending removal, and had been asked to come and say goodbye, and to bring such clothing and toilet necessities as she thought I might need. I remember asking for Darwin's 'Origin of Species' and Wallace's 'Natural Selection', as it occurred to me that there was likely to be time ahead, in which to pursue reading sufficiently worthwhile to help me escape from the depressing present.

The Inspector seemed tired, harassed and in low spirits. He complained to me, and again later to my wife, that he could not think what the country was coming to, and that he had not become a policeman in order to be the instrument of persecution of those poor women who had howled all night, nor to lock up persons of whose bona fides he was assured.

When my wife arrived with my hand-luggage she recounted how the previous evening, after the news of my arrest had got around, an army officer with the insignia of a colonel had pushed his way into the house. She described him as visibly trembling with emotion, and obviously in an over-wrought state. He had raved at her in a voice so quavering as to be incoherent; but from his facial contortions, and accompanying gestures, she gathered that he was trying to tell her that he did not like her.

At length he managed to gain sufficient control over himself to make known his message that she and her husband ought to be shot, and the house burnt down. When my wife asked him if he knew anything at all of British Union policy or of its views on the war, he replied that he neither knew nor wanted to know anything about either. On this highly intellectual and impartial level, the conversation was terminated by a lady, presumably the officer's wife, who finally succeeded in drawing him away.

The police promised that so far as they were able, there would be no recurrence of such intrusion. They asked my wife to give them a ring immediately if anything untoward happened, or seemed about to happen. I felt that the worst likely to occur would be for some zealous citizens to break the windows with stones; but that would have been an unpleasant enough experience for three small children with only their mother at home.

After she had bidden me farewell she returned to 6 St. Alphege Lane, and packed a bag with necessaries for herself and the children, and then waited with inward trepidation but as much outward calm as she could muster in the unpleasant circumstances, for the Detention Order consigning her to Holloway Gaol, so sure was she of her place on the list of those to be arrested. As the daughter, grand-daughter, and great-grand-daughter of British soldiers she felt that in the present ordeal any attitude other than that of external composure would be a betrayal of her military stock.

She had the mistaken idea that she could take the children to prison with her; but such would not have been the case. They would have been handed into the care of the nearest workhouse-master, until alternative arrangements could have been made with other members of the family, all of whom lived at a distance. Fortunately in the hit and miss operation of 18B, my wife was not one of those whose names appeared on the detention roll; she was left free to enjoy with the children the liberality of the Local Public Assistance Board.

When I was handed over to my escort, I was delighted but at the same time grieved to find that my fellow prisoner was "Smithie" from the "King William IV". Our escort proved to be two as decent "Bobbies" as ever "bashed a beat". From the start of our journey by rail to Liverpool, they behaved with consideration, but after an hour or two they became even more friendly and communicative.

"You can thank malicious tongues for putting you in this mess," observed the senior of the two. To this comment the other added: "Pens, too. There have been letters about you."

As we took our seats in the Liverpool express at Euston Station, we were aware of a stir and commotion on the platform. People were stopping and staring; then they stood back to make way for a line of men handcuffed together. The prisoners were not manacled in pairs in the usual manner, but in single file, each man shackled by his right wrist to the left wrist of the fellow in front, and by his own left wrist to the right of the man next in line behind. They were being hustled along by a strong guard of police.

"What the hell - !" exclaimed one of our escort, staring in amazement. I was about to observe that they must be captured enemy agents, and evidently dangerous, when with a sense of shock I recognised one of them as Sidney Crosland, a leading member of British Union in Sussex, and a man well known in that county. He was a County Councillor, a fellow of irreproachable character, and the Movement's prospective parliamentary candidate for one of the Sussex constituencies.

I then recognised one or two others without being able immediately to attach names to them. With feelings of renewed shock I realised that this file of men being publicly humiliated, was a more or less haphazard selection of members of British Union from Sussex, ranging from an elderly retired senior officer of the Colonial Service to husky young farm workers.

In this "chain-gang" being openly exhibited were also men whom I knew later to be, respectively, a chartered accountant, a retired officer of the Regular Army, a shop-keeper, a commercial traveller, an estate agent's clerk, house painter, a shoemaker, and others from almost every walk of life.

Later, I learned too that these men had been thus marched through the streets of Horsham, and instead of being conveyed across London from one main line station to the other in chartered buses or army lorries, had been taken on the Underground shackled together exactly as I had seen them. Hundreds of persons must have viewed them thus, and either gaped in amazement or glared in aversion.

It has been suggested that this public parading of political prisoners was done purposely to raise morale on the Home Front, and to show that despite the defeats suffered on the Continent the Government of Great Britain was still able to wield a big stick at home.

As Smith and I were being conducted to Walton Gaol with politeness that was almost kindness, other members of our organisation from all parts of the country were converging on that same place, many of them making the journey, as in the case of the Sussex Blackshirts, under conditions that while painful and humiliating to the victims, in actual fact disgraced the authorities responsible for the outrages.

In Sheffield, on 3rd June, 1940, a dozen or more leading Mosleyites were arrested at work or at their homes, and were taken to Sheffield Central Police Station.

One of their number, S.W. Turner, a Master Cutler, at the same time a London club man, who was a veteran of the First World War during which he had attained the rank of Captain, and been twice decorated with the Military Cross, was well past his prime. Another was a schoolmaster, F.J. Hamley, who after having had his desk, locker and attaché-case publicly searched by plain clothes officers, was arrested in front of his class at Whitby Road School.

Finally but by no means least was an ex-Regular soldier, T.W. Buttery, a sixty-six year old veteran of the First World War, the Boer war, and campaigns on the North West Frontier of India, whose naturally short temper and fiery disposition, Indian and African suns had rendered dangerously combustible. He was an utterly fearless and indomitable Englishman of a breed that is almost extinct, who took unkindly to the term "traitor" when applied to himself, and with whom bullying policemen and hectoring prison warders after one brief clash, hesitated to risk another.

On account of his tongue, profane and corrosive enough to blister the paint off a guard-room door, old Buttery earned for himself the almost respectful cognomen of "Old Buggery".

Some time after having been brought to the Central Police Station, Sheffield, two C.I.D. officers cross-examined in turn each of the prisoners, who were made to stand beneath a glaring light while the rest of the room remained in darkness.

Next they were herded six to a cell for the night. It was a warm night; the windows of each of the cells had been permanently blacked-out, the lights were left on, the water-closets were out of order and would not flush, and were already stinking when the new arrivals were shown in. The only ventilation was through the grilles in the doors so the atmosphere became increasingly thick and fetid as the night wore on.

There were no mattresses; there was not room for all the occupants on the wooden shelves intended for sleeping, so some had to stretch out on the tiled floor, one poor unfortunate with his head resting beside the reeking pan of the water closet.

For breakfast they were each given a mug of tea and one slice of bread, then they were handcuffed and chained in threes, and taken to the passage outside their cells, and were left standing for more than four hours, chained together all the time, and with nothing to sit on but the stone floor. Repeated requests to see their solicitors were refused.

At noon they were loaded into two small Black Marias, and driven to Liverpool. It was not until after their arrival at Walton Gaol at 3 p.m. that their chains were removed. At 9 p.m. they were given one slice of bread apiece, and a mug of cocoa to be shared between three, which was their first food since their slice of bread and mug of tea at 7.30 that morning.

Four members of British Union arrested in Buckinghamshire were taken from police headquarters at Aylesbury to Bletchley junction to catch the train for Liverpool; they were handcuffed, and escorted by six policemen. One of these manacled prisoners, of the name of Palmer-Thompson, was not only aged seventy-six, but was a very sick man. He was suffering from cancer in an advanced form.

When one of the other prisoners, C.W. Elliot of Slough protested against this harsh treatment of an already suffering old man, he was ordered to "shut his mouth". Elliot later described the journey:

"Whilst waiting for the train, Palmer-Thompson asked for water, which after a lot of argument with the accompanying police we persuaded a porter to get." On arrival at Lime Street Station, Liverpool, Palmer-Thompson had to be lifted down from the train. At the prison he was admitted immediately to the hospital, to die there within three weeks.

Thus, in order to appease the fears and spite of the Left, did a law-abiding and upright old Englishman who wished only to see his country great and strong, honoured and respected, die like a felon in one of the most notorious penal establishments in Britain.

When Smith and I were turned over by our escort to the prison authorities at Walton, it was to find ourselves among scores of other newcomers, all brought in under Defence Regulation 18B, who, with one or two exceptions, were members of Mosley's Movement. The reception cells could not accommodate such an influx; the routine for receiving new prisoners broke down. While the first-comers had had to submit to the full regulation bath and check-up, those who arrived a little later walked through the bath cubicles without bathing or undressing, but those who came later still by-passed the ablutions altogether on their way to be examined by the doctor.

As we stood waiting our turns packed tight in the reception block, prisoners continued to arrive. If some took their arrest in feigned light-heartedness, others were seething and contained themselves with difficulty. There was one Devonshire farmer in particular, Frederick Hooper, a strong, stout, hale man of middle age, who greatly resembled John Bull; like his prototype he had broad, ruddy features adorned with what are now called "side burns".

This typical yeoman was seething, firstly that he, an ex-Serviceman who was also a South American volunteer, should be suspected of intending treachery, secondly that he should have been apprehended by the police in the middle of his sheep-shearing, and given no opportunity to arrange the working of his farm in his absence.

A tall elderly fellow was brought in by a young policeman of the Dorsetshire County Constabulary, the constable carrying the prisoner's luggage. The newcomer staggered a few steps, then collapsed groaning on a stool, his face buried in his hands. He explained brokenly that he had only just risen from a sick-bed, where he had lain for a very long time. He was a retired master mariner, Maurice Fitzgerald from Dorchester, where he had been District Leader of British Union until compelled to resign through ill health.

Fitzgerald, too, was taken to the prison hospital moribund, but was later allowed to go home in time to die in his own bed.

Some of the new arrivals were sailors, soldiers and airmen who had been arrested in camps and barracks, and were still in uniform. One of these was "Ned" Instone, a corn and seed merchant from Bridgnorth in Shropshire who, previously, had been District Treasurer of the local B.U. formation. He had held the old-fashioned view that "when my King is at war, then I am at war," and had therefore enlisted in the Army as a volunteer; but for all that the Home Secretary ordered his arrest.

His mother, well known locally as officer of the Conservative Constituency Association wrote in indignant protest to a Conservative Member for Parliament, who replied not at all sympathetically but to suggest that those who infiltrated the Services would be likely to be the most dangerous traitors of all.

Among those held in Walton Gaol were four clergymen of the Church of England, the Reverends Nye Thomas, Yates-Allen and Tibbs, some half-dozen schoolmasters and even schoolboys taken from their classes. There were two or three doctors of Medicine, including Dr. H.M. Stephenson who was a country G.P. from Maiden Newton, Dorsetshire, and who in common with all other 18Bs was not allowed to brief whoever was going to carry on his practice. One does not need much imagination to think of the possible disastrous consequences of this prohibition to certain unfortunate patients. Among the imprisoned medicos was one Harley Street specialist.

There were locked up that day several policemen representing the Metropolitan, Brighton and Hull forces, and one Inspector of colonial police, and there was at least one lawyer.

Other prisoners of State were Colonel Cherry, a retired commanding officer of the Durham Light Infantry, Captain Luttman-Johnson, an ex-Indian cavalryman, two Military Intelligence officers, Major N. Bacon and Captain "Tug" Wilson who, it would seem, knew things which it would have been better for them not to have known, and a monocled young officer of the Colonial Service. Sir John Anderson's bag that June during the big drive since the opening of 18B, included Captain Frank

Clifford of the Cunard line, "Skipper" Oddsson, an Arctic trawlerman from Hull who had also commanded a naval mine-sweeper in the First World War., and several merchant seamen of all ranks from deck officers to stokers.

Small businessmen such as Thomas, a one-legged ex-Serviceman from Poole where he was a tailor and outfitter, were dragged from their desks and counters and loaded into police cars and Black Marias to be driven off without being given any opportunity to safeguard their affairs.

Prisoners were brought in exactly as they had been arrested. Labourers taken from building sites and construction works, entered the gaol in their hob-nailed boots and clay-encrusted corduroys; Parsons, a merchant seaman from Southampton, continued to have to wear his thigh-length sea-boots for weeks. There were tradesmen and mechanics in their stained working clothes and overalls, who complained that they had not been allowed to lock up their expensive kits of personal tools, but had to leave them on their benches for unscrupulous workmates to plunder.

Those political prisoners, who, thrown into Walton Gaol in the first days of June, 1940, ranging from George Pitt-Rivers, one of the largest hereditary land-owners in Wessex, who was a famous anthropologist, also an eccentric, to F. Davies, a builder's labourer from Longsight, Manchester, and H.C. Trengrove, a village postman from Cornwall, were a representative cross-section of English life.

At last it was my turn to go through the by now shortened formalities of being received into prison; when these were completed I was passed to a quiet, pleasant featured warder to be conducted to my cell. As we went through the main building, and what I assumed to be the administrative centre I was edified to see displayed Ministry of Information posters, proclaiming:

"Freedom is in Peril: Defend It with All Your Might;" and "Lend to Defend the Right to be Free."

The warder led the way through seemingly endless iron doors which had to be unlocked to let us through, then locked again behind us, until we came to a vast, silent hall, its walls lined with tier upon tier of cells, the metal-faced doors of which opened on to iron galleries reached by staircases also of iron. The place was impressive in its size, silence, and seeming emptiness.

I was taken to the fifth and topmost landing, where after studying the cards outside one or two doors, only to find there were occupants behind them, my escort at length found one that was untenanted. He showed me in; but before locking me in for the night, he turned to me with a smile, and wished me goodnight.

This particular prison officer was named Biggs or Briggs, I forget which. I learnt later that he held his master mariner's certificate, but through the prolonged slump in trade he had remained without a berth for so long that he had entered the prison service in despair. He it was who spoke to me some weeks later, on the morning following the German peace offer broadcast to the world on 19th July, when Hitler had said:

"In this hour I feel it to be my duty before my conscience to appeal once more to reason and common sense to Great Britain... I see no reason why this war must go on."

Briggs (or Biggs) told me the gist of Hitler's speech which he had listened to on the German wireless. He thought that the terms being offered by the Fuhrer, taking into consideration the strength of his position, were fair and reasonable, and that he hoped Government would consider them. He added that he could see no reason why Britain should disregard them.

The cells at Walton were much the same as those at Brixton, but conditions generally were tougher, as Walton was a convict prison, whereas Brixton was for remand prisoners and debtors.

The cell furnishings at Walton were even more austere than those described by Charlie Watts; my habitation had neither table nor chair, the triangular wash-stand in a corner, no more than eighteen inches in length, had to serve also as dining table and desk, and in lieu of a chair there was a little stool. There were no sheets to the bed, only three frowsy and ominously stained blankets.

For several days I had no mirror, but I did have a spoon and fork, and later a tin knife, (tin so as to render it useless for the stabbing of a "screw".) Some detainees were not issued with cutlery for weeks, but had to make shift with their fingers or splinters of wood picked up in the exercise yard. They complained of the difficulty of eating porridge or stew with their fingers. The previous tenants of my abode obviously had been pigeons.

All our toilet things were taken from us; it was days before we had access to our tooth-brushes, combs and clean handkerchiefs. For a long time there was no issue of toilet paper, and as at the beginning of our imprisonment we were not allowed newspapers, and all letters and papers had been impounded, the consequences were unpleasant.

Photographs of herself and the children which my wife sent me were likewise impounded; my request to the Governor that I might have the postcard-size portraits with me was refused. It was never explained to me in what way I would have been helping Hitler to win the war if I had been allowed to look on the likenesses of my family; but there it was, the regulations forbade it.

A photograph of myself at Walton was something I would not have liked my wife to have seen. It was ten days or a fortnight before any of us were permitted to shave. At length we were allowed to remove our beards, under the eyes of a warder with communal razors and brushes dipped into a pail of some tepid, slimy mixture. Our beards were thick, each blade had to suffice for at least a dozen persons; so it was as a painful and bloody operation.

It was, to the best of my memory, three weeks before I bathed or changed my underclothes and socks. Those first weeks of imprisonment under Defence Regulation 18B were a degrading and searing experience.

The prison staff who, with one or two exceptions, had at first been surly and hostile, or at the best coldly correct, soon descended to human level and became friendly, even sympathetic. Warders confided to some of us later that immediately prior to our arrival they had been warned that they were about to become responsible for the safe custody of "some of the most dangerous men in England".

When on the morning after our arrival we were let out to empty slops, the "screws" threw open our doors, then quickly stepped back in much the same manner as animal-keepers might enlarge a pack of dangerous beasts. When the door of the cell which contained the former heavyweight boxing champion of Great Britain, and contestant for world title, Joe Beckett, was opened, three apprehensive warders stood in readiness to deal with almost any eventuality. Instead of some berserk creature rushing out, one the kindest and most thoroughly decent fellows to have represented his country in the boxing ring strolled out to take his place at the tap and sink in the recess.

This "most dangerous in England" became something of a joke shared between gaolers and 18Bs; and the process of establishing better rapport with the prison officers became known, with due apologies to the late William Shakespeare, as "the taming of the screw".

There were, it must be recorded, one or two members of the prison staff, nature's bullies, who remained consistently nasty and always ready to gibe and hurt. Warder Watson, in particular, was accused by several detainees of continued brutish behaviour; apparently when meals were being served he delighted in kicking the filled mess tins across cell floors. Another warder who had been transferred from Hull prison to Walton was in the habit of stopping outside cell doors at night to call out to the inmates:

"It won't be long now before we get orders to shoot you. Probably tomorrow. Have a good night's sleep. It might be your last." Brutes and bullies were the exceptions; most prison officers were tough, but decent.

There was one true friend and comforter – the Church of England chaplain, an ascetic-looking man of early middle-age. To those of our number whom he visited in their cells he spoke with understanding; he admitted to knowing and admiring the Movement's programme for social betterment, and its policy for peace.

His sermons in the prison chapel were at once a consolation and an inspiration. On the Sunday that he preached from the Sermon on the Mount, several hundred political prisoners were so moved that many of them murmured audibly, to the obvious embarrassment of the warders on duty.

"Blessed are the peace-makers...

"Blessed are they which are persecuted for righteousness sake...

"Blessed are ye, when men shall revile you, and persecute you, and shall say all manner of evil against you falsely..."

The well-remembered words of the Beautitude were for the political prisoners an emollient of extraordinary significance, they were so singularly appropriate. When later one of the detainees apologised to the padre for the sounds of what was uncommonly like applause which greeted his sermons, he replied that he was gratified at the reaction to his words, and wished that he could always make similar contact with his congregations.

I never learnt the name of this priest who was such a good spiritual friend at that time when most of the political prisoners, forced from their families and dependents, were undergoing mental as well as physical distress.

Outstanding in the mind of every 18B gaoled at Walton, was the filth and hideous squalor of the place as they remember it. The dirty bedding, the foetid smells, the decomposing food and nameless things such as swabs of cotton wool smeared with blood and pus that strewed the ground beneath the countless little windows. There were constant complaints to the Governor concerning the sordid and dangerously unhealthy conditions prevailing in his domain. The request made to him with the most frequency was for disinfectant; but this reiterated plea was rejected on the ground that the Prison Commissioners did not consider its use necessary.

Philip Shelmerdine, later a missionary in Africa but in those days a leading member of British Union in Manchester, where he owned an atelier for the production of statuary, appeared to have contracted a foul and unsightly skin disease but which proved to be a massive rash of bug-bites.

George Raymond Merriman, a newspaperman employed by the 'Hulton Press' in Southampton, while held in Walton Gaol developed "Sycosis Barbae", or "devil's beard", from the communal shaving arrangements already described. The story of Merriman's arrest is unusual: he was one of those who answered the call to man the little ships for the Dunkirk evacuation. He was actually picked up by the police aboard the motor-yacht Dorbetta, on the point of departure for Dunkirk.

Probably the worst feature of imprisonment in Walton was the solitary confinement. In the early part of their incarceration, prisoners were shut up in their cells for twenty-two or more hours out of the twenty-four, with only brief periods for exercise, and the opening of cell doors for slopping out and receiving meals. It was some time before arrangements could be made for the purchase of newspapers from outside, and days before any reading matter from the prison library became available.

At length there was an improvement, when newspapers could be purchased, and once or possibly twice a week two books at a time, one serious, one fiction, were placed in the cells by "star" prisoners, while their occupants were enjoying one of their all too short periods of exercise and restrained conversation. As for this prison library service, there was no choice of reading matter; some of the books, such as the collected sermons of some evangelically inspired divine of the time of William IV were, from a twentieth century point of view, somewhat heavy and indigestible, not to say well-nigh unreadable.

The bright summer days crawled by until all sense of time was lost; then after about seven weeks rumour became rife that a mass transfer from Walton was impending. Members of Parliament and journalists of the Left had been urging that the fascists should be deported; so it was felt generally among detainees that they were about to be shipped to Canada.

Hooper, the Devonshire farmer who resembled John Bull, and who had not ceased to fume at his arrest and the allegations of treacherous intent being made against him by persons and parties who, in reality, were more concerned in saving international socialism than in preserving Britain and the Empire, approached me as a senior officer of British Union. He fell in step with me during one exercise period to discuss the probable deportation, and to make known his view. He wanted to know if we, as loyal and law-abiding subjects of King George VI, were to allow ourselves to be loaded like cattle into some transport vessel, to be sent into exile at the very time when our country faced its gravest danger since Napoleon Buonaparte threatened invasion.

These were my sentiments entirely, so we agreed that should we be marched to the docks for embarkation we would lead a resistance. We realised that if at a pre-arranged signal we were suddenly to throw ourselves on our military guards and to grapple with them for their weapons, some of us would be sure to lose our lives. The alternative, tame submission, seemed craven and unworthy of Englishmen. We knew that there could be only one possible end to such an unequal fight, even if we did succeed in overpowering our guards, which was by no means impossible, but we were moved by the hope that the public commotion attending the incident might influence those Parliamentarians and others who retained respect for the time-honoured rights of Englishmen, and still had some regard for their country's good name.

The rumour of a transfer proved correct; only the destination was not to be Canada but a military prison camp at Ascot, Berkshire, which before the war had been the winter quarters of Bertram Mills' circus.

Between seven and eight hundred men held under 18B travelled by special train from Liverpool to Ascot under military guard. Immediately prior to entraining at Lime Street Station there were unpleasant scenes, when the young officer commanding the soldiers who lined the platform with rifles and fixed bayonets, seeing that a number of the prisoners were in naval, military and Air Force uniforms, went up to the nearest, who happened to be an army officer, to pluck off his buttons and insignia of rank.

The perpetrator of this outrage could not have been cognisant of military law, for an officer can be broke, that is deprived of the King's Commission, only after trial and sentence by court martial. As there was nothing wherewith to charge those commissioned officers arrested on the Home Secretary's orders, in most cases against the recommendations of the Admiralty, the War Office and the Air Ministry, not one of them had faced court martial. Therefore the officer in charge of the escort had placed himself in what could have been an extremely awkward position.

The stupid and histrionic exhibition on the railway platform evoked angry shouted protests and gestures from the hundreds of fellow prisoners who witnessed it. The soldiers came to what I assume to be the "on guard" position, and threatened the mass of thoroughly riled 18Bs with their muzzles and bayonets.

Someone near me snarled at a youth in battledress who faced him with a raised rifle, "Don't you dare threaten me with your Belisha bayonet!"

Later, I asked my indignant friend what he had meant by a "Belisha bayonet". He answered that the particular weapon to which he had objected was streaked with rust, and therefore could not possibly have belonged to a soldier of the pre-Belisha era of British military history.

One Canterbury member, serving with No. 138 Battery, 16th Regiment, Royal Artillery, was taken from his gun-site in the Kent countryside, and thrown in Brixton Gaol, after being informed that the King had no further use of his services.

27 - The Government Wields The Big Stick

Lady Pearson's Hollingbourne Manor was raided by the Kent police, and she herself carried off to police headquarters at Maidstone, where she was locked in a cell and kept virtually incommunicado for several days, not being allowed even to send for her solicitor.

When Brigadier-General Sir Henry Page Croft, Conservative Member for Bournemouth, learned of his sister's arrest, his amazement was exceeded only by his wrath. He demanded to see the Home Secretary, Sir John Anderson, immediately. There was an angry scene when he confronted the "Bengal Tiger"; he stormed at him for his "outrageous act", and for the stupidity and indecency of authorising the arrest of a woman, no longer young, who was completely devoted to her country, and wished only to serve it. Sir John produced some papers, presumably the dossier on Lady Pearson, and read to his fuming visitor a report on the incriminating evidence uncovered at Hollingbourne Manor, the most damning being the discovery of a stock of fascist uniforms.

"How," asked the Minister, "could you have expected me to act otherwise, in view of this report from the Kent police?"

Sir Henry, now even more concerned for his sister to whom he was deeply attached, hastened to Maidstone, and with the Home Secretary's authorisation was able to gain access to her at police headquarters.

He found the prisoner serene, and not in the least perturbed at the shocking things being said about her. He was a little put out by her calmness, and upbraided her for what he called her 'incredible folly' in having a store of fascist uniforms, presumably to be issued to the "storm-troops" when the moment came for a coup, timed to coincide with the Nazi invasion.

Lady Pearson could not think what her brother was talking about, until suddenly she remembered that in a corner of her room were several cardboard dress-boxes, one of which was inscribed on the outside, in thick crayon, with the word "Uniform". That particular box, she now recollected, contained a black leather belt with a B.U.F. chromium buckle of a type obsolete since 1936, and an unfinished black woollen knitted pullover.

This was the evidence on which an elderly lady of blameless character was confined for days in a cell intended to hold a prisoner for no more than a few hours, or one night at the most. However, she had no complaints, and told me afterwards that her enforced solitary confinement was an unforgettable spiritual experience.

Not for one moment do I suggest that there was any direct connection between the two events; but subsequently the Chief Constable involved committed suicide. I mention this tragedy in order to indicate that the harshness of the Kent police, their distortion of facts, and their hysterical behaviour throughout, might have been induced by a lack of mental balance at the top.

The great witch-hunt was pursued throughout June and July with undiminished vigour. Hundreds of our friends and companions were rounded up and thrown into prison forthwith, or kept for days in horrible little cells at police stations "pending enquiries".

At the same time, thousands of luckless aliens, mostly inoffensive refugees, were thrown into strongly guarded and heavily wired camps, erected originally to house those masses of prisoners of war which the fighting so far had failed to produce. More than a thousand of these poor fellows, including a number of Italian ice-cream vendors, fruiterers and restaurateurs, who wished Britain no ill, and German merchant seamen, all in transit to Canada for internment there, were drowned, trapped helplessly behind steel doors and festoons of barbed wire, when on 2nd July, 1940 the torpedoed Arandora Star went to the bottom amid scenes of indescribable horror.

It was in June that Special Branch Police arrested Captain Charles Bentinck-Budd, who had been commissioned in the field during the 2nd Battle of Ypres, at the age of seventeen, by the Commander-in-Chief in person. Bentinck-Budd who had served Mosley since the earliest days of the Movement, eventually to receive the appointment of National Inspector, had been asked by the War Office, months before the outbreak of the Second World War, to rejoin the Army. He volunteered, and was thereon commissioned as Captain and Adjutant of the 12th Divisional Royal Engineers, a new unit which he helped to form in Sussex.

"At the time of my arrest," says Budd, "I was serving as captain and second in command of a training company, Royal Engineers, at a barracks in Colchester, Essex. On 15th June, 1940, in the morning I was asked to go to the Orderly Room as my Commanding Officer wanted to speak to me. When I arrived, he informed me that there were two police officers waiting for me in my bedroom. He escorted me to my room, and there the two police officers read to me the warrant for my arrest under 18B."

"I was in full uniform and armed with a .45 Colt revolver which I handed over to the police, having taken it out of the holster on my belt, together with my ammunition. After a short drink with my colonel who protested against my arrest, and who had previously been on to the War Office by telephone without success, I was taken by train to London, thence to Brixton Prison, in full uniform, together with empty holster on my belt."

I heard the story of Budd's arrival at Brixton from another source. It was told me by the District Leader of Bognor Regis, the late Commander Charles Hudson O.B.E., R.N. Retd. who, himself arrested that same morning, and almost at bursting point with controlled rage, had just been ushered into that horrid place.

He was waiting his turn to undergo the humiliating formalities of reception, when he saw coming down the corridor Bentinck-Budd, in uniform, accoutred and, he assumed, armed. Immediately he jumped to the conclusion that Budd, who he knew well, was there on duty and in the role of military gaoler. Chin out-thrust and grey torpedo beard bristling, the old sailor glared, then exploded: "Budd!!! You here!! By God – this is too much!"

It was some moments before he could accept that the "Sapper" captain, apparently in full panoply of war, who had been his former brother Blackshirt, was in fact a fellow victim. With his First World War record, his qualities of leadership and command, and his pleasant, whimsical personality, Bentinck-Budd had won many friends in Eastern Command. His sudden arrest on suspicion of treachery was regarded as ridiculous as well as iniquitous. General Sir Guy Williams, G.O.C. Eastern Command, wrote to the Secretary of State for War upholding Budd. The then Minister for War was Sir Anthony Eden, (Lord Avon), who at no time was noted for his partiality for fascists!

Someone, somewhere, suppressed that letter, so that it never reached the Home Secretary's Advisory Committee looking into Budd's case. Such suppression of favourable evidence suggests that the Foreign Office was not the only Government Office to shelter hidden communists or pro-Red agents.

All commanding officers did not behave like the colonel of the 12th Divisional Royal Engineers. When in another part of the country the police came to arrest another soldier, Captain Richard Hamer, another Blackshirt, his commanding officer allowed that edifying spectacle to take place while Hamer was actually on parade. He was taken away between police officers before the astounded eyes of the men whom until that moment he had been commanding.

It is worth mentioning en passant that "Dick" Hamer had a brother-in-law who was a bright and promising Conservative Member of Parliament. Somehow, Hamer contrived to brief his connection by marriage concerning a few of the worst injustices and hardships attending Defence Regulation 18B; but the reply that reached him was that any Member of Parliament found to be interesting himself in 18B on behalf of the victims would be prejudicing his own political career.

The Dependants of Detainees

The sudden, forcible removal of breadwinners brought not only consternation, but all too often hardship and penury to the families concerned.

Edith Charnley, wife of the District Leader of Hull, was left wholly without means when her husband was arrested. She was compelled to give up her home, sell most of her possessions in order to defray the cost of removal of the remainder of her furniture to her native Southport, where she made application to the Public Assistance Board for relief for herself and her two children, a tiny tot of a girl and a baby boy of five months.

She was told by the officer who examined her case: "Your husband is a bloody traitor, and should be shot. You will get nothing from us, neither you nor your children. As far as I am concerned you can either go to work or starve."

John Charnley's imprisonment lasted for three and a half years, during the whole of which time his family received not one penny of public money, despite their desperate plight and the legal and moral obligation of the Assistance Board to relieve hardship.

The authorities seemed to be quite without compassion. In Barnsley they arrested a member of British Union who was over seventy years old age; they took him away, leaving his wife who was blind, helpless and alone, to fend for herself.

Dependants of detainees found themselves all at once treated like lepers, shunned by former friends, insulted by neighbours, threatened with violence, or even subjected to actual bodily harm.

Mrs. F. Cunningham of Rotherham whose husband had been taken into custody on the 3rd of June 1940, was set upon not far from home and in a neighbourhood where she was known, by a party of ruffians who knocked her down and kicked her as she lay on the ground. This took place shortly after her husband's arrest. She was pregnant at the time, and suffered a severe haemorrhage. Two years later she still had intermittent internal bleeding; her physical condition deteriorated, and she became tubercular. Until the attack she had been a strong, healthy young woman.

From the foregoing it can be seen that those Mosleyites picked up under 18B were by no means the only ones to suffer. Few members of our Movement, either in gaol or out, had a more hideous time than that experienced by Miss L.M. Reeve, a leading member of British Union in East Anglia, who had been nominated the Party's prospective parliamentary candidate for South West Norfolk.

Miss Reeve, a friend of my wife and myself, was a woman of quite extraordinary talents. She was of humble rustic origin, and had started her working life as a domestic servant but good looks, good sense and good manners had been her natural heritage. She was a keen and discriminating reader, and thus began to educate herself. She rose steadily in the world until she became one of the very few qualified women Land Agents, possibly the first in Britain, and was appointed Agent for Lord Walsingham's Merton Estate, on which she had been born.

When my wife and I came to know her, she was a woman of considerable charm, culture and erudition, and being gay, witty and hospitable, was very good company. She drove with verve a scarlet super-sports car, which she had nicknamed "Red Angel"; but others who viewed its impetuous passage with apprehension, preferred to style it "Red Devil". She was also a good shot, and the leading member of a Norfolk shooting syndicate; yet there was nothing masculine in her make-up. She dressed fashionably and well, and was not at all averse to the company of attractive and eligible males.

When, in the agricultural decline of the 1930s, farms on the Merton Estate fell tenantless Miss Reeve took them in hand, and in the interests of her employer pioneered new enterprises, such as the large scale rearing of ducklings for the table. She herself assumed the tenancy of one large neglected farm, which had reverted almost to rabbit-infested heath, and set about its reclamation. She erected thousands of yards of rabbit-proof fencing, and within the protection of the fences planted tens of thousands of young conifers to become, in time, windbreaks without which the light sandy blow-away soil of the Norfolk Brecklands is almost impossible to bring under cultivation.

The war with its evil propaganda transformed our friend from local heroine to local outcast; then with Dunkirk and its frenzied aftermath she was denounced repeatedly as a German agent. Troops were sent to apprehend her; she was seized, put in a truck and driven off under armed guard. Her valuable gundog, which was also her devoted companion, was admired by the non-commissioned officer in charge of the party. Telling her that she was probably about to be shot, he asked if he could keep the dog. However, after the usual search and interrogation, Miss Reeve eventually regained her freedom and returned to her ransacked home.

The estate became part of a military training area. Tanks tore gaps in the netted fences, the rabbits poured back and killed the young trees without which the cultivation of the fields was useless, and Miss Reeve was evicted from her home, a charming Tudor cottage with steep-pitched roofs and tall chimneys, which subsequently became an unauthorised artillery target.

With courage still high she took up more land outside the Battle Training Area, as most of Lord Walsingham's estate had now been denoted, and set about improving and farming it. She devoted herself, all her resources and all her energies to her new project, until the day she was notified that the Battle Area was to be extended and that her farm and dwelling were to be included in the scheme. It was too much. Harried, reviled, shunned and persecuted, and twice evicted, she hanged herself from a beam in one of her out-buildings.

28 - Ascot P.O.W. Camp No. 7

"No freeman shall be fined or bound;
Or dispossessed of freehold ground,
Except by lawful judgment found,
And passed upon him by his peers,
Forget not after all these years."

- Rudyard Kipling.

Prisoner of war Camp No. 7 was found to be a number of shabby brick-walled, iron-roofed huts of varying shapes and sizes connected by long dank corridors. This range of buildings was set in a sandy clearing in pinewoods not far from the village of Ascot in Berkshire. Camp and compound were surrounded by tall double fences and aprons of barbed wire; between the fences ran a sentry walk. By night this perimeter was illuminated by arc lights; at intervals along this boundary of barbed wire were observation towers facing inwards, out of which machine guns commanded the enclosure.

On arrival, the 18B detainees, surrounded by guards with rifles and bayonets, were marched into this open space to be medically examined. A retired admiral in his seventieth year, an Austrian prince who was also a naturalised British subject, men who had commanded His Majesty's warships, battalions of the Regular Army, and squadrons of the Royal Air Force, master mariners, doctors, parsons, schoolmasters, directors of companies, business men, and men from almost every walk of life (including gangsters of Italian origin from Soho) were paraded in two inward-facing lines. In full light of day, screened from the main road by the camp buildings, but plainly visible to any passers-by on the other three sides, these men were ordered to drop their trousers and raise their shirts.

The toughest and least sensitive of the prisoners resented this farce of a health check; but for those who were naturally modest or shy it was a searingly degrading experience.

After this "medical inspection" which seemed to have been purposely humiliating, the new arrivals were drafted to their respective quarters where they found that they were to sleep in crude three-tier wooden bunks on straw-filled palliases. The feeding was in a large ceilingless iron-roofed hall, cheerless enough in summer but doubly so in winter.

For those who were young and healthy, and had Service experience, or had knocked around the world, this rough communal existence was galling but bearable; but for those who were elderly, or had led sheltered and comfortable lives it was misery. There were one or two unfortunate men, well past the prime of life, and with bodily ailments that should have spared them from the rigours of a place intended for the confinement of fit and active enemy soldiers taken in battle. How many lives were shortened by such privation it would be impossible to say.

Old Kiddell-Monroe, a British Union official of York, and a former Conservative Party election agent, who had held his white head gallantly throughout his sojourn in Walton and Ascot, and who was one of the comparatively few liberated early in 1941, went home only to collapse and die. Some time later Professor S.F. Darwin-Fox, another elderly fellow, died in confinement.

Bryan Smith, a middle-aged ex-Serviceman and prosperous City merchant, was arrested shortly before what was to have been his wedding day. Although he took pains to conceal his distress, it was obvious to those who knew him that psychologically he had been hit hard. He was released after some five or six months, but did not long survive his return home; he dropped dead one Sunday morning in the porch of Sheringham Church, leaving his bride a widow.

18B also proved too much for Albert Potter, who had served in the Boer War and in the First World War, when he had been wounded three times; he had also roughed it in the colonies. Late in life he had married a girl, an attractive London secretary, many years his junior. They had turned their backs on urban ways, and with a tiny capital bought a few acres of semi-barren heath alongside a main road in Norfolk, not far from the little market town of Swaffham. There they kept pigs and poultry, raised feeding-stuffs and vegetables on their poor blow-away soil, and opened a transport cafe.

After a long struggle out of poverty and through adversity, they had won through. Their transport cafe with an added wing containing dormitory cubicles for long distance drivers, grew to become their main source of income. There was no mistaking their politics. The walls of the cafe, along with portraits of the King and Queen, were adorned with photographs of Mosley and fascist posters. If a minority of their customers objected and ceased calling, most accepted this propaganda without emotion, and a number were converted.

Then came disaster in the form of 18B. Potter was dragged off to prison; his wife was conveyed to Holloway Prison where to her dismay her infant son, whom she had weaned only recently, was taken from her arms and handed to a policeman's wife who had accompanied her, to take back to Norfolk for consignment to some institution. Meanwhile young "patriots" from neighbouring villages visited the deserted cafe and smallholding, smashing windows and doors, and wrecking all that they could reach.

These accumulated misfortunes finished the old veteran, who fell ill and was removed from Ascot camp to a military hospital at Aldershot. He was released a wreck of his former sanguine self, and not long after, died.

In the hut, officially styled "B" Room, of which I took charge, there was one poor prisoner, Bertram Hoare, far from young, who suffered from miserable internal disorders, chronic colitis and a weak bladder, that allowed him no peace at night, and rendered him unpleasant to live with. He, poor old chap, was painfully

Ascot POW Camp where 18B Detainees were imprisoned.

aware how uncongenial was his company. It was disgraceful that a man of his age and disability should have been confined under those conditions, particularly as his only crime (he was not a member of British Union), appeared to be that he had a German wife who owned property in Germany and had relatives who were Nazi Party members.

Of the one hundred and two occupants of "B" Room approximately two-thirds were followers of Mosley; the remainder were largely Italian ice-cream vendors, restaurateurs and waiters, three or four active Sinn Feiners, a couple of well-to-do business men who had had family or commercial connections with Germany, and one or two seedy characters whose stories of how they came to be held under Defence Regulation 18B were decidedly unconvincing.

Of the Blackshirts in "B" Room at least six were commissioned officers of the three fighting Services, including one holder of the Military Cross and an officer of the Royal Air force who had already been wounded in the current war. There were also two Chief Petty Officers R.N., two former Chief Petty Officers R.N., a Colour Sergeant of the Royal Northumberland Fusiliers, a young soldier straight from Dunkirk, and a dozen or more young fellows from the Navy, Army and Air Force who had not seen active service.

Paul Cope, senior British Union officer in Shropshire, and Burgess, a master cobbler with a business near Ardwick Green, Manchester, had both been prisoners of war in Germany during the First World War; it was interesting to hear them compare their present life in an English P.O.W. camp with their experiences in German camps. Burgess always maintained that his German camp commandant was a pleasanter person to deal with than the Governor of Walton gaol, and that he was more accessible than the commandant at Ascot.

Life behind the barbed wire soon settled into a wearisome and seemingly endless routine of musters, roll calls, and meals so scant that stomachs rumbled with chronic emptiness. It was learnt later, but never officially, that there had been a misunderstanding between the Home Office and the War Office as to the actual number of persons being transferred from Walton gaol to P.O.W. Camp No. 7. It was in consequence of the inability of someone to count that the quantity of rations issued fell far short of the regulation requirement.

For most 18Bs this was their first experience of real hunger. They learnt that the term "pangs" when applied to perpetually empty bellies is no misnomer. After a time the error as to the real ration strength was discovered and rectified; but even so, no one got enough to eat.

The Army, figuratively speaking, pitch forked the food raw and in bulk over the wire, leaving the prisoners to see to its preparation and distribution. The military did not concern themselves whether the prisoners distributed the victuals fairly, formed rackets, or came to blows over them.

If the detainees' hunger was far from satisfied by the size of the servings on their plates, there were no complaints concerning the manner of preparation of their meals. Santarelli, maitre d'hôtel of the Savoy took charge of the catering, and appointed as head cook a man who had been chef de cuisine of Reece's Restaurant, Liverpool. John Charnley, District Leader of Hull, who was a master baker and confectioner, became senior assistant cook. They were helped by others who had had hotel and restaurant experience. Alfred Smith with his service in the Army Service Corps was made storeman.

Apart from providing the inmates of P.O.W. Camp No. 7 with the basic necessities of life, even if in inadequate quantity the camp guards fulfilled their duty by seeing that their charges remained behind the barbed wire. They were largely indifferent to what went on inside the enclosure, and held no communication with the prisoners.

In the camp administrative offices, situated by the guardroom outside the camp gate, were several Intelligence Officers, some of whom were harmless, even pleasant enough persons, others whom it would be difficult to define as pleasant, and one, a brilliant linguist who behaved as if unbalanced. This officer claimed to have Churchill's ear, and from time to time, to dine with him. He said that Churchill was always interested to hear about the 18B detainees. This officer suggested that if only the 18Bs would "play ball" with him, he would see that the highest in the land was informed of their good behaviour and amenability, all of which would be to their ultimate benefit.

As none of the 18Bs, at least those who followed Mosley, had anything to hide, all this Intelligence Officer heard in response to his invitation to confess, was moral indignation expressed with fluency and strong language, in some cases with such heat that guards had to be called to remove the incensed Blackshirt.

There were two sergeants of the Rifles, a sergeant of a line regiment, and a corporal of cavalry, all Regular soldiers, and all first class fellows, courteous, patient and obliging. Their duties were probably internal security; at any rate they spent much of their time inside the camp, where most inmates eventually came to regard them as friends.

Several of the military personnel, ex-Regulars, were not only courteous and correct but went out of their way to demonstrate how odious they found their duties as custodians of fellow countrymen imprisoned for their political beliefs.

They never addressed their charges but as "gentlemen", and prefaced any orders that had to give with the word, "Please, gentlemen." At least two of their number were on the wrong side of the barbed wire; one was an old supporter of Cheltenham District, the other identified as a friend of the Movement elsewhere. One of these two officers once went so far as to apologise publicly for the distasteful nature of the duty he had been called on to perform.

There were from time to time other embarrassing encounters as when Rimmington, a former officer of the British Union well known on Merseyside, was seen in the uniform of an Army lieutenant, loaded revolver in his belt, standing on the kerbside as a column of 18Bs was marched past under escort. On another occasion when a party of Blackshirt prisoners, including Jim Battersby, Harry Jones, the District Leader, and other members of Stockport District, was being conveyed from a concentration camp in York to another outside Liverpool, the unhappy officer in charge of the escort was also a member of Stockport District.

Squadron Leader Thomson R.A.F., while held in Huyton camp had for neighbour on the other side of the barbed wire his own son, who was an officer in a Scottish regiment at that time stationed in Huyton. When eventually the Squadron Leader was released, he walked out through our heavily guarded main gate and in through that of the "Jocks", to be the guest of their mess.

After two months of what had been virtually solitary confinement in the sordid cells of Walton gaol, life in a prison camp did offer one welcome amelioration. Prisoners now had the opportunity to mingle with their fellows, and to have hours of unrestricted conversation; at last they could swap stories of recent incidents and of the events leading to their arrests.

Unthinkable and shocking episodes concerning the manner in which some of their number had been taken were disclosed for the first time. There were revelations of stupidity, callousness, vindictiveness and even downright dishonesty on the part of the authorities.

It was at Ascot that I first heard from Burrows, who was in "B" Room, the almost incredible story of neglect on the part of the Shrewsbury police to his wife, the shock of whose arrest and imprisonment had led to the loss of the child she was carrying, and to her own critical ill health.

For the first time too, we learnt the story attending the arrests of C.P. Dick and Eric Hamilton-Piercy, two well-known Blackshirts, who with one other companion had taken Dick's forty-foot motor yacht Advance to Dunkirk. Having embarked more members of the B.E.F. than the little vessel could carry with safety, they had returned to England to no heroes' welcome but to a reception organised by the Home Secretary who had given orders for their immediate apprehension and imprisonment.

So scandalous were some of the incidents which now came to light, that several detainees grouped together and resolved to record the worst cases, so that whatever the future might hold for the hapless victim of 18B, posterity would learn the truth. They decided that depositions of instances of rigged evidence, the use of agents provocateurs, and of dishonest and brutal police methods should be obtained, signed and witnessed and secreted in some safe place.

This was done despite the difficulties attending life in prison camps in 1940 and 1941, when there were shortages of most things, including writing materials. These statements were taken down on all manner of bits and pieces of paper. When later the 18Bs were transferred to Huyton near Liverpool and ultimately deported to the Isle of Man, these testimonies were conveyed from place to place secreted in clothing and hidden in baggage.

Later they were buried in a damp-resistant container in a remote place in the Manx countryside. It was nearly twenty years before John Wynn, one of the original burial party was able to return to the Isle of Man to unearth his cache. So well had he memorised the bearings, that he had no trouble in locating the site. He found the contents of the container not only intact, but unaffected by damp.

John Wynn's own story of how he was arrested, and how his property was treated, is disgraceful enough in all respects to merit recapitulation.

Wynn, an infantry officer in 1914, and a pilot of the Royal Flying Corps, was Managing and Technical Director of Gyrotone Ltd., a firm making specialised electrical equipment for the Admiralty. He lived at the Aerial, a bungalow at Balsall Common, Coventry.

Early one morning in June 1940, he was visited by the police who seized him and took him away; some of the party remained behind to ransack the place thoroughly. When they had concluded their search, they went away but neglected to secure the front door behind them.

Neighbours anxious to see for themselves what a fifth column lair contained, walked in and took away trifles as souvenirs of so exciting an interlude in their dull prosaic lives. When after some days and finally weeks the owner failed to return, so sure were they that John Wynn was by that time pushing up daises from out of his traitor's grave, they helped themselves to furniture and furnishings, until they had all but stripped bare what had been a comfortable bachelor home.

In the atmosphere current in England in the summer and autumn of 1940, a number of people would not have greatly blamed Wynn's neighbours for appropriating for themselves the property of a man known to be a fascist. The popular press and persons prominent in the influencing of public opinion had inferred that anyone whose views on the war conflicted with those of the then Left-inclined Establishment was automatically out-lawed, and could be hunted and harried with impunity.

In fact, not to join the popular hue and cry was almost tantamount to admitting to dangerous and heretical thinking in one's own self.

Wynn's manufacturing business was brought almost to a standstill through the absence in gaol and later in prison camps of its chief controller and technical head. His co-directors kept making long and fruitless journeys to his various places of detention, so that he could elucidate technical points known only to himself, but the camp and prison authorities were adamant in refusing them access to their prisoner.

Meanwhile the Admiralty grew restive at the ever lengthening delay, for which the Home Secretary and his underlings were responsible, and who in their way were helping the enemy quite ably and well, which was something no British Blackshirt ever did.

From time to time small parties of selected prisoners vanished mysteriously. One ex-Serviceman who was also a man of forceful personality and of strongly held views as to the intolerable injustice of 18B, refused to surrender himself for removal without first being told where he was being sent.

An Intelligence Officer who possessed neither one soldierly bone in his physical being nor one shred of psychological understanding in his make-up, expostulated excitedly, blustering and shouting at the immobile figure. Seeing that he was making no impression, he ordered soldiers to manhandle the prisoner into the waiting truck. There was an unseemly scuffle and Captain George Henry Lane Fox Pitt-Rivers, late of the First Royal Dragoons, a cripple for life from wounds received in the First World War, who was also an anthropologist of international repute, was dragged along rough ground by his heels.

As their custodians would not divulge the reasons for these sudden transfers of selected prisoners nor state where they were being sent, imaginative 18Bs not unnaturally saw something sinister in these disappearances, obscured in secrecy and silence. They wondered if the Corneliu Codreanu and Jose-Antonio

Primo de Rivera tragedies were being re-enacted in an English setting.

Today it must seem extraordinary that any balanced person could have harboured such ridiculous fears; but England of that brief unhappy period was far from her composed and normal self. There was hysteria in high places, particularly where those high places were occupied by prominent persons of the political Left, such as Ernest Bevin and Herbert Morrison, who had been throwing out hints about people who ought to be shot. There were far too many jittery authorities who listened to denunciations emanating from twentieth century rivals of Titus Oates, and half-trained, trigger-happy soldiers and Home Guards who shot without ado motorists and passers-by who had the misfortune to be deaf. All these combined to create an overall atmosphere of fear, panic, suspicion and malice.

At one period of our detention, actually it was while we were at Huyton, we came under surveillance of a provost-sergeant with glaring eyes, fiercely upturned moustache and a complexion like raw beef, whose boast it was that during the First World War he had shot more than a thousand deserters, mostly Australians, while either resisting arrest or escaping from custody. One of our number, Captain John St. Barbe-Baker, who had served in Intelligence in the previous war, recognised the soi-disant killer and was shocked into exclaiming: "My God! B----! What are you doing here?" The provost-sergeant leered, dropped two hands on his revolver butts (he wore two in open holsters on his belt), and replied that he was there to do his "usual job of course".

The popular press with its scares and outcries did nothing to allay the general nervous tension, but exacerbated that war-psychosis which already gripped large sections of the populace.

In conditions like these, perhaps the overwrought fears of a number of the political prisoners who, it must be remembered, were powerless, voiceless, friendless and without redress, can be understood. What may appear silly today by no means seemed silly in 1940.

However, the fascists and others who were driven off under armed guards for unknown destinations were not being "shot while escaping", like the Rumanian Iron Guard leader and his officers, but were delivered safely to an address on Ham Common about 12 miles from London.

This place, Latchmere House, was a large country house standing in its own grounds. It had been requisitioned by some undisclosed authority for the conditioning and interrogation of suspects, both national and alien; but who or what secret body controlled it, was never discovered. There were questions in Parliament concerning this establishment, nor was it mentioned in the newspapers; but most 18Bs suspected that it functioned beneath the aegis of the unmentionable Swinton Committee. It remained a top military or political secret, any reference to which in the outside world was absolutely forbidden.

At Ham Common, prisoners underwent continuous solitary confinement on rations about half the normal prison scale; no newspapers were allowed, nor letter received. Any letters that the prisoners wrote home, to their lawyers or their Members of Parliament, never reached their destinations. No news of the outside world reached the captives in their shuttered cells, none of home, nor might they speak a word to the silent soldiers who brought them their tiny meals. They had all day and all night in which to brood on their helplessness.

Admiral Sir Barry Domville's younger son, Compton Domville, a former deck officer of the P&O. Company, who was kept incommunicado at Ham Common for a time, declared that the Medical Officer (there was actually a resident M.O.) told him that "the treatment was intended to produce a state of mental atrophy and unreserved loquacity".

It all seemed to be without purpose and without end; until suddenly late one night, or in the small hours, the prisoner would wake to find armed soldiers in his cell. A senior N.C.O. wearing a revolver in an open holster on his belt, bid him rise and dress, then having fumbled into his clothes wondering the while if he

We Marched with Mosley

was to be led to some yet more horrible place of confinement, or a stake in front of a firing squad, the victim would be marched along passages and corridors, then ushered into a darkened room where two or three officers sat at a lamp-shaded table. All else was in obscurity except for one pool of blazing light, in which the blinking prisoner was made to stand.

Prominent on the table, close to the right hand of the centrally seated officer who was presumably the senior, was a loaded revolver pointing at the prisoner.

The questioning would begin, loud voiced and threatening, then insinuating, the officers pretending to a close knowledge of Mosley's treacherous intentions and of the treasonable activities of British Union. Sometimes they seemed even to sympathise with the man they were grilling, and to express regret for the situation in which he now found himself due to his unwise participation in politics in which he had unwittingly got out of his depth.

The interrogation would continue for hour after hour, one officer taking up the attack when another had exhausted himself. There would be threats of summary execution, and promises of lenience if only the prisoner would prove accommodating. The victim would find his head reeling, and his mind in confusion, but still the hateful voices persisted.

One can almost spare a mite of sympathy for the interrogators. It must have been exhausting work, and quite fruitless as there was nothing, absolutely nothing, to be extracted from those Blackshirts whom they battered with their accusations and challenges.

Water cannot be drawn from a stone, nor can incriminating evidence be drawn from a man who has nothing to hide.

Among those to undergo that midnight ordeal was the irrepressible Charlie Watts, who terminated his session by blandly telling his inquisitors that they must have read too many

Sexton Blake stories. Next, springing to attention he gave them the fascist salute and a resounding cry of "Hail! Mosley!" which he followed with an unrepeatable observation of his own to mark his contempt for what he considered their childish histrionics.

After a time, those responsible for administering Ham Common discontinued their hospitality to Mosley's friends and followers. Military intelligence may have continued to use that particular establishment to reduce unfortunate aliens to "unreserved loquacity", but no more 18Bs were invited to partake of its simple life.

As well as at Ascot, political concentration camps were established later at York and Huyton, Lancashire; also in addition to Brixton and Walton gaols, H.M. prisons at Stafford and Durham came to be utilised as places of detention. In the spring of 1941 the bulk of the 18Bs were deported to Peel in the Isle of Man; although a handful of the more important prisoners remained at Brixton until the end. Mosley, Major de Laessoe, and T.F. Swan were transferred to Holloway Gaol where they joined respective wives in a section of the prison set aside for married couples.

Most of the women detainees who had had a harrowing time in Holloway during the "blitz", eventually were sent to a camp at port Erin in the Isle of Man.

At York, two or three hundred prisoners were housed beneath the grandstand and among other buildings on the race-course; conditions generally were more tolerable than at Ascot, as the military personnel were friendly and gave a little latitude.

At Huyton, which was on the outskirts of Liverpool, an estate of recently completed council houses had been encircled with barbed wire, and converted into a prison camp. This could have been one of the less unpleasant places of confinement, the houses being new and fully equipped with bathrooms, water closets, and hot water systems; but in actual fact it was the most depressing and sordid place of the lot. Whereas the previous occupants of P.O.W. Camp No. 7 at Ascot had been German merchant seamen who left their barracks and surroundings spotless, most of those at Huyton had been refugees from Germany rounded up during the Dunkirk panic, and were neither house-trained nor decent. In the room which I shared with a B.U. friend, Ronald D'Alessio, a former naval officer and District Leader of Cheltenham, was a notice in German requesting inmates not to urinate on the floor.

The houses were surrounded by trampled mud, a stiff yellow water-logged clay, in which rotting mattresses, pillows, blankets and clothing lay in sodden heaps; everywhere, indoors and out, were garbage and filth. An advance party of detainees from Ascot spent days endeavouring to render some of the cottages fit for human habitation again. In one house, amid an assortment of rubbish in a built-in cupboard, they discovered the mouldering remains of a former tenant; the corpse might have been that of a suicide, although it could equally have been that of a victim of neglect by the authorities, or even of murder by fellow internees.

29 – You Must Have Done Something Wrong!

*"... but innocence shall make
False accusation blush."*
'Winter's Tale, Act 3, Scene 2. William Shakespeare

One of the provisions of Defence Regulation 18B was that the Home Secretary would appoint an Advisory Committee to examine each case of detention, and allow those held in custody the opportunity to answer the "reasons for their detention", as set out in the document ordering their confinement. On completion of each hearing the Committee was instructed to report back to the Home Secretary, making such observations and recommendations as they saw fit.

Mr. Norman Birkett K.C., later Lord Birkett, was appointed chairman; but as the task of examining exhaustively each of the nearly two thousand detainees was immense and seemed like to drag into eternity, two or three subsidiary committees were formed and prominent lawyers and other persons were invited to sit on them. Among those who sat in appraisal of the victims of detention orders were Messrs. Morris, Mallon, Cockburn, Stuart-Bunning, Mrs. Low, and others.

Even with these auxiliary courts, the delays in obtaining hearings were great. In some instances men and women who had been apprehended in early June, were not informed as to the real reasons for their being selected and gaoled, nor were given the opportunity to reply to those charges until well into the following year.

One of the first persons to appear before Mr. Norman Birkett was Sir Oswald Mosley himself, whose hearing, continuing over several days, totalled sixteen hours. Richard Stokes, Labour Member for Ipswich, who was not only unhappy about 18B, but had the courage to say so both within and outside the House of Commons, informed Parliament on 10th December, 1940, of the dialogue between prisoner and chairman which had terminated Mosley's appearance before the Advisory Committee.

Mosley: "There appear to be two grounds for detaining us...

> 1. A suggestion that we are traitors who would take up arms and fight with the Germans if they landed; and...
> 2. Our propaganda undermines civilian morale."

Birkett: "Speaking for myself you can entirely dismiss the first suggestion."

Mosley: "Then I can assume that we have been detained because of our campaign in favour of a negotiated peace."

Birkett: "Yes, Sir Oswald, that is the case."

In connection with the alleged enormity of having preached in favour of ending the war by mutual agreement, it was enlightening to read in the 'Evening Standard, 15.10.1966:

"Mr John Gordon, editor-in-chief of the 'Sunday Express' says Sir Winston Churchill would have gone to Parliament with a German offer of peace in 1941 had Deputy Prime Minister Attlee not advised the immediate rejection of the proposal."

Churchill, great parliamentarian that he was, who there is no reason to believe disliked 18B intensely, had made appeasement of the Left the lynch-pin of home policy; therefore in order to keep the Labour party sweet, Mosley and his friends continued behind bars in flagrant contravention of those liberties previously regarded as the finest and fairest expression of the English way of life.

The first rank and file fascists to appear before the Advisory Committee were subjected to nebulous accusations of treasonable intent. These hypothetical charges were made not against them personally but against British Union and its leadership. The inquisitors hinted at all sorts of underhand and subversive activities.

"If you only knew as much about the inner workings of your Party as we know, you would soon reconsider your attitude to your leader," was the theme of the examiners during many of the hearings in the summer and autumn of 1940.

Such innuendoes were useless. The prisoners for their part repeated their demands to be shown the proof positive that would confirm the suggestions and allegations; the Committee members on the other hand regretted their inability to specify or even to discuss those shameful secrets which they claimed their investigators had uncovered.

Later they changed their tactics and instead of bandying vague hints of treason, contented themselves in seeking to learn the prisoner's attitude to the war, and what he would do if at liberty in the event of German invasion. By that time they were beginning to understand better the kind of men with whom they were dealing, and to realise that Mosley's followers were inspired by a fervent patriotism which, although at utter variance to that "liberal" internationalism to which most of their own kind subscribed, prohibited those British Blackshirts from thought or deed harmful to the land of their birth.

The Advisory Committee varied its approach according to the background, antecedents and outlook of the person whom they were grilling. For instance, they were not long in discovering that Joe Beckett's views on Jewry were strong and unflattering.

"Surely, surely, Mr. Beckett," exclaimed one of the suave gentlemen who was examining him, "you must admit that there are some good Jews?"

"There may well be some," replied simple, steadfast old Joe, "but I've never met any, leastways not in the boxing world."

W.G. Barlow, ex-R.F.C. pilot and former racing motorist returned from his Committee seething. He was angered by the inability of those who were examining him to understand how a wealthy man could come to join a political party at variance with the Establishment and most unlikely ever to benefit his own pocket from the association. The members of his Committee had inferred that his motives for joining Mosley were deeply suspect, and that they considered his explanation not at all satisfactory.

Barlow felt insulted by this cross-examination by persons apparently so small-minded that they could not accept that a man of means could put his country before his purse, or be the possessor of a social conscience.

It was at these tribunals that many 18Bs had their first inkling of exactly what they were supposed to have said or done, and to be able to guess with reasonable accuracy the identities of the persons who had denounced them. The Advisory Committees were careful never to name those informers who, remember, had been promised anonymity by the Government; but from the very nature of the allegations made, and from the sometimes intimate details supplied, it was often possible to deduce who it was who had distorted simple acts or expression of opinion, making them appear mysterious, sinister or danger.

For example, Sidney Crosland, the Sussex County Councillor who was a bachelor still living beneath the parental roof was told, besides the usual rigmarole about being a member of a political party, etc. etc., that he was also a member of a suspicious household. The peculiarity which gave rise to mistrust was that his father, an elderly parson, and his mother, slept in different rooms. This fact prompted the deputy grand inquisitor to observe: "That, you must agree Mr. Crosland, is a very strange circumstance," or words to that effect.

Poor Crosland, who was a devoted son, had to explain with deep embarrassment that the snores of one of his parents had driven the other from the marriage bed.

This particular item of information concerning what had been a close-kept family secret, could only have emanated from someone with inside knowledge of the ménage. Puzzling afterwards over this extraordinary evidence of "suspicious activities", or whatever the intelligence people classed it, suddenly it occurred to Crosland that there was one possible person who could have supplied such detailed information. Without doubt his accuser was a maid who had left the house in spiteful mind after having been summarily dismissed by his mother in connection with the disappearance of money from the dining room mantelpiece.

A friend of my wife, Mrs. Robert Burk, then living at Herne Bay, was honoured by a visit from the British "Gestapo" who proceeded to search her house. Their endeavours were rewarded by the discovery of a slip of paper bearing a message concerning "black Italian". This document which seemed to them pregnant with esoteric meaning, happened to be a docket from a local shop relating to the purchase of cotton cloth suitable for black-out material.

Apart from the notorious traitor Anthony Blunt, other strange individuals managed to secure congenial employment for themselves with M.I.5 at that time. The joint authors of the book [56] exposing "Kim" Philby mention the wartime activities of a certain Brian Howard, Old Etonian, and homosexual, who utilised his Military Intelligence appointment not only to smell out fascists in Mayfair, but to blackmail several of his many acquaintances who had found him loathsome, and had not hesitated to tell him so. Someone who knew him well described him as "the leading arrogant swine of his generation".

The authors of the Philby book also contrived to contact some former members of M.I.5 staff, who had been typists, secretaries and filing clerks in the heyday of that department during its occupancy of H.M. Prison, Wormwood Scrubs, and before enemy air raids obliterated forever its tons (literally) of files and dossiers. The ladies questioned by the writers were not only

---

56   Philby: The Spy Who Betrayed A Generation, p.102.

quite forthcoming, but showed by the nature of their replies and by their unsolicited observations that they had been considerably unimpressed by the methods, sagacity and commonsense of many of those then engaged in counter-espionage.

One of the former M.I.5 girls told how [57] "quite by accident she discovered that her mother was listed as suspect because she had once held a musical evening, and among her guests had included an Austrian couple, who were refugees from the Nazis." This same lady learnt of "another dangerous person... a woman living... in Lowestoft who was recorded thus: 'She is always gazing out to sea and has a German friend.'"

One may well ask how those officers of M.I.5, and of the Special Branch, and the worthy members of the Advisory Committee, could possibly have lent themselves to such absurdities. The answer is that deafened, dizzied and bemused by the clamour of the Ministry of Information, the B.B.C., the press and Parliament, and by all the nonsensical uproar and din of Britain's not-so-finest hour, they no longer acted like reasonable men, but had allowed themselves to be swept away in the general hysteria.

In October, 1940, Churchill reshuffled his cabinet. Sir John Anderson left the Home Office to become Lord President, and was succeeded by Herbert Morrison from the Ministry of Supply.

Herbert Morrison, who a few years before had obliterated the Army Cadet Corps in the schools of the London County Council in 1940 charged Neville Chamberlain, John Simon and Samuel Hoare with lukewarmness to the war effort which, he told an audience in Southampton, he held primarily responsible for the Norwegian fiasco.

When in May, 1940, he had been made Churchill's Minister of Supply, Morrison wrote in The Listener, 30.5.1940:

---

57   Idem, pp.134-5.

"But do not forget that our task today has to be a bigger, a different, an even mightier effort, than that of the last war. The job of my Ministry is to turn the wealth of the nation into bullets, and shells, and guns, and tanks; to take the raw material and forge it into a sword of victory... more shells, more tanks, more guns; these are the swords we can place in the hands of our brave sons..."

Fine words indeed from that man who during 1914-18 had written against that war, derided the war effort, and encouraged others to shirk duty. It was not surprising that 'Truth' should have observed with a shudder: "A conchie turned salamander is a repellent spectacle."

Possibly he had not been turning out his instruments of death and destruction fast enough, for all his brave words; because in October of that same year Churchill transferred this Wayland with soft hands and a quiff to the Home Office where he could direct his crusading fervour into fresh channels. Herbert Morrison, gaoler, jangled his keys with gusto.

That Herbert Morrison loved the job we have on the authority of Winston Churchill who told Robin Maugham, writer and newspaper correspondent, in the annexe to No. 10 Downing Street in July, 1945:[58] "That wretched man Morrison... delighted and revelled in the power of 18B."

Morrison claimed that during his term in the Home Office he treated his old enemies, the British Blackshirts, now his personal prisoners, with complete impartiality; but it is difficult to reconcile this pretension with either his views as expressed in his published memoirs, or by his actions in office.

It was not long after Morrison's translation to the Home Office that Alfred Richards, a Pembrokeshire farmer, and his daughter came before the Advisory Committee. Birkett after studying the evidence and hearing the prisoners' version of events, said that the accusations were obvious lies, that the Richards had been

---

58   *Daily Telegraph*, 26.1.1965.

badly used, and that he was recommending their immediate release. Nevertheless Richards and his daughter were both notified subsequently that the Home Secretary had ordered their "further detention".

Within his first few months of office, Herbert Morrison turned down no less than fifty-five[59] similar recommendations for release made by Birkett and his colleagues. He admitted to the House of Commons on 26th November, 1941, that in the cases of 894 men and women imprisoned under Defence Regulation 18B, whose releases his own Advisory Committee had advocated he had over-ridden their expressed opinions and had ordered those particular prisoners be kept locked up indefinitely.

This admission prompted Mr. Ernest Evans, Member for the University of Wales, to protest that apparently the Home Secretary had no confidence in the judgement of a body of men appointed by himself. That, he pointed out, was a position of anomaly, the concomitant of which could only be that the Advisory Committee would have little confidence in the Home Secretary.

When in May, 1941, Bentinck-Budd applied for a writ of habeas corpus against the Home Secretary, the High Court judge on studying the Detention Order under which Budd had been incarcerated, referred witheringly to that document as a worthless bit of paper, and ordered his immediate release.

Herbert Morrison reluctant to part with a valued guest, promptly issued another Order and within ten days had Budd back in gaol where he remained until October 1942, when his First World War wounds became troublesome, deteriorated, and necessitated his removal to Queen Mary's Hospital, Roehampton. The actual physical hardships experienced during our imprisonment were slight, except for those who were infirm or aged; but the scant rations brought chronic hunger, particularly to the young and

59 According to the publication *It Might Have Happened to You* p.3, the actual figure should have been 128.

Britain's wartime Home Secretary - Herbert Morrison

active. At Ascot we were recommended by the several medical men among us to exert ourselves as little as possible, and to conserve our energies. At Huyton any cat that strayed into the camp did so at peril of its life; and at Peel, where seagulls were trapped for the table, snails which were only remotely related to escargots were esteemed not as delicacies but as relief from hunger.

Salted herring, which but for the war would have been exported to the eastern shores of the Baltic, appeared on our dietary with unwelcome frequency. They were incredibly salty. One former prisoner, who later in life developed a chronic and finally fatal heart condition, was asked by a heart specialist whom he consulted, if for any period he had taken an excess of salt that could account for his condition.

There were however the psychological effects of detention that left the deepest scars. It would be almost impossible to indicate without fear of contradiction any single prisoner held under Defence Regulation 18B whose mental and physical health and prospects of life were unaffected in some way by the stress and anxieties of political confinement.

The worst sufferers were those poor fellows to whom detention had brought smashed businesses, ruined careers or broken homes. Nor in many cases did eventual release, not even the end of the war, terminate their troubles when they found themselves reproached or even disowned by their own next of kin. I could name at least two ex-18Bs, not weaklings but men of faith and courage who, rejected by their families, were driven to suicide. Other former detainees found themselves shunned by pre-war friends, and refused employment commensurate with their abilities. This was persecution and it went on for years.

Of course there was no comparing the rigours of like in a British gaol or concentration camp with, say the horrors of a Japanese prisoner of war camp; but whereas the British prisoners in the Far East could comfort themselves with the certain knowledge that all Britain thought of them, prayed for them and longed for the day of their deliverance, the 18Bs were constantly reminded that they shared the almost universal contempt of their propaganda-deluded fellow-countrymen. This scorn and condemnation heaped on us by our own people, often by our own families, was what hurt the most.

For centuries Englishmen have been imprisoned only on conviction for proven crime. So long has it been since men in Britain were locked up for their way of thinking, that to most people imprisonment has become synonymous with conviction for felony. To the general public, therefore, it was axiomatic that if Mosley and his followers had been gaoled, then they must be guilty of some heinous wrong.

"You must have done SOMETHING wrong!" was the parrot-cry.

This was the attitude of my own parents to the news of my arrest when given out by the B.B.C. The letter I received from them in Walton gaol was reproachful rather than sympathetic, and blamed me greatly for whatever it was I had done which had necessitated my arrest. A sister-in-law wrote to my mother to say that I "deserved to be shot"; nor was her observation considered out of place. Few people could believe that men and women who were innocent could be thrown into prison solely on account of their views.

In other and less ordered lands where it is not unusual for public opponents to be put out of the way before becoming too troublesome, there is no stigma attached to imprisonment for political ends. In fact to be locked up by the government of the day, frequently is regarded as the conferment of an honour.

There is no such cachet to be gained from having done a stretch in an English gaol, where to have been held in custody for whatever reason can carry a life-long smear, as not a few former victims of 18B have found to their cost and even ultimate ruin.

Lord Jowitt, who was Solicitor General in Churchill's wartime administration and Lord Chancellor in Atlee's Labour Government between 1945 and 1951, reminded the House of Lords on 11.12.1946: "After all, let us be fair to those people who were imprisoned under Order 18B, and let us remember that they have never been accused of any crime; not only have they not been convicted of a crime, but they have never been accused of a crime."

Jowitt's words did little or nothing to vindicate publicly the former political prisoners; for whereas the entire press had carried the stories of our arrests with bold headlines and lengthy columns, the Lord Chancellor's exoneration was ignored by some newspapers and relegated to obscure corners by others.

30 - The Swan Song of the British Empire

"Winston, brilliant as he is does not listen to the opposite side, and is impatient of opinions that do not coincide with his own. This is a fatal defect in a civilian minister who has to consider the initial moves in a great war. If Winston is going to wield the armed forces of the Empire, he should cure himself of this grave fault." - Lord Esher, in 1912 [60]

"He (Churchill) was, we all considered, a danger to the Empire." - Admiral the Hon. Sir Stanley Colville, to H.M. King George V.[61]

"Heaven forbid that Churchill should ever become Prime Minister of this country! It would be an event of unparalleled disaster. Winston, for all his brilliance, is completely irresponsible and regardless of consequences." - Oswald Mosley, in 1938.[62]

"We sometimes longed for a leader with more balance and less brilliance." - Major-General Sir John Kennedy, in 1941 [63].

Churchill's dramatic phrases and stirring words caught the popular imagination and rekindled those fires of patriotism long stifled by the Left, which permitted those flames to glow again so long as they were kept burning for his own political ends. Even the dreadful creatures who ruled Russia had to reshape their propaganda for home consumption. Metaphorically they exhumed past military heroes from their imperialist graves where they had long lain shunned or defamed patriots, who had served bygone Tsars, had their names invoked so as to inspire

60   *Winston Churchill and the Dardanelles*, p.31, by Trumbull Higgins, pub. Heinemann.

61   *From the Dreadnought to Scapa Flow*, Vol. 2, p.288, by A.J. Moore, pub. O.U.P.

62   In conversation with the author.

63   *The Business of War*, p.115.

"comrades" of Stalin's era to defend with their life blood, not Lenin's heritage, but the sacred soil of Mother Russia.

The British people, emasculated, pacifist and utterly negative for two decades, then thrown into confusion by the disasters in Norway and in Northern France, began at Churchill's bidding to recall their heroic past and to brace themselves for whatever shocks might yet come. After the seemingly endless defeats, retreats and evacuations, the brilliantly daring implementation of General Sir Archibald Wavell's [64] strategy in the western desert by Major-General Sir Richard O'Connor who achieved a series of victories, swift and decisive, over a vastly superior enemy, and pursued the routed hosts of Marshal Graziani for five hundred miles from inside Egypt to El Agheila in Libya, was a timely tonic. After eighteen months of war, fraught the most part with bitter humiliation, Britain had been presented at last with a spectacular triumph.

However, the resultant elation was all too transient, for the fruits of victory were to be promptly dissipated. On orders from Whitehall, O'Connor's advance was halted; the bulk of his troops and equipment was diverted to Greece in pursuance of aims which were political rather than military, and which were contrary to the advice of General Brooke who [65] "considered that our participation in the operation in Greece was a definite strategic blunder... and could only result in the most dangerous dispersal of force."

The expedition to Greece proved to be almost as mortifying as the Norwegian fiasco, but was even costlier in material, some 104 tanks, 400 guns, 1,800 machine guns and 8,000 motor vehicles being lost. All the recent conquests in North Africa were completely cancelled out when Rommel and his Afrika Korp emerged unexpectedly out of the desert dust, and started to roll back what remained of O'Connor's army, sadly depleted by Churchill in pursuit of his Greek gamble, until once again Egypt and the Suez Canal were threatened.

---

64   Commander-in-Chief, Middle East.

65   *The Turn of the Tide*, p.235

There was anxiety edged with anger at the War Office where the Director of Military Operations, Major-General Sir John Kennedy recalls: [66]

"At that time, criticism of Churchill was bitter and general, and it was said that all was not well with machinery for the military control of the war. The gist of the criticisms was that we were living from hand to mouth on a diet of improvisation and opportunism; that no clear cut military appreciations were being laid before the War Cabinet, for their discussion, and approval or rejection; that from their very inception, military opinions were being distorted and coloured by the formidable advocacy of the Prime Minister; the fact that he was not only advocate, but witness, prosecutor, and judge. He was also criticised for sending personal directives to the Commanders-in-Chief without professional advice, and for exhausting the Chiefs-of-Staff to the point of danger."

As Prime Minister-cum-Defence Minister, Churchill was making exactly those same mistakes that had cost him his office of First Lord of the Admiralty in 1915, when on more than one occasion he had sent war signals, with often dire results, to admirals commanding fleets, without the knowledge of the Sea Lords.

Concerning the allegation that Churchill was "exhausting the Chiefs-of-Staff to the point of danger", Dill, who was Churchill's Chief of Imperial General Staff from 27th May, 1940, until near the end of 1941, and on whom devolved the unpleasant duty of exposing the weaknesses or impossibilities of Churchill's multitudinous brain-waves, showed unmistakable signs of reaching the limit of endurance. Later when he was sent to Washington to represent Great Britain on the Combined Chiefs of Staff Committee, he expressed his fervent wish "never to have to work with that man again".

Dill, who was esteemed by his brother officers as an outstanding strategist, and who came to be highly regarded at the Pentagon,

66   *The Business of War*, p.235

was Churchill's bête noire; the man who nipped in the bud many beautiful ideas. It was suggested to Churchill that Dill should be rewarded with a peerage; the Prime Minister neither assented nor disagreed, but nothing came of it. Winston must have been deeply irritated not to have publicly honoured the departing Chief of Imperial General Staff.

Overwhelmed with work, personal tragedy, and his Prime Minister's scorn, Dill died in Washington, a worn-out wreck.

The First Sea Lord, too, old Sir Dudley Pound, was giving indications of imminent physical collapse. He sat in his chair apparently little more than semi-conscious during Churchill's interminable midnight conferences, known as the "Midnight Follies", although he would wake up quickly enough if some matter concerning the Royal Navy was mentioned. Eventually he succumbed to a stroke; like Dill he died in harness.

Kennedy, writing of those crowded years, states:

"One of my first impressions of the War Office was that a heavy strain was being put on the Chiefs-of-Staff by the Prime Minister's habits. He worked in bed in the morning, slept in the afternoon, kept the Chiefs-of-Staff up at night, and went off to the country for long weekends. This suited him if no one else; and it certainly enabled him to remain fresh...

His usual hour for meeting the Chiefs-of-Staff was 9.30 p.m., and he kept them until one or two in the morning. Further he had collected round him a number of men who gave him independent advice, which was sometimes irresponsible and often unsound and their ideas had to be discussed and debated."

Elsewhere in his memoirs, Kennedy mentions the possibility of the war being lost in Whitehall. He wrote: [67]

"The Chiefs-of Staff were being over-driven, and were having

---

67   *The Business of War*, p.93.

to compete for the Prime Minister's attention with a group of independent advisers with whom he had surrounded himself."

Liddell Hart writing in the 'Daily Express', 3.3.1940, had given warning:

"The real defeatists throughout history have been the men who defeated their country's true purpose by pushing their countrymen to attempt more than was practicable, thereby paving the way to exhaustion, if not defeat."

The former Australian Prime Minister, Sir Robert Menzies, then in London, and the only man not subordinate to Churchill and who could therefore talk to him as an equal, which apparently he did with colonial forthrightness, was uneasy concerning the war leadership. Mindful of the lives of his young Anzacs, he was reluctant to entrust them to the very man who by that same reckless irresponsibility that he still manifested, had sent their fathers to die in their thousands on Gallipoli in an ill-pledged and bungled adventure.

When Churchill said scathing things about British troops and their poor performances in the field, it was Menzies who stood up for them, telling Staff Officer: [68]

"He does not seem to realise that men without proper equipment, and with nothing but rifles, do not count in modern war – after all we are not living in the age of Omdurman."

In Menzies' opinion it was only Churchill's magnificent and courageous leadership that compensated for "his deplorable strategic sense".

At the time of the German airborne attack on Crete, the British were once again worsted, but only after stubborn resistance. In the rescue of the remnants of what had once been O'Connor's victorious desert troops, the Royal Navy suffered terrible losses,

---

68   Idem, p.115.

with 4 cruisers, 6 destroyers sunk, 3 battleships, 1 aircraft-carrier and 3 cruisers heavily damaged. This was the fifth such rescue operation mounted by the Navy.

The Luftwaffe again demonstrated to the world that whoever had supremacy of the air above the sea also held supremacy of that sea.

All this time a spate of signals was passing between Churchill and Wavell, and there was such continual interference in Wavell's planning that Kennedy was driven to observe: [69]

"If I were in Wavell's shoes, I should reply that interference in the details of my Command had become intolerable and that unless I could be assured that it would cease... I would prefer to give up my command."

Kennedy says:[70] "Whenever an idea, however wild, was thrown up, he ordered detailed examinations, or plans, or both to be made at high speed. Our stables were so full of these unlikely starters that we were hard put to it to give the favourites the attention they deserved. To cope with the situation adequately, it would have been worthwhile to have two staffs: one to deal with the Prime Minister, the other with the war. His domination over the Chiefs of Staff seemed greater than ever; and Dill, on whom fell the brunt of opposing him, now began to show signs of great exhaustion.

When Churchill's projects were finally thrown aside after the useless expenditure of much labour and energy, he obviously did not realise that he had been saved from disaster. On the contrary he seemed to think he had been thwarted by men who lacked initiative and courage."

On such occasions he would inveigh against his generals whom

69   Idem, p.122.

70   Idem, pp. 173-174.

he described as defeatists and [71] "only too ready to surrender, and who should be made examples of like Admiral Byng", which, unintentionally was a singularly apt comparison as poor Byng was shot in order to cover up the ineptitude of politicians, especially that contemptible bungler, the Duke of Newcastle, who headed the Government.

It was á propos Churchill's constant interference in details that Alan Brooke, some time after he became Chief of Imperial General Staff towards the end of 1941, on studying a memorandum which Kennedy was preparing for the Prime Minister, picked up a pencil and crossed out nine-tenths of the draft at the same time remarking: [72]

"The more you tell that man about the war, the more you hinder the winning of it."

On 22nd June, 1941, Hitler launched "Barbarossa", the German attack on Russia. Churchill promptly declared full alliance with the Soviet Union, to the horror of tens of thousands of persons who regarded the U.S.S.R. the joint ravager of Poland with Germany, with even stronger aversion than they felt for Hitler's Germany. In view of her pledge to Poland solemnly made little more than two years before, many Englishmen felt Churchill's new alliance to be incompatible with honour, and asked themselves what was the moral point of going to war to overthrow tyranny if one entered into compact with even viler tyranny to do so. This was siding with Satan to cast out sin.

Dill, still Chief of Imperial General Staff at that time, voiced the opinion of many of his fellow-countrymen when he informed colleagues on the day that Churchill welcomed Russia: [73] "that he regarded the Russians as so foul that he hated the idea of any close association with them".

---

71   *The Turn of the Tide*, p.254.

72   *The Business of War*, p.108.

73   Idem, p.147.

Hannen Swaffer of the 'Daily Herald' recapitulated his dismay on overhearing two senior Staff Officers lunching at a neighbouring table at the Savoy Grill, or wherever that oracle of the working classes chewed his frugal crust, rejoicing at the rout of the Red Army and hoping that the Germans would soon bomb it to blazes. That, said Swaffer, was deplorable and not at all the way to speak of a great and gallant ally.

The German advance into Russian-held territory, then into Russia, exposed happenings which showed the Bolsheviks of 1941 to be no better than they had been in the early days of the Revolution, when they had butchered officers of the Imperial Army and Navy in batches of hundreds, possibly thousands. Someone, having talked out of turn, led Germans to the Katyn Wood in the Smolensk area and there indicated a spot, which when opened by the spade, proved to be vast grave containing almost 5,000 corpses of Polish officers who had been taken prisoner at the time of the "stab in the back" campaign in the autumn of 1939.

This inconvenient discovery hardly seemed to confirm George Lansbury's innocent-minded claim that: [74] "Bolsheviks are more humane, more civilised in warfare, and in their treatment of prisoners than any other government I know... the communist leaders of Russia have hitched their wagon to a star... the star of love, brotherhood, and comradeship."

The Germans and the Polish Government in Exile wanted the International Red Cross to investigate; but the Kremlin developed unexpectedly tender susceptibilities, and declared that the very suggestion of inviting the Red Cross was a stain on the shining bright honour of the Soviet Union. In Britain the horrible story was played down lest it spoil the beautiful friendship being fostered between the freedom-loving democracies of Churchill and Stalin. It was suggested that the Germans were the real authors of the massacre of the Polish Officer Corps and were utilising it to defame the Soviets.

---

74   *Daily Herald*, March 1920.

Anthony Eden, constant in his regard for Russia, sprang to her defence, telling Parliament on 4th May, 1943, that [75] "His Majesty's Government have no wish to attribute blame for those events to anyone except the common enemy". Churchill, too, ignoring the fact that Britain had gone to war to save Poland, turned a cold shoulder to his 1939 ally but rallied to the new, declaring that the Katyn "issue should be avoided"

Actually the Katyn Wood discovery was only the beginning of the uncovering of a hideous mass extermination of Poles of the upper and professional classes in Russian hands. In all, some 15,000 [76] Polish Officers captured by the Russians in 1939 were never seen alive again.

The victories of the Wehrmacht in the earlier part of the campaign in Russia were spectacular in their magnitude and completeness. The numbers of prisoners taken and the miles of territory seized were immense. The whole of the rest of the world watched, and gasped in amazement. Not since Alexander had extended his empire from Europe into India had such conquests been known.

For all their overwhelming victories in the field the German military planners were responsible for one major tactical blunder which was costly in the extreme. For while their armour was on tracks and could travel where it wished, even crossing the Bug and other major rivers by crawling totally submerged across their beds, with engines sealed, crews in oxygen masks, and gun muzzles tamponed, their transport was on wheels and thereby restricted to the roads. Elsewhere in Europe wheeled transport would have been a minor hindrance; but in Russia where the roads were virtually non-existent, towns and villages being linked for the most part by earth tracks across the steppes which after rain and the passage of a few vehicles resembled bogs and as about as hazardous to traverse, this oversight was a catastrophe.

---

75   *The Katyn Cover-up*, p.77, by Louis Fitzgibbon, pub. Tom Stacey.

76   *Death in the Forest*, by J.K. Zawodny, pub. University Press of Notre Dame.

In many areas the Germans were received not as enemies but as liberators. Older women threw flowers to the invaders, the national flag of the Ukraine was flown in Kiev, and priests of the Orthodox Church officiated at public worship in Smolensk cathedral for the first time since its desecration by the Bolsheviks during the Revolution.

It was the attitude of many of the victors that nullified in time the friendly approaches of the people; and for this, German propaganda forever harping on the beastliness of the Russians, without attempting to distinguish between the monsters on top and the mute masses beneath, was to blame. Told again and again that the Russians were no better than savages, which charge seemed ocularly confirmed by the Katyn Wood horror, Germans felt revulsion and contempt for the Russian people. Nor did they trouble to conceal their feelings but by their overbearing behaviour rejected all overtures of future friendship.

Possibly it was a minority of German soldiers who behaved with ill-considered arrogance or inhumanity, but by their disregard for the feelings of the populace they threw away the only opportunity that ever presented itself for the overthrow of communism in Russia from within.

Even so, thousands of Ukrainians, White Russians, and Cossacks went over to the invaders, freely joined the German armed forces, and continued to serve in them with loyalty and devotion until the end of the war, when they and 2 million other Russians – including many who had never lived in Soviet Russia – were handed over to Stalin to face arrest, torture and death.

Churchill's Russian alliance was responsible for a swing yet further to the Left in Britain. Russians were not only our "brave Allies" – they were fantastically brave – but they became respectable. The British communists basked in the reflected glory of their co-ideologists, shared the general glow of approbation, and exploited, as only they knew how, the new situation with psychological skill. In no time they were at work burrowing into the Services, industries and professions. The Special Branch police may have been alarmed at the way things were going; but no one in authority attempted to put a stop to the treason and subversion that were brewing.

In the Second World War, in contradistinction to the First, money and effort were spent on educational services for the members of the armed forces. This was a heaven-sent opportunity for the Left to indoctrinate a generation of young men, more literate than their fathers in 1914-1918, but with less respect for tradition, and consequently infinitely more receptive to Marxian philosophies. One of the war ministers or some other authority in high place must have been responsible for the appointment of those officers of the Army Education Corps who led the Army up left-hand garden paths during the last war. This fact did not entirely escape notice at the time; General Martel comments: [77]

"The teaching profession has always been a hotbed of communism. Many officers with a communist trend succeeded in gaining important posts in the Army Education Corps."

The Royal Air Force seems to have been similarly afflicted. An old Blackshirt friend, Flight Lieutenant F.R. C_ _ _ _ _ D.F.C. assures me that the same pro-communist views were being expounded to the personnel by many R.A.F. educationalist. In his opinion it was this widespread indoctrination, apparently officially sponsored, which caused the General Election of 1945 to become a landslide to the Left.

"The 1945 election has often been regarded as the Army Education Corp's only battle of honour." ('*Daily Telegraph*, 14.9.1970)

The Royal Navy seems to have been rather more particular about whom it recruited for the instruction of its ratings, and preferred officers of more patriotic outlook and who still retained some respect for tradition.

---

77 *An Out-Spoken Soldier*, p.326.

30 - The Swan Song of the British Empire

From even before the outbreak of war in Europe until the debacle in Pearl Harbour, President Roosevelt had been assuring the American people that he was not going to allow them to become involved in war; but even as he repeated his pledges to keep his country neutral, he schemed how he could slowly edge it into the conflict without the onus of himself declaring war on the Axis.

In October 1940, when he knew that war was inevitable, he told his people: [78]

"We will not participate in foreign war; we will not send our Army, Navy and Air Force to fight in foreign lands... I have said this before, and I shall say it again, and again, and again. Your boys are not going to be sent into any foreign wars. Your President says this country is not going to war."

"But," as General Fuller observed, "he left no stone unturned to provoke Hitler to declare war."

Dr. Barnes quotes Clare Boothe Luce, America's first woman ambassador, as charging Roosevelt with having "lied the United States into war".[79] This, declared Barnes, was "one of the most restrained understatements of the wartime period. While he (Roosevelt) was publicly insisting that he favoured peace and was assuring American fathers and mothers that their sons would not be sent into any foreign war, he was engaged in secret intrigue with Winston Churchill [80] planning how the United States might rapidly be brought into the war..."

"This,' [81] wrote Ambassador Bullet, 'was a low-watermark in Presidential morality; but the President won the election.'"

---

78   *The Decisive Battles of the Western World*, Vol. 3, p.416.

79   *Revisionism: A Key to Peace*, in Rampart Journal, Vol. 2, No. 1, p.30

80   Ref. Page

81   *War at the Top*, p.253, by General Sir Leslie Hollis, KCB, KBE, edited by James Leasor, pub. Michael Joseph.

At some time in 1941, thanks to an unlikely accident in the Aleutian Islands, a million to one chance, the Americans had broken the Japanese code, since when all Japanese signals by wireless were being intercepted and decoded. President Roosevelt was being kept informed of Japanese movements and preparations in the Pacific; but he refrained deliberately from warning the naval, military or civil authorities in Hawaii.

Captain L.F. Safford, U.S. Navy, at that time in charge of the Security Section of U.S. Naval Communications, Washington subsequently stated: [82] "On December 4th, 1941, we received definite information from two independent sources that Japan would attack the U.S. and Britain, but would maintain peace with Russia. At 9.00 p.m. Washington time, December 6th, 1941, we received positive information that Japan would declare war against the United States at a time to be specified thereafter. This information, Safford testified, was unmistakable and was made available to Military Intelligence virtually at the moment of its decoding. Finally at 10.15 a.m. Washington time, December 7th, 1941, we received positive information from the Signal Intelligence Service, War Dept., that the Japanese declaration of war would be presented to the Secretary of State at 1.00 p.m. Washington time that date; when it was 1.00 p.m. in Washington it would be daybreak in Hawaii and approximately midnight in the Philippines, which indicated a surprise air raid on Pearl Harbour in about three hours."

No alarm was flashed to Hawaii. At dawn that day, exactly as predicted by those American Intelligence Officers, some 150 Japanese bombers and torpedo-carrying aircraft and approximately an equal number of fighters took off from their carriers, and flew in to the attack. As the planes approached they were picked up on the screens of the recently installed radar station at Opana on Oahu, and were instantly reported; but as radar was a new 'Limey' contraption which hitherto had inspired little confidence, the report was ignored.

---

82   Wedemeyer Reports, pp. 429-30.

Minutes later the storm of war broke over the slumbering base. Eighteen warships, including 3 battleships, were sunk or very heavily damaged, 177 aircraft were destroyed on the ground, and 4,575 American citizens were killed or wounded.

The warning signal from General Marshall, Chief of Staff, Washington, which could have been dispatched instantly, had been delayed, then transmitted deliberately by ordinary commercial cable, and delivered by a messenger on a bicycle to General Short and Admiral Kimmell as they stared in incredulous horror at blazing barracks, hangars, workshops and stores, and a shambles of sunken warships. At that same time, the raiders, mission completed, were returning to their carriers out of sight over the northern horizon.

Admiral Theobald, U.S.N., who commanded the destroyers in Pearl Harbour at the time, affirmed that: [83]

"By holding a weak Pacific fleet in Hawaii as the invitation to a surprise attack, and by denying the Commander of that fleet the information which might cause him to render the attack impossible, President Roosevelt brought war to the United States on December 7th, 1941. He took a fully aroused nation into the fight, because none of its people suspected how the Japanese attack fitted into their President's plans."

In Washington, [84] "on receipt of the first news of the terrible losses at Pearl Harbour, Roosevelt called for the deeply shaken American Naval Secretary, looked smilingly at him as he stood white with shock at the door of his room, then burst into roars of laughter."

In London that same night, Winston Churchill relaxed in pleasure and relief. He described his feelings[85] "being saturated

83   *The Final Secret of Pearl Harbour*, by Rear Admiral Robert A.Theobald, USN, foreword by Fleet-Admiral William F. Halsey, USN.

84   *Union*, 8.3.1952, beneath the caption "The Happy Hyena".

85   *The Second World War*, Vol. 3. p.540

and satiated with emotion and sensation, I went to bed and slept the sleep of the saved and the thankful".

Shortly before Pearl Harbour, Churchill supported by Anthony Eden at the Foreign Office, but opposed by others, ordered a naval squadron, including capital ships, to demonstrate in Malayan waters with the object of deterring the still neutral Japanese from adventure in those parts. Because of recent heavy losses at sea and commitments elsewhere, the Admiralty was unable to supply a single aircraft-carrier to give air cover to H.M. Ships Prince of Wales and Repulse, two battleships detailed for the task.

Naval opinion was vehemently opposed to the dispatch of great ships to the Far East without air cover. Dudley Pound, tough and seasoned old sailor that he was, but lacking that granite-like quality of Alan Brook against which the wrath of Churchill beat in vain, allowed himself to be talked into reluctant compliance with a strategic move that he viewed with misgiving.

On their outward passage Prince of Wales and Repulse called at Cape Town, where Marshal Smuts saw with concern the two vessels at anchor in Table Bay. He sent an urgent signal to London pointing out the danger to which those two great ships were about to be exposed unless they could be allowed an escorting carrier with its fighter protection; but Churchill refused to reconsider his decision.

The squadron reached Singapore on 2nd December, 1941, but by the evening of the 10th both battleships rested on the bottom of the South China Sea, with Admiral Sir Tom Phillips and a large proportion of their companies, sunk by Japanese airmen using strictly orthodox tactics, and almost at their leisure.

This was a re-enactment of the sinkings of H.M. Ships Aboukir, Cressy and Hogue in 1914, and it was doubly blameworthy as the man responsible for the disaster in the China Sea had not heeded the lesson of the vulnerability of unprotected warships to air attack as demonstrated by the recent losses off Crete.

Winston Churchill remained heedless of the experiences of the past, whether of centuries ago or only yesterday. Thus, within the space of three days, the combined statecraft of Churchill and Roosevelt had contrived to establish the Japanese as Lords of the Pacific. In no time, too, Japan dominated the eastern side of the Indian Ocean, and at the same time Australia and New Zealand were directly threatened. It was to take years of bloody and ferocious fighting, and immense sacrifice of life and wealth, to clear those thousands of miles of ocean, the myriad islands set in it, and the rich countries on its shores, of the fanatically brave little men who had overrun them.

In popular belief it was the explosions over Hiroshima and Nagasaki of the first two atom bombs on 6th and 9th August, 1945, respectively, that finished Japan. In actual fact the Emperor and his advisers had already realised that their country had lost the war, and had offered to surrender two days [86] before the first nuclear device exploded. This was described by Fleet-Admiral William Leachy, Chief of Staff to both Presidents Roosevelt and Truman as "... a modern type of barbarism not worthy of Christian men".

This was how Britain came to be tied by the bond of alliance to two great powers whose leaders, Roosevelt and Stalin, were united in their detestation of the British Empire and in their resolve that having made the utmost use of it in the war against the Axis, they would smash it. At the same time too, they were determined to utilise the war to bring to an end the overseas empires of France and Holland.

The American President nursed a deep-seated hatred of the British Empire and of most things British. As a legacy of their own heroic early history many Americans disliked and distrusted the Imperial concept, but Roosevelt's detestation went deeper. Whatever the source of his phobia it was apparently something he had nurtured most of his life; on his own admission, when as a schoolboy on a visit to London at the time of Queen Victoria's

---

86   *Japan's Decision to Surrender*, by Robert J.C. Burton.

diamond jubilee, he saw the old queen driving in state through the streets of her capital, he had prayed for her assassination so that the world might be rid of an oppressive tyrant.

It was more than ironic that Hitler, the common enemy, should have esteemed Britain and her Empire, considered the Pax Britannica essential to world peace and stability, and should have gone to an extraordinary length at Dunkirk to preserve it.

Churchill, from having directed the war in person and as a complete autocrat, was reduced to the perturbed and often indignant but nevertheless helpless appendage of Roosevelt and Stalin, who had ganged up on him from the outset of their alliance. General Sir Leslie Hollis, K.C.B., K.B.E., who was at the very centre of the inter-allied councils, states: [87]

"American policy was 'to make the Russians trust us', and the implementation of that policy sometimes necessitated the cutting of the throats of the British."

The President, probably America's greatest ever political "fall-guy" was being steered on a pro-communist course by those economic experts and other ill-chosen advisers of Leftish views with whom he had surrounded himself. General Hollis[88] tells us:

"Roosevelt's greatest weakness – and shared by that band of 'tragically ignorant progressives' who had guided American policy in the crucial years – was a passion for flirtation with the Kremlin. His claque of faithful supporters – General Marshall, Ambassador Joseph Davies, Harry Hopkins (known to a number of Republicans as 'the Rasputin of the White House'), and his own son, Elliott, missed no opportunity to praise the Soviet Union, in and out of season."

When during the last months of the war in Europe, the German armies in the west retreated and fell back before the irresistible

---

87   *War at the Top*, p.283

88   *War at the Top*, p.279

weight of men and material put into the continent by America and Britain, and as the allied soldiers swept forward in triumph and were about to snatch the full fruits of victory, they were halted short of their objectives, in some areas they were even made to fall back, on the orders of Roosevelt, anxious as always to give no offence to Stalin, with whom he felt that he alone was competent to negotiate.

According to Hollis it was Feodor Gusev, one time Russian Ambassador to Great Britain, and Russian representative, at the European Advisory Commission at Lancaster House, London, who was largely responsible for persuading the President to halt the allied armies on their victorious eastward march, and to allow the Red Army to reach Berlin first, there to capture "upwards of 50,000 German technicians, scientists and electronic experts who had been working on V.1 and V.2 guided missiles near Berlin, and to transport them to Russia. The emergence of Russia as a space-power barely thirteen years after the war owes much to the eminent services of Feodor Gusev who could say nothing in several languages with unruffled immobility."

On 8th May, 1945, Britain and the United States celebrated their victory in Europe ("V.E. DAY"), but as General Fuller observed, the fruits of victory proved to be but "apples of Sodom, which turned to ashes as they were plucked."

He continued his jeremiad: [89] "The western frontier of Russia had been advanced from the Pripet Marshes to the Thüringerwald, a distance of 750 miles, and as in the days of Charlemagne, the Slavs stood on the Elbe and the Böhmewald. A thousand years of European history had been rolled back. Such were the fruits, fructified by inept strategy and a policy of pure destruction."

From the time of Munich we worked night and day to avoid conflict with Germany. Despite the frenzied rearmament the British public was in a far from bellicose mood, and right up to May 1940 we received a far more sympathetic hearing than those who had spoken against war in 1914.

---

89   *War at the Top*, p.279.

Yet we were greatly hampered in a way that has not hitherto been remarked on. A substantial proportion of our members were of military age – army, navy and air force reservists, many of whom had been called up in 1938 and who were again called up in 1939. From April 1939, our younger members were being conscripted in increasing numbers into the Militia. We were losing the services of our most active members at a growing pace. Many of our 400 branches had to suspend their activities because all the branch officials and active members had been called up. This was particularly noticeable at the July 1939 meeting at Earl's Court. At this the largest indoor gathering that had ever been held in the world a great many members of the 30,000 strong audience were in uniform.

Two things about the BUF have surprised some historians. One was the appeal of what they had been led to believe was a reactionary organisation to such pioneer feminists and leading suffragettes as Mary Allen, Mary Richardson, Olga Shore and Norah Elam. The other was its strongly pacifistic nature. The BUF did not contain timid types; a substantial proportion of its membership consisted of battle-hardened veterans of the First World War – no wilting violets or pansies these.

The fact is that Mosley, Henry Williamson, General Fuller and indeed the generality of members had learned a most important lesson: that war – the Twentieth Century's "Total War" – has become too immensely destructive for national objectives to be achieved by resorting to it.

The BUF did not believe in interventionism in European affairs. It considered that Britain's national and imperial interests would be best served by avoiding all foreign entanglements and concentrating on the development of an insulated, isolationist, self-sufficient British Empire.

The BUF was by no means alone in advocating an honourable, negotiated peace after 3rd September 1939. Many other organisations wanted the war to end before real hostilities began, including the Independent Labour Party, the British People's Party and the Peace Pledge Union.

30 - The Swan Song of the British Empire

Even the British Government, after the Fall of France, put out feelers to seek terms. In Washington, Lisbon and Berne British diplomats made appropriately discreet contact with the Germans. Lord Halifax suggested to the War cabinet that a favourable reply should be prepared if Hitler offered peace on fair terms. But Churchill was now Prime Minister. So instead of proposing peace Halifax was given the task of firmly rejecting Hitler's peace offer.

Churchill himself realised that in the end he would be judged by results. In his autobiography, Churchill's Parliamentary Private Secretary, Lord Boothby records: "He (Churchill) once talked to me, when the war was over and he was out of power, about the position he would ultimately occupy in history; and I said that nothing could take from him the fact that he had saved Britain in 1940. He then said, rather sadly: "Historians are apt to judge war ministers less by the victories achieved under their direction than by the political results which flowed from them. I am not sure that I shall be held to have done very well." [90]

Lloyd George, whom many men of clear vision and moderation would have preferred as Prime Minister and war leader, confided to Earl Winterton, Conservative Member for Worthing, who was his guest at Churt, that he took a dismal view of the future, and that whoever won the war he could foresee that: [91]

"The end of it would see Western civilisation in ruin, with little chance of the re-emergence of Britain as a great power within the lifetime of the youngest person alive."

So perished the British Empire.

---

90   *My Yesterday, Your Tomorrow*, by Lord Boothby

91   *The Decisive Battles of the Western World*, Vol. 3, p.589.

www.ingramcontent.com/pod-product-compliance
Lightning Source LLC
Chambersburg PA
CBHW070555270326
41926CB00013B/2324